Key to map pages

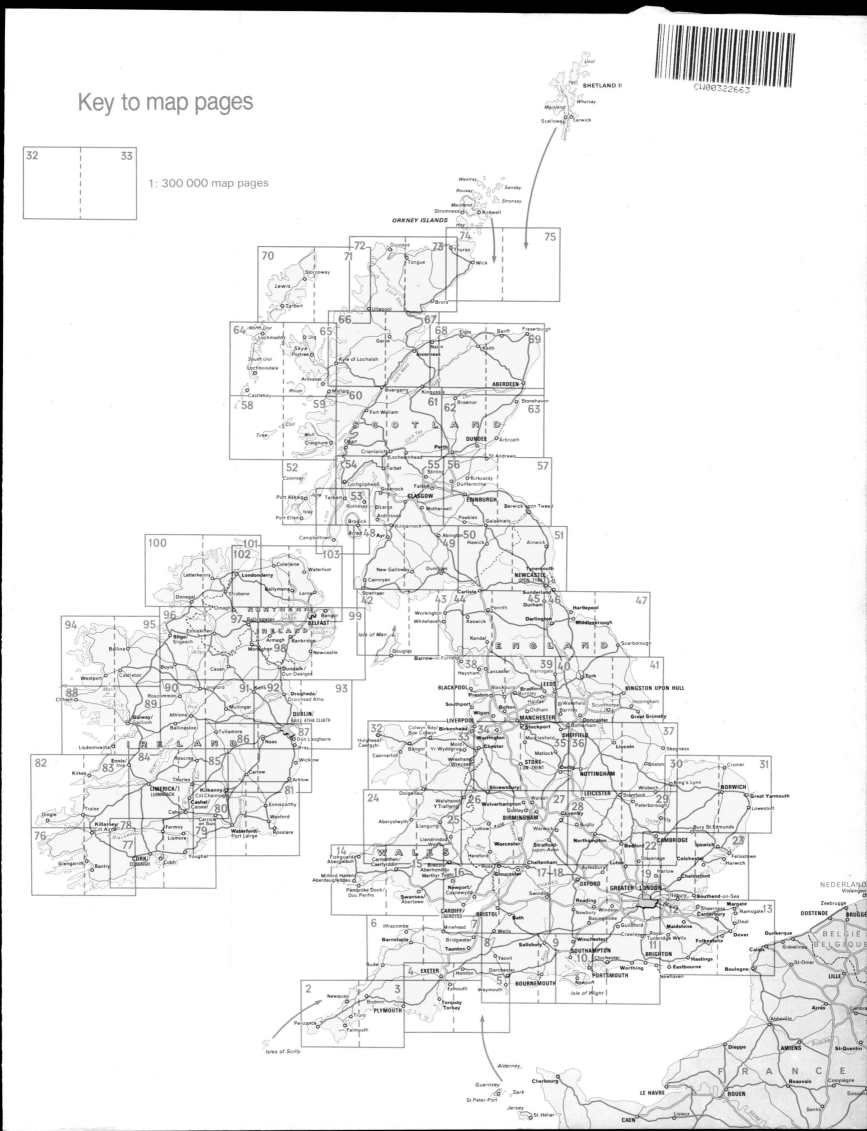

32 33

1: 300 000 map pages

MICHELIN®
Road Atlas of
Great Britain and Ireland

Tourism Department
MICHELIN

MICHELIN the world's leading manufacturer of tyres, is also a well known name in the field of tourist publications; its annual sales of maps and guides exceed 16 million in over 70 countries.

Acting on the belief that motoring would have a great future, the Michelin brothers decided to offer the motorist a touring service, an innovative step at the turn of the century : free or inexpensive publications designed to provide information, assistance and encouragement.

At the wheel, touring, on holiday – these three aspects of travel were met by a simple response – a trio of complementary publications to be used together.

The first of these, the Red Guides, which are published annually, present a selection of hotels and restaurants, with a wide range of prices and facilities. It is, however, probably their award of the stars for good cooking that has established their international reputation ; as well as the wealth of essential touring information included in them. There are several guides covering Europe, including the Red Guide to France which alone has sold over 20 million copies to date. Readers have such faith in their reliability that the Red Guides are foremost among reference books in this field.

The role of the Michelin Green Guides is to provide tourists with an introduction to the regions of France and other foreign countries. The guides describe the sights, the countryside and picturesque routes ; they also contain maps, plans and practical information as well as illustrations and photographs which whet one's appetite for travel. There are over 70 titles covering Europe and North America, which are published in French and other European languages and are revised regularly.

The mapping of this Atlas of Great Britain and Ireland is an enlargement of the 1:400 000 sheet map series covering these countries. There are 102 pages of mapping, 48 town plans and an index of approximately 10 000 place names. Uniquely, in this Atlas we have used the same grid system as on the maps so that it can be used in conjunction with our Hotel and Restaurant Guide Great Britain and Ireland and our Green Guides to Scotland, London and the West Country.

It is our intention to continue our service to our readers by annually updating the information contained within the Atlas. We should welcome your comments and suggestions in order that we may take your wishes into account when preparing the next edition.

Thank you in advance. May we wish you a safe journey.

MICHELIN maps and guides
complement one another :
use them together !

Contents

Inside front cover

Key to map pages

II   Michelin

IV   **Route Planning**

VII   **Distances** in Great Britain and Ireland

VIII   **Key to symbols :** Welsh and Irish

1   **Key to symbols :** English and French

2   **Great Britain** at a scale of 1:300 000

20   **Greater London** at a scale of 1:200 000

76   **Ireland** at a scale of 1:300 000

104   **Key to town plan symbols**

105   **Index of place names :** Great Britain

132   **Index of place names :** Ireland

Inside back cover

Shipping Services

Plans of cities and principal towns

63 ● Aberdeen	110 ● Chester	41 ● Kingston upon Hull	124 ● Norwich
105 ● Bath	79 ● Cork/Corcaigh	117 ● Leeds	124 ● Nottingham
133 ● Belfast	111 ● Coventry	117 ● Leeds area	125 ● Oxford
132 ● Belfast area	111 ● Derby	118 ● Leicester	3 ● Plymouth
107 ● Birmingham	13 ● Dover	82 ● Limerick/ Luimneach	125 ● Portsmouth
106 ● Birmingham area	134 ● Dublin/ Baile Átha Cliath		127 ● Sheffield
38 ● Blackpool	135 ● Dublin area	118 ● Lincoln	127 ● Southampton
107 ● Bournemouth	63 ● Dundee	119 ● Liverpool	128 ● Stoke on Trent
108 ● Bradford	47 ● Durham	118 ● Liverpool area	128 ● Stoke on Trent area
11 ● Brighton	112 ● Edinburgh	120 ● London	128 ● Stratford upon Avon
108 ● Bristol	112 ● Edinburgh area	123 ● Manchester	129 ● Sunderland
109 ● Cambridge	113 ● Exeter	122 ● Manchester area	129 ● Swansea/Abertawe
109 ● Canterbury	114 ● Glasgow		130 ● Winchester
109 ● Cardiff/ Caerdydd	115 ● Glasgow area	47 ● Newcastle upon Tyne	130 ● Wolverhampton
110 ● Carlisle	23 ● Ipswich		131 ● York

● Town plan on map page   ● Town plan on index page

Route planning

	Motorway
	Major road
	Other route
A 38	Road number
24	Mileage
- - -	Shipping route

The Primary Road network in England is currently under review.
Certain roads may therefore change their status during the currency of this publication.
The classification and numbering of roads in Ireland are subject to modification.

SHETLAND ISLANDS

Unst

Yell

Whalsay

Mainland

Scalloway○ ○Lerwick

Kirkwall *Aberdeen*

ORKNEY ISLANDS

Westray

Rousay *Sanday*

Stronsay

Mainland

Stromness○ ○Kirkwall

Hoy *Scalloway*

Durness 16 ○Thurso
27 A 836
31 Tongue A 882 ○Wick
A 836 39 58
A 897 A 9
89 ○Brora

Stornoway

Lewis

THE MINCH

72

Loch Shin

Tarbert○ 31 A 835
○Ullapool

North Uist

Lochmaddy○ ○Uig
49 Garve 26
A 890 Elgin 35 Banff ○Fraserburgh
Skye 17 Keith 21 A 98
Portree○ 57 Nairn 39
Kyle of Lochalsh 43 **Inverness** 68
South Uist A 82 *Loch Ness* 40 A 9 A 95 64 A 96 51
Lochboisdale○ 50 A 93
Ardvasar 52 Kingussie 59 ○Stonehaven
Rhum Mallaig○ Invergarry *Dee* **ABERDEEN** *Lerwick*
Castlebay○ 25 A 86 105 72 Braemar A 92
46 A 830 51 A 94 68
Fort William 67
A 9

Sea of the Hebrides

Coll

Tiree

S C O T L A N D

Mull

Craignure○ 41 A 82 52 *Loch Tay* A 93 **DUNDEE** ○Arbroath
Oban A 85 53 A 85 **Perth** 22
Colonsay Crianlarich 17 Lochearnhead 33 A 9 29 77 ○St. Andrews
38 49 Tarbet 43 Stirling A 91 30
A 816 A 83 41 *Firth of Forth*
Lochgilphead○ 29 Falkirk A 90 14 ○Kirkcaldy
Jura Greenock Dunfermline
Port Askaig○ Tarbert○ Rothesay **GLASGOW** 39 13 **EDINBURGH** 56
Islay Largs 69 8 Motherwell M 8 39 Berwick upon Tweed
Port Ellen○ Ardrossan A 77 31 A 721 41 A 7 34 A 1
Brodick Kilmarnock A 702 63 Peebles Galashiels 45
51 *Arran* **Ayr** 13 M 74 Abington A 72 17 A 698 Alnwick
Campbeltown○ A 713 Hawick A 68 62 63
51 58 60 43
35 46 A 701 A 7

NORTH SEA

NORTH CHANNEL

Bergen
Stavanger
Kristiansand
Oslo
Göteborg
Hirtshals
Esbjerg

Londonderry A 2 Coleraine
Waterfoot
31 A 26 25 New Galloway A 702 Dumfries 39 A 74 Tynemouth
14 A 6 90 Cairnryan 44 14 18 32 A 75 A 696 **NEWCASTLE-UPON-TYNE**
Ballymena 55 A 75 Carlisle A 69 59
Strabane Larne Stranraer A 69 34 20 **Sunderland** A 19
20 28 34 Penrith **Durham** 45 **Hartlepool**
NORTHERN 38 A 596 49 M 1 **Middlesbrough**
magh 26 Ballygawley A 66 Workington A 66 **Darlington** 24 A 171
IRELAND *Lough Neagh* ○Bangor Whitehaven Keswick A 66 A 19 51
31 53 M 1 **BELFAST** 55 M 6 38 65 ○Scarborough
17 Armagh Banbridge 42 *Isle of Man* Kendal A 1 59 A 165
A 3 37 A 25 21 E N G L A N D A 64
Monaghan A 1 52 Newcastle Douglas *Wharfe* 40 *Swale* 47
67 T 24 13 A 2 **Barrow-in-Furness** 12 A 65 64 Harrogate **York** A 1079
Dundalk/ Heysham Lancaster 26 A 63 **KINGSTON UPON HULL**
Dun Dealgan 37 *Ouse* 31
Kells 22 **BLACKPOOL** 20 Blackburn **Bradford LEEDS** A 63 Immingham
60 71 **Southport** 27 **Bolton** Halifax **Wakefield** Scunthorpe 16 Rotterdam Zeebruge
Drogheda/ **Preston** Burnley 38 Barnley 19 M 180 17
Droichead Átha **Wigan** 25 10 Oldham 39 9 **Doncaster** A 15 A 16
Mullingar 43 **LIVERPOOL** **MANCHESTER** **Great Grimsby**
DUBLIN/ Colwyn Bay/ **Birkenhead Stockport** 43 Rotherham 28 A 159
BAILE ÁTHA CLIATH Bae Colwyn **SHEFFIELD**

IRISH SEA

Distances in Great Britain and Ireland

All distances are quoted in miles and kilometres.

miles in red

kilometres in blue

The distances quoted are not necessarily the shortest but have been based on the roads which afford the best driving conditions and are therefore the most practical.

Example:

Oxford – Killarney:

	Oxford – Fishguard	218 m.	or	351 km.
+	Rosslare – Killarney	162 m.	or	261 km.
		380 m.	or	612 km.

Ireland

Kilometres

Belfast		402	116	166	80	315	439	37	328	113	109	309	203	212	317
	Cork		291	248	321	196	87	439	93	452	397	198	321	190	117
		Drogheda		50	35	225	351	203	240	196	134	167	214	111	204
250			Dublin		85	217	304	204	193	235	158	103	240	161	214	97	154
72	181			Dundalk		246	359	153	248	158	103	240	171	132	237
103	154	31			Galway		214	352	103	283	238	307	145	132	227
50	200	22	53			Killarney		476	111	483	428	261	348	227	180
196	122	140	135	153			Larne		365	116	121	365	240	249	359
273	54	218	189	223	133			Limerick		372	317	204	237	116	124
23	273	126	127	95	219	296			Londonderry		55	397	138	262	389
204	58	149	120	154	64	69	227			Omagh		343	111	208	335
70	281	122	146	98	176	300	72	231			Rosslare		330	175	80
68	247	23	112	64	148	266	75	197	34			Sligo		153	283
192	123	104	100	149	191	162	227	127	247	213			Tullamore		130
126	200	133	133	106	90	216	149	147	86	69	205			Waterford	
132	118	69	60	82	82	141	155	72	163	129	109	95			
197	73	127	96	147	141	112	223	77	242	208	50	176	81		

Miles

Great Britain

Kilometres

		711	991	846	805	877	389	1025	108	209	967	864	241	1493	753	639	172	304	589	592	898	584	532	378	798	848	695	290	819	1157	1031	972	938	399	872	386
Aberdeen		290	146	177	323	603	484	267	333	483	294	246	224	753	784	191	166	196	138	285	331	90	259	80	644	101	457	331	238	204	497	219	969
	Birmingham		253	188	307	603	135	883	764	291	486	763	201	526	402	1033	1063	422	446	85	418	513	562	204	274	311	924	169	483	357	77	98	777	365	1249
		Brighton		267	74	459	320	739	619	135	251	618	331	381	370	888	919	338	301	195	274	430	478	175	362	240	779	117	325	200	161	127	632	132	1104
442			Bristol		322	417	193	697	539	397	539	499	576	126	414	220	846	877	237	335	88	262	322	370	87	98	142	737	161	587	462	214	206	591	380	1062
616	180			Cambridge		489	375	769	650	195	183	648	386	346	401	919	949	368	278	249	304	460	508	230	417	267	809	172	385	259	230	196	663	64	1134
526	91	157			Cardiff		637	282	163	579	475	161	541	364	249	431	462	200	204	510	196	145	95	404	459	306	386	431	769	644	584	550	175	483	647
500	110	117	166			Carlisle		917	739	451	552	796	206	560	422	1067	1097	438	479	122	452	523	570	238	278	344	957	235	640	515	228	245	811	433	1282
545	110	191	46	200			Dover		101	859	756	134	821	645	531	216	293	481	484	790	476	425	270	685	740	587	187	711	1049	924	864	830	291	764	430
242	201	375	285	259	304			Dundee		740	636	74	702	525	372	251	328	322	365	671	357	235	169	565	581	428	198	592	930	805	745	711	212	644	465
637	201	84	199	120	233	396			Edinburgh		372	739	460	502	491	1009	1039	453	422	325	394	550	599	306	492	360	899	248	182	74	227	193	753	253	1223
67	375	549	459	433	478	175	570			Exeter		634	563	272	471	906	935	381	277	426	309	488	536	377	556	796	381	562	436	407	373	648	122	1120
130	301	475	385	335	404	101	459	63			Fishguard		700	523	409	277	290	359	364	669	356	304	253	563	618	465	150	591	928	803	743	710	140	642	492
601	166	181	84	247	121	360	280	534	460			Glasgow		531	344	970	1001	360	451	127	425	446	494	209	108	265	861	225	650	526	257	270	714	444	1184
537	207	302	156	310	114	295	343	470	395	231			Harwich		360	795	824	270	166	433	198	377	425	327	528	288	685	354	692	566	507	473	537	307	1009
150	300	474	384	358	403	100	495	83	46	459	394			Holyhead		681	457	98	211	294	159	143	203	254	238	151	571	301	681	555	410	404	425	442	895
928	183	125	206	78	240	336	128	510	436	286	350	435			Hull		132	631	634	940	626	574	420	835	890	737	190	861	1200	1073	1014	980	415	914	214
468	153	327	237	257	215	226	348	401	326	312	169	325	330			Inverness		916	665	970	656	605	497	864	920	767	203	891	1229	1104	1044	1010	426	944	346
397	139	250	230	137	249	155	262	330	231	305	293	254	214	224			Kyle of Lochalsh		121	328	69	106	312	222	280	119	521	269	648	523	430	423	375	410	845
107	468	642	552	526	571	268	663	134	156	627	563	172	603	494	423			Leeds		352	56	227	274	246	378	209	525	274	611	486	426	393	378	301	850
189	487	661	571	545	590	287	682	182	204	646	581	180	622	512	284	82			Liverpool		325	386	444	111	176	217	830	95	515	389	126	140	684	307	1155
366	119	262	210	147	229	124	272	299	200	285	237	223	224	168	61	392	569			London		175	224	220	306	116	516	246	584	459	399	365	370	346	842
368	103	277	187	208	173	127	298	301	227	262	172	226	280	103	131	394	413	75			Manchester		66	315	365	212	465	360	740	615	523	515	319	502	700
558	122	53	121	55	155	317	76	491	417	202	265	416	79	269	183	584	603	204	219			Middlesbrough		362	412	259	415	409	788	662	570	563	234	550	634
363	86	260	170	163	189	122	281	296	222	245	192	221	264	123	99	389	408	43	35	202			Newcastle		185	113	726	68	496	370	214	206	578	296	1049
331	177	319	267	200	286	90	325	264	146	342	303	189	277	234	89	357	376	66	141	246	109			Northampton		628	158	550	425	320	312	481	309	951
235	206	349	297	230	316	59	354	168	105	372	333	157	307	264	126	261	309	95	170	276	139	41			Norwich		751	1089	964	904	870	288	805	405
493	56	127	109	54	143	251	148	426	351	190	234	350	130	203	158	519	537	138	153	69	137	196	225			Nottingham		438	312	137	103	605	230	1076
527	161	170	225	61	259	285	173	460	361	306	370	148	553	572	174	235	109	190	227	256	115			Oban		126	418	385	942	442	1143
432	50	193	149	88	166	190	214	365	266	224	221	289	165	179	94	458	74	130	135	72	132	161	70	120			Oxford		293	259	817	317	1289
180	400	574	484	458	503	240	595	116	123	559	495	93	535	426	355	118	126	324	326	516	321	289	258	451	485	390			Penzance		34	758	288	1229
509	63	105	73	100	107	268	146	442	368	154	218	367	140	220	187	535	554	167	170	59	153	224	254	42	160	98	467			Plymouth		724	254	1195
719	284	300	202	365	239	478	398	652	578	113	349	577	404	430	423	746	764	403	380	320	363	450	490	308	424	342	677	272			Portsmouth		658	629
641	206	222	124	287	161	400	320	574	500	46	271	499	327	352	345	667	686	325	302	242	285	382	412	230	346	264	599	194	78			Southampton		1128
604	148	48	100	133	143	363	142	516	442	141	253	462	160	315	255	630	649	267	265	78	248	325	354	133	192	199	562	85	260	182			Stranraer	
583	127	61	79	128	122	342	152	516	442	102	232	441	168	294	251	609	628	263	244	87	227	320	350	128	188	194	541	64	239	161	21			Swansea	
248	309	483	393	367	412	109	504	181	132	468	403	87	444	334	264	258	265	233	235	425	230	198	167	359	394	299	179	376	586	508	471	450			Thurso	
542	136	227	82	236	40	300	269	475	400	157	76	399	276	191	275	568	587	255	187	191	215	312	342	184	295	192	500	143	275	197	179	158	409		
240	602	776	686	660	705	402	797	267	289	760	696	306	736	627	556	133	215	525	528	718	523	435	394	652	686	591	252	669	878	801	764	743	391	701	

Miles

Eochair   Allwedd

Bóithre — Ffyrdd

Mótarbhealach agus ionaid seirbhíse	Traffordd a mannau gwasanaethu
Carrbhealach dúbailte le saintréithe mótarbhealaigh	Ffordd ddeuol â nodweddion traffordd
Acomhail mótarbhealaigh : iomlán - leath - teoranta	Cyfnewidfeydd : wedi'i chwblhau - ar ei hanner - rhannol
Uimhir	Rhif
Mórbhóthar : carrshlí dhéach	Prif ffordd gysylltu : ffordd ddeuol
4 lána - 2 leathanlána	4 lôn - 2 lôn lydan
2 lána - 2 chunglána	2 lôn - 2 lôn gul
Líonra réigiúnach bóithre : carrshlí dhéach - 2 leathanlána	Rhwydwaith ffyrdd rhanbarthol : ffordd ddeuol - 2 lôn lydan
2 lána - 2 chunglána	2 lôn - 2 lôn gul
Bóithre eile : réidh - gan réitiú	Ffyrdd eraill : â wyneb - heb wyneb
Bóthar á dhéanamh	Ffordd yn cael ei hadeiladu
Data sceidealta um oscailt	Dyddiad agor
Cosán - Cosán fadslí	Llwybr troed - Llwybr hir neu lwybr ceffyl
Timpeall - Bearnas is a airde (i méadair)	Cylchfan - Bwlch a'i uchder (mewn metrau)
Faid ar mhótarshlíte, ar bóithre : i mílte - i giliméadair	Pellter ar ffyrdd a thraffyrdd : mewn milltiroedd - mewn kilometrau

Aicmiú oifigiúil bóithre — Dosbarthiad ffyrdd swyddogol

An Ríocht Aontaithe :	Y Deyrnas Gyfunol :
Mótarshlí	Traffordd
Priomhbhealach	Prif ffordd
Bóithre eile	Ffyrdd eraill
Ceann scríbe ar ghréasán bóithre priomha	Cyrchfan ar rwydwaith y prif ffyrdd
i bPloblacht na hÉireann :	Gweriniaeth Iwerddon :
Mótarshlí	Traffordd
Priomhbhóithre agus fobhóithre náisiúnta	Prif ffordd genedlaethol a ffordd eilradd
Bóithre eile	Ffyrdd eraill

Constaicí — Rhwystrau

Bóthar cúng le hionaid phasála (in Albain)	Yn yr Alban : ffordd gul â mannau pasio
Bóthar : toirmeasctha - faoi theorannú	Ffordd : gwaharddedig - cyfyngiadau arni
Bacainn dola - Bóthar aonslí	Rhwystr Toll - Unffordd
Réimse achrannach nó contúirteach bóthair	Darn anodd neu beryglus o ffordd
Ar phríomhbhóithre agus ar bhóithre réigiúnacha :	Ar brif ffyrdd a ffyrdd rhanbarthol :
Teorainneacha airde (faoi 15′6″ IRL, faoi 16′6″ GB)	Terfyn uchder (llai na 15′6″ IRL, 16′6″ GB)
Teorann Mheáchain (faoi 16 t) (teorannu - inathraithe)	Terfyn pwysau (llai na 16 t) (y cyfyngiadau'n agored i gael eu newid)
Grádán : (suas treo an gha)	Graddiant (esgyn gyda'r saeth)

Iarnróid — Rheilffyrdd

Leithead caighdeánach - Staisiún paisinéirí	Lled safonol - Gorsaf deithwyr
Iarnród thraein ghaile - Ráille tionsclaíoch	Rheilffordd ager - Trac diwydiannol
Crosaire comhréidh, iarnród ag dul faoi bhóthar, os cionn bóthair	Croesfan rheilffordd : rheilffordd yn croesi ffordd, o dan ffordd
Cáblashlí thionsclaíoch - Cathaoir cábla	Lein gêbl ddiwydiannol - Cadair esgyn

Longsheirbhísí — Llongau ceir

Seirbhísí séasúracha : dearg	Gwasanaethau tymhorol : mewn coch
Bád - Árthach foluaineach	Ilong - Ilong hofran
Fartha (uas-ualach : tonnaí méadracha)	Fferi (llwyth uchaf : mewn tunelli metrig)
Coisithe agus lucht rothar	Teithwyr ar droed neu feic yn unig

Bailte - Riarachán — Trefi - Gweinyddiaeth

Bailte a bhfuil a bplean in Eolaí Dearg Michelin	Trefi â map ohonynt yn Llyfr Coch Michelin
Bailte a chuimsítear san Eolaí Michelin sin	Trefi a gynhwysir yn Llyfr Michelin uchod
Teorainn chontae nó régiúnach	Ffin sirol neu ranbarthol
Teorainn na hAlban agus teorainn na Breataine Bige	Ffin Cymru, ffin yr Alban
Teorainn idirnáisiúnta - Custam	Ffin ryngwladol - Tollau

Ambleside

Comharthaí Eile — Symbolau eraill

Crann teileachumarsáide - Teach Solais	Mast telathrebu - Goleudy
Stáisiún Giniúna - Cairéal - Mianach	Gorsaf bŵer - Chwarel - Mwyngloddio
Monarcha - Scaglann	Ffatri - Purfa
Ráschúrsa - Láthair champa, láthair charbhán	Rasio Ceffylau - Leoedd i wersylla
Timpeall rásaíochta - Cuan bád aeraíochta	Rasio Cerbydau - Harbwr cychod pleser
Machaire Gailf - Páirc Fhoraoise Náisiúnta, Páirc Náisiúnta	Cwrs golff - Parc Coedwig Cenedlaethol, Parc Cenedlaethol
Éire : Iascaireacht - Brú chumann na hóige - Ráschúrsa con	Iwerddon : Pysgota - Hostel ieuenctid - Maes rasio milgwn
Siúlóid fhoraoise - Páirc thuaithe - Aill	Llwybr coedwig - Parc gwledig - Clogwyn
Bealach Aoibhinn	Ffordd olygfeydd
Aerfort - Aerpháirc	Maes awyr - Maes glanio

Príomhionaid inspéise : féach Eolaithe Michelin — Prif Olygfeydd : gweler Llyfr Michelin

Foirgneamh Eaglasta - Fothrach - Séadchomhartha	Adeilad eglwysig - Adfeilion - Cofadail
Caisleán, teach stairiúil	Castell, tŷ hanesyddol
Leacht meigiliteach - Pluais	Heneb fegalithig - Ogof
Éire : Cros Cheilteach - Cloigtheach	Iwerddon : Croes Geltaidd - Tŵr crwn
Zú - Caomhnú nádúir, tearmannéan mara	Parc saffari, sŵ - Gwarchodfa natur
Gáirdíní - Amhairc éagsúla	Gerddi, parc - Golygfeydd amrywiol
Lánléargas - Cothrom Radhairc	Panorama - Golygfan
Bailte nó áiteanna inspéise baill lóistín	Trefi neu fannau o ddiddordeb, mannau i aros

Rye · Elgol

Roads / Routes

Motorway and service areas	Autoroute et aires de service
Dual carriageway with motorway characteristics	Double chaussée de type autoroutier
Interchanges: complete - half - limited number	Échangeurs : complet - demi - partiel numéro d'échangeur
Major road: dual carriageway	Route de liaison principale : à chaussées séparées
4 lanes - 2 wide lanes	à 4 voies - à 2 voies larges
2 lanes - 2 narrow lanes	à 2 voies - à 2 voies étroites
Regional road network dual carriageway - 2 wide lanes	Routes de liaison régionale : à chaussées séparées - à 2 voies larges
2 lanes - 2 narrow lanes	à 2 voies - à 2 voies étroites
Other roads: surfaced-unsurfaced	Autre route : revêtue - non revêtue
Road under construction	Route en construction
Scheduled opening date	Date de mise en service prévue
Footpath - Long distance footpath or bridleway	Sentier - Sentier de grande randonnée ou piste cavalière
Roundabout - Pass, altitude (in metres)	Rond-point - Col, altitude (en mètres)
Distances on motorways or roads in miles - in kilometres	Distances sur autoroute et route : en miles - en kilomètres

8-1990

Official road classification / Classement des itinéraires

United Kingdom:	Royaume-Uni :
Motorway	Autoroute
Primary route	Itinéraire principal
Other roads	Autres routes
Destination on primary route network	Localité jalonnant les itinéraires principaux
Republic of Ireland:	République d'Irlande :
Motorway	Autoroute
National primary and secondary route	Itinéraire principal
Other roads	Autres routes

M 5   A 38   A 155   B 142   YORK   M 1   N 5   N 59   R 313   L 34

Obstacles / Obstacles

In Scotland: narrow road with passing places	En Écosse : route très étroite avec emplacements pour croisement
Road: prohibited - subject to restrictions	Route : interdite - à circulation réglementée
Toll barrier - One-way road	Barrière de péage - Sens unique
Difficult or dangerous stretch of road	Parcours difficile ou dangereux
On major and regional roads:	Sur liaisons principales et régionales :
Height limit (under 15'6'' IRL, 16'6'' GB)	Hauteur limitée (au-dessous de 15'6'' IRL, 16'6'' GB)
Weight limit (under 16t) (restrictions liable to alteration)	Charge limitée (au-dessous de 16 t) (Peuvent avoir été modifiées depuis la date d'édition)
Gradient: (ascent in the direction of the arrow)	Montées - Descentes : (les flèches dans le sens de la montée)

11'9   10   1: 7–1: 5   +1: 5   14–20%   +20%

Railways / Voies ferrées

Standard gauge - Passenger station	Voie ferrée - Gare voyageurs
Steam railway - Industrial track	Voie touristique - industrielle
Level crossing, railway passing under road, over road	Passage de la route : à niveau - supérieur - inférieur
Industrial cable way - Chair lift	Transporteur industriel aérien - Télésiège

Car ferries / Transport des véhicules

Seasonal services: in red	Liaisons saisonnières : signe rouge
boat - hovercraft	par bateau - par aéroglisseur
ferry (maximum load in metric tons)	par bac (charge maximum en tonnes)
Pedestrians and cycles	Transport des piétons et cycles seulement

15

Towns - Administration / Localités - Administration

Town having a plan in the Michelin Red Guide	Localité dont le plan figure dans le Guide Rouge Michelin
Town included in the above Michelin Guide	Localité ayant des ressources sélectionnées dans ce même guide
County or regional boundary	Limite de Comté ou de Région
Scottish and Welsh borders	Limite de l'Écosse et du Pays de Galles
International border - Customs	Frontière internationale - Douane

Ambleside

Other symbols / Signes divers

Telecommunications mast - Lighthouse	Émetteur de télécommunication - Phare
Power station - Quarry - Mine	Centrale électrique - Carrière - Mine
Factory - Refinery	Industrie - Raffinerie
Racecourse - Caravan and camping site	Hippodrome - Camping, caravaning
Racing circuit - Pleasure boat harbour	Circuit automobile - Port de plaisance
Golf course - National Forest Park, National Park	Golf - Parc forestier national, parc national
Ireland: Fishing - Youth hostel - Greyhound racetrack	Irlande : Pêche - Auberge de jeunesse - Cynodrome
Forest walk - Country park - Cliff	Sentier signalisé - Parc de loisirs - Falaise
Scenic route	Parcours pittoresque
Airport - Airfield	Aéroport - Aérodrome

Principal sights: see Michelin Guides / Principales curiosités : voir Guides Michelin

Ecclesiastical building - Ruins - Monument	Édifice religieux - Ruines - Monument
Castle, historic house	Château, manoir, palais
Megalithic monument - Cave	Monument mégalithique - Grotte
Ireland: Celtic cross - Round tower	Irlande : Croix celte - Tour ronde
Zoo - Nature reserve, seabird colony	Parc animalier, zoo - Réserve d'oiseaux
Gardens - Miscellaneous sights	Jardin, parc - Curiosités diverses
Panorama - Viewpoint	Panorama - Point de vue
Towns or places of interest, places to stay	Localités ou sites intéressants, lieux de séjour

Rye (▲)   Elgol

Isles of Scilly

6°20
50°
Round Island
St. Martin's
Bryher
Tresco
34
Hugh Town
St. Mary's
Penzance
Bishop Rocks
St. Agnes
Isles of Scilly
6°20

D
E

Pentire Point
Padstow Bay
Trebe
Trevose Head
Trevone
Constantine Bay
Padst
Treyarnon
St. Merryn
Porthcothan
Little
Park Head
Petherick
B 3276
St. Isse
Bedruthan Steps
Trenance
B 3274
Mawgan Porth
Watergate Bay
Tregurrian (Λ)
A 39
32
B 3276
St. Co
A 3059
Ma
Newquay
(Λ ▲)
A 392 7½
(Λ) Crantock
A 3058
Holywell Bay
13·9
Penhale Point
Holywell
Trerice
Fraddon
A 3075
Summercourt
212
Cubert
A 3016
2½
Ligger or
Newlyn
A 3058
Perran Bay
6
Mitchell
13
(Λ) Perranporth
Gonnhaven
A 3075
B 3285
St. Agnes Head
12
Perranzabuloe
Ladock
15
The Beacon
St. Agnes
B 3284
Trispen
192
Mithian
5½
7½
St. Ste
B 3277
21
B 3284
Probus
Porthtowan
13
A 590
6
A 39
A 3078
Trew
Portreath
(Λ) Blackwater
B 3284
Chacewater
Truro (Λ)
Tin Streaming
6
Hell's Mouth
Illogan
5 15·3
St Michael
Penkevil
B 3300
A
St. Day
(Λ)
Fal
St. Ives
23 37
Redruth (Λ)
Kea
(Λ)
St. Ives Bay
Gwithian
3½
Come-to-Good
Ruan High
Zennor
Gwennap
Lanes
Carbis
Camborne
Trelissick
B 3289
Bay
A 3074
Hayle (Λ)
Perranarworthal
Garden
Veryan
Halsetown
(Λ)
252
Feock
Gurnard's Head
247
6
Praze-an-
Stithians
Mylor
Nare I
Pendeen Watch
B 3311
St. Erth
B 3302
Beeble
B 3280
Bridge
B 3280
A 393
10
Penwith
B 3309
Leedstown(Λ)
B 3303
(Λ)
Portscatho
33
B 3306
9
10½
Penryn
St Just in Roseland
Madron
A 30
Ludgvan
B 3280
Carleen (Λ)
Lamanva
205
St. Mawes
B 3308
Hayle
B 3291
Cape Cornwall
A 3071
Marazion
Relubbus
Wendron
10
Zone Point
Trengwainton
Rosudgeon 194
B 3302
Mawnan
(Λ ▲)
St. Just
6½
Sithney
Constantine
Smith
Falmouth
Sancreed
14 Breage
A 394
Glendurgan
Falmouth Bay
△ 224
St Michael's
Praa
Helston
Mawnan
Whitesand Bay
Mount
Sands (Λ)
Gweek
9 Penzance
Newlyn
Culdrose
Helford
Cross-an-Wra
Cudden Point
Gunwalloe
Mawgan
Gillan
Sennen
(Λ)
Porthleven
(Λ)
Manaccan
B 3283 (▲)
St. Buryan
Mousehole
A 3083
Lizard
Porthallow
Longships
B 3315 (Λ)
Mount's Bay
B 3293
Manacle Point
Lamorna
11 113 △
St. Keverne
Land's End
A 3083
Porthcurno
Gwennap Head
Poldhu Point
Peninsula
Porthgwarra
(Λ) Mullion
Coverack
B 3296
Isles of Scilly (St. Mary's)
Mullion Cove
Black Head
Ruan Minor (Λ)
Kynance Cove
Wolf Rock
Lizard
34
Lizard Pt.

C
D
E

Main map labels

F · G · H

Tintagel Head
Tintagel
308 △
Boscastle
Cornwall Coast
B 3263
Warbstow
Boyton
256 △
N. Petherwin
Werrington
Broadwoodwidger
St. Giles-on-the-Heath
Bratton Clovelly
Thrushel
Sourton
621 △ High Willhays
Delabole
B 3314
B 3263
B 3266
Camelford
47
29
A 39
Davidstow
Laneast
Egloskerry
Yeolmbridge
Castle
A 395
Lifton
Lewdown
15
24
Lydford
Lydford gorge
Lyd
281 △
11
Dartmoor Fo
604 △ Cut Hill
Dartmoor
Port Isaac Bay
Port Gaverne
Port Isaac
Pendoggett
St. Teath
Allen
A 39
Altarnun
A 30
Launceston
S. Petherwin
A 388
Lewannick
Chillaton
N. Brentor
Brent Tor
Mary Tavy
Wistman's Wood
St. Endellion
St. Key
10½
St. Tudy
Michaelstow
St. Breward
Bolventor
Brown Willy
420 △
Bodmin Moor
North Hill
Kilmar Tor
390 △
Lezant
B 3254
B 3257
Milton Abbot
12½
Lamerton
A 384
539 △
Great Mis Tor
debridge
St. Minver
B 3314
St. Mabyn
6½
Pencarrow
A 389
Blisland
34
21
301
De Lank
Dozmary Pool
The Cheesewring
Bray Shop
Stoke Climsland
A 388
Gulworthy
A 384
Tavistock
Whitchurch
B 3357
Two Br
Dartmoor Priso
Princetown
Wenn
St. Breock
Bodmin
Cardinham
Colliford Lake
The Hurlers
Caradon Hill
369 △
Kelly Bray
Callington
A 390
Gunnislake
12
13
Morwellham
Horrabridge
14 3
National
32
St. Neot
St. Cleer
St. Ive
18
St. Dominick
Cotehele House
Calstock
Yelverton
Buckland Abbey
Meavy
Plym
492 △
Lanivet
19
12
A 389
A 308
12 19
A 38
Dobwalls
Liskeard
8½
162 △
St. Mellion
Bere Alston
Bere Ferrers
Plymouth-Roborough Airport
Bickleigh
Cornwoo
Roche
St. Dennis
312 △
Carthew
Lanhydrock
Restormel Castle
21
E. Taphouse
14 6
A 390
B 3359
Menheniot
Landrake
27
17
13
A 38
Pillaton
Landulph
Tamerton Foliot
Plympton
27
17
St. Austell
A 3058
Bugle
Luxulyan
St. Blazey
Par
Lostwithiel
Duloe
Morval
B 3252
B 3251
Widegates
St. Germans
Hessenford
Saltash
Antony House
Torpoint
20
Devonport
PLYMOUTH
Plymstock
Brixton
Dunstone
Ermington
Sticker
Carlyon Bay
Charlestown
St. Austell Bay
Pentewan
Mevagissey
Gribbin Head
Pywardreath
Golant
Fowey
Polruan
Lanreath
Pelynt
Downderry
Crafthole
Antony
Stonehouse
Mt. Edgcumbe
Cawsand
Millbrook
B 324
The Sound
Plymstock
Wembury
Newton Ferrers
Holbeton
Black Head
St. Ewe
Boswinger
Gorran Haven
Veryan Bay
Dodman Point
Mevagissey Bay
Chapel Point
Lansallos
Polperro
Talland-by-Looe
W. Looe
E. Looe
E. Cornwall Coast Path
Whitsand Bay
Rame Head
Wembury Bay
S. Devon
Stoke Point
Bigbury-on-S
Burg
Island
Bigbury Bay
Santander
Roscoff
33

PLYMOUTH inset map

Ferry Rd
B 3396
A 386
A 374
DEVONPORT PARK
Molesworth Rd
Stuart Rd
Fitzroy Rd
Stuart Rd
PLYMOUTH
Clifton Pl.
North Rd East
A 3230
North Hill
Greenbank Rd
Armada Rd
Avenue
Wilton
VICTORIA PARK
North Rd
West
Saltash Rd
North Cross
Cobourg St
North Road
Regent Street
Lipson Rd
A 3236
Z
Park
Fore Street
Devonport
Paradise Place
Mill Bridge
Cecil Street
Approach
Cornwall St.
DRAKE CIRCUS CENTRE
POL
Ebrington
Beaumont Road
Z
King's Road
Clarence Pl.
Stoke Rd
King St.
Royal Parade
Exeter St.
B 3240
Exeter Side
Sutton Rd
A 374
Chapel Street
Duke St.
George St.
James St.
Cumberland Rd
Devonport Hill
High St.
Richmond Walk
A 374
Union Street
Martin St.
Union St.
The Crescent
Lockyer St.
Notte St.
SUTTON HARBOUR
Teats Hill Rd
Richmond Walk
Durnford Street
Caroline Place
Millbay Rd
West Hoe Rd
Citadel Rd
The Barbican
Southside St.
GREAT WESTERN DOCKS
THE HOE
Grand Parade
Hoe Rd
Madeira Rd
ROYAL CITADEL
Smeaton's Tower
The Promenade
THE SOUND
ROSCOFF SANTANDER

400 m
400 yards

PLYMOUTH street index

Armada Way . . . . BZ 2
Cornwall Street . . . . . BZ
Drake Circus Centre . . . . BZ
New George Street . . . BZ 27
Old Town Street . . . . . BZ 32
Royal Parade . . . . BZ

Buckwell Street . . . . . BZ 3
Charles Cross . . . . BZ 6

Charles Street . . . . . . BZ 7
Derry's Cross . . . . . BZ 10
Drake Circus . . . . . . BZ 12
Eastlake Street . . . . BZ 13
Eldad Hill . . . . AZ 15
Great Western Rd . . . AZ 18
Kinterbury Street . . . BZ 21
Mayflower Street . . . BZ 25

Providence Place . . . AZ 34
Quay Road . . . . BZ 35
St. Andrew's Cross . BZ 37
St. Judes Road . . . . BZ 38
S. Sebastian Sq. . . . . BZ 39
Southside Street . . . BZ 40
Stonehouse Bridge . AZ 42
Vauxhall Street . . . . BZ 44

H I J

Ashley
Wembworthy
A 377
Winkleigh
Lapford
DEVON
A 396
Willand
B 3181
B 3211
Iddesleigh
Morchard Bishop
Cheriton Fitzpaine
Bickleigh
A 373
Petrockstowe
B 3220
Cullompton
Black Torrington
Sheepwash
Monkokehampton
Copplestone
Sandford
Bradninch
B 3185
Plymtree
Hatherleigh
B 3216
Exbourne
N. Tawton
A 3072
Bow
Coleford
Thorverton
Silverton
B 3181
Clyst Hydon
A 3176
Jacobstowe
Colebrooke
Killerton
18
Talaton
A 3072
Inwardleigh
Sampford Courtenay (△)
6
Crediton
15
A 30
Whimple
27
Halwill Junction
Northlew
Newton St. Cyres
Stoke Canon
M5
Broadclyst
Folly Gate
Spreyton
Tedburn St. Mary
EXETER
Pinhoe
EXETER AIRPORT
29
Okehampton
Sticklepath
S. Tawton
Cheriton Bishop
28 45
Ide
A 396
Clyst Honiton
Venn Ottery
Bratton Clovelly
Belstone
S. Zeal
Whiddon Down
Spinster's Rock
Drewsteignton
Dunsford
Alphington
A 3052
Clyst St. Mary
15
Newton Poppleford
Bridestowe (△)
Sourton
Throwleigh
Sandypark
Castle Drogo
Fingle Bridge
Kennford
Topsham
Exminster
Woodbury
Bicton garden
Lewdown
15 24
Lydford
281
High Willhays
621 △
Scorhill
Easton
A 382
△ 356
B 3212
B 3193
Lympstone
A La Ronde
Hayes Barton
Withycombe
Lydford gorge
Chagford
Shovel Down
Moretonhampstead
Christow
Kenton
Starcross
Littleham
Chillaton
N. Brentor
Dartmoor Forest
N. Bovey
A 382
Lustleigh
Hennock
△ 250
Exmouth
Milton Abbot
Brent Tor
Mary Tavy
604 △ Cut Hill
Grey Wethers
Manaton
Becka Falls
529
Bovey Tracey
39 24
Chudleigh
Ideford
Dawlish
Lamerton
Dartmoor
435
Postbridge
Haytor Rocks
Ilsington
Bishopsteignton
Teignmouth
A 384
Gulworthy
539 △ Great Mis Tor
Wistman's Wood
Widecombe-in-the-Moor
476 △
B 3387
Kingsteignton
Shaldon
B Combeinteignhead
32
Tavistock (△)
Two Bridges
Buckland-in-the-Moor
Bickington
Newton Abbot
Babbacombe Bay
Whitchurch
B 3357
Dartmoor Prison
Princetown
Dartmeet
River Dart
Ashburton
Abbotskerswell
Maidencombe
Gunnislake
Morwellham
National
Ryder's Hill
Holne
Staverton
Kingskerswell
TORQUAY
Horrabridge
515 △
Buckfast
Ipplepen
Compton
Babbacombe
Calstock
Meavy
Buckfastleigh (△)
Dartington
Cockington
TORBAY
Bere Alston
Yelverton
Buckland Abbey
492 △
Park
S. Brent
A 385
Castle
Berry Pomeroy
Paignton (△)
Bere Ferrers
Bickleigh
PLYMOUTH ROBOROUGH AIRPORT
Cornwood
Totnes
Goodrington
Tamerton Foliot
PLYMOUTH
Plympton
27 17
Ivybridge
Avonwick
Harberton
Ashprington
Stoke Gabriel
Churston Ferrers
Berry Head
Saltash
Diptford
Cornworthy
Dittisham
Brixham
Torpoint
Devonport
A 379
Brixton
Ermington
Ugborough
Harbertonford
Halwell
Blackawton
Kingswear
Stonehouse
Mt. Edgcumbe
Plymstock
Yealmpton
Dunstone
Modbury (△)
B 3207
Dartmouth (△)
Cawsand
Wembury
Newton Ferrers
Holbeton
Aveton Gifford
Goveton
Stoke Fleming (△)
S. Devon Coast Path
Kingston
Bigbury
W. Alvington
Kingsbridge
A 379
Stokenham
Torcross
Burgh Island
Bigbury-on-Sea
Thurlestone
W. Charleton
Chillington
Slapton (△)
Hope
Malborough
S. Pool
Hallsands
Bolt Trail
Salcombe
E. Portlemouth
Start Point
Sharpitor
△ 138
Bolt Head
Prawle Point
Alderney Guernsey Jersey
Santander Roscoff
33

H I J

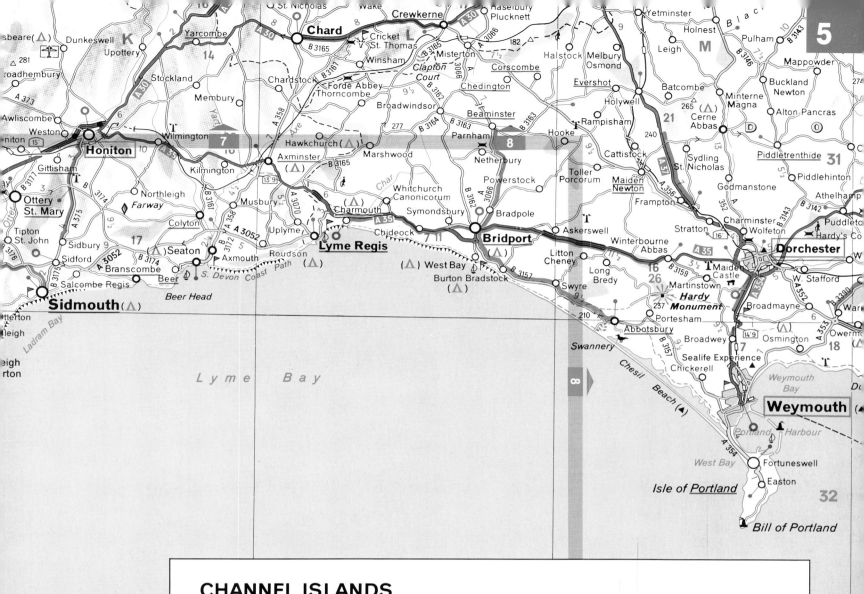

CHANNEL ISLANDS

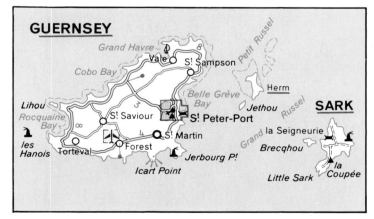

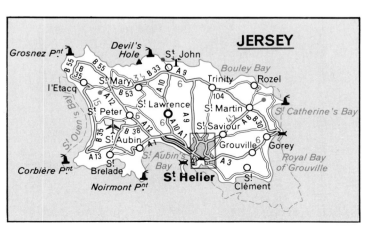

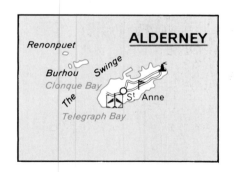

Lundy

(▲) **Ilfracombe** · Berrynarbor · *Heddon's Mouth* · Woody Bay · **Lynton** · Lynmouth

Lee · Combe Martin · Hunter's Inn · *Valley of the Rocks*

Morte Point · Mortehoe · Chambercombe · A 399 · Parracombe · A 39

Woolacombe · B 3343 · W. Down · 262 · 13 · B 3343 · Blackmoor Gate · 480 · **Exmoor** △ 487

Morte Bay · B 3231 · 210 · 15 · A 361 · 13 · 12 · A 39 · Challacombe · B 3358

Baggy Point · Putsborough · Georgeham · Muddiford · Arlington Court · 9 · B 3226

Croyde (▲) · B 3231 · (▲) · Bratton Fleming · Brayford · 493 △

Saunton · Braunton · Punchardon · **Barnstaple** (▲) · E. Buckland

Braunton Burrows · Wrafton · 6 · A 361 · Goodleigh · B 3226 · N. Molton

Barnstaple · Fremington · A 39 · 8 · Bishop's Tawton · W. Buckland · A 361 · 9

or · Appledore · Instow (▲) · Swimbridge · 27 · 43 · S. Mol

Bideford Bay · Westward Ho! · Northam · 69 · Newton Tracey · Chittlehampton · B 3227 · South Mo

Hartland Point · Abbotsham · **Bideford** · Atherington · B 3226

Hartland Quay · Hartland · Clovelly · Fairy Cross · Landcross · Umberleigh · Alswear · Bish Nym

Horn's Cross · Woolfardisworthy · Parkham · Buckland Brewer · High Bickington · Chittlehamholt · A 373

40 25 · 233 △ · △ 216 · St. Giles · King's Nympton

Welcombe · W. Putford · Great Torrington (▲) · Burrington · 40

Cliffs · Morwenstow · Bradworthy (▲) · Stibb Cross · Lit. Torrington · Beaford · Chulmleigh

Kilkhampton · Milton Damerel · Dolton · Ashreigney · Ashley · Eggesford · Chawleigh

Tamar Lake · *Waldon* · Merton · A 377 · Lapford

Poughill (▲) · Shebbear · Petrockstowe · Winkleigh (▲) · Wembworthy

Bude · Stratton · Chilsworthy · Thornbury · Iddesleigh

Launcells 5 · Holsworthy · Bradford · Black Torrington · Sheepwash · Monkokehampton

Marhamchurch · Bridgerule (▲) · A 3072 · Hatherleigh · Bow · Colefor

Widemouth Bay · Clawton · Halwill Junction · Northlew · Inwardleigh · Jacobstow · Sampford Courtenay (▲) · Colebroo

Cambeak Point · Poundstock · Whitstone (▲) · N. Tamerton · Folly Gate · Spreyton

St. Gennys · Week St. Mary · Ashwater (▲) · Okehampton · Sticklepath (▲) · S. Tawton

Crackington Haven · Jacobstow △ 166 · Belstone · S. Zeal · Whiddon Down · Spinster's Rock

Boscastle · Warbstow · St. Giles-on-the-Heath · Bratton Clovelly · Sourton · Throwleigh · Sandypark · Castle Drogo

N. Petherwin · Werrington · Broadwoodwidger · Bridestowe (▲) · High Willhays 621 △ · Scorhill · Easton

Margate (▲)   Cliftonville
B 2051

Westgate-on-Sea   *Foreness Point*
Herne Bay   Reculver   (▲) Birchington   6   Kingsgate
B 2051
itstable (▲)   B 2205   *North Foreland*
16·3   St. Peters   5½
salter   15·6   St. Nicholas-at-Wade   7½   I. of Thanet   **Broadstairs** (▲)
11   A 299   (▲)   Sarre   B 2050
Yorkletts   A 28   A 29I   Chislet   11   Abbey   7   A 253   Minster   253   **Ramsgate** (▲ △)
7   Blean   Sturry   B 2046   Pucks Gutter   A 256   7   B 2048   *Pegwell Bay*
n Street   Fordwich   (△)   5   — *Dunkerque*
Harbledown   7   **CANTERBURY**   Preston   Ash
7   Wingham   A 251   *Sandwich Bay*
42   A 257   Littlebourne   5   Woodnesborough   **Sandwich** (△)
Chartham   24   17   Patrixbourne   B 2046   Eastry   A 258   1
39   Bridge   5½
hilham   Lower Hardres   8   Aylesham   6½   *The Downs*
14   Petham   Barfreston   A 256   Ringwould   B 2057   **Deal** (▲)
Barham   12   Eythorne   Martin Mill   8½   Kingsdown
Stelling   Lydden   Whitfield   A 258
Waltham   Minnis   Lydden   10½   B 2058   St. Margaret's-at-Cliffe   B 2058
177   Circuit   6½   B   B 2058   *St. Margaret's Bay*
B 2068   B 2065   A 260   2060   *South Foreland*
Elham   Temple Ewell   13
bourne Lees   Lyminge   Swingfield   B 2060   8   **DOVER**
Acrise   Alkham   A 256   — *Zeebrugge*
Sellindge   Stanford   Place   Capel le Ferne   — *Oostende*
1   B 2065   A 20
16·3   11   16   12   13
Westenhanger   A 261   The Warren
B 2067   9½   *E. Wear Bay*   **FOLKESTONE**
Lympne   6   Sandgate   (▲ △)
Hythe   10
Marsh
Dymchurch
St. Mary's Bay
21   34
Littlestone-on-Sea
Greatstone-on-Sea
Lydd-on-Sea
Dungeness

Channel Tunnel under construction

STRAIT OF DOVER

CALAIS
Blériot-Plage
Sangatte   D 940   19.5   N 1
Cap Blanc-Nez   Coquelles
(134)   114   90   D 243E
26   Escalles   13   N 1 E 402   10
42   D 246   21   6
Wissant   D 244   D 215
S! Inglevert   9½   D 244   Guînes
Cap Gris-Nez   163   15   D 127
(50)   3.5   D 238   D 127
Audresselles   D 191   D 231   168   D 127
D 191E   Marquise   Rinxent   Hardinghen
Ambleteuse   D 238   D 121E   120   Herbinghe
8   11
Wimereux   13   D 238
N 1   PAS - DE - CALAIS   Colembert
6   233   N 42   160
BOULOGNE   D 940   Belle   D 224
S-MER   S! Martin   N 42   Crémarest
le Portel   la Capelle   D 254   Selle
les Boulogne   12
Pont-de-   19   D 254E
Briques   Wirwignes   Desvres
Equihen-Plage   Ecault   206

DOVER

Bench Street	3	Charlton Green 6
Biggin Street	4	Crabble Hill 7
Cannon Street	5	Eaton Road 10
High Street		Ladywell, Park Street .. 15
King Street	13	London Road 17
Pencester Road		New Bridge 18
		Priory Road 19
Barton Road	2	Priory Street 20
		Sandwich Road 21
		Tower Street 24
		Worthington Street 25

CONNAUGHT PARK
Castle Avenue   Connaught Road
Frith Rd
Bridge St   Park Avenue   PLAYING FIELD
Maison   Godwyne Rd   Leyburne Rd
High St   Dieu   **CASTLE**
Dour   POL.
Pencester Rd   Castle Hill Road
DOVER COLLEGE   PENCESTER GARDENS
PRIORY   York Street
Folkestone Rd   25   13
North Military Rd   DROP REDOUBT   Townwall Street
Snargate St.   Marine Parade
A 20 *HOVERPORT*

STRAIT OF DOVER

30

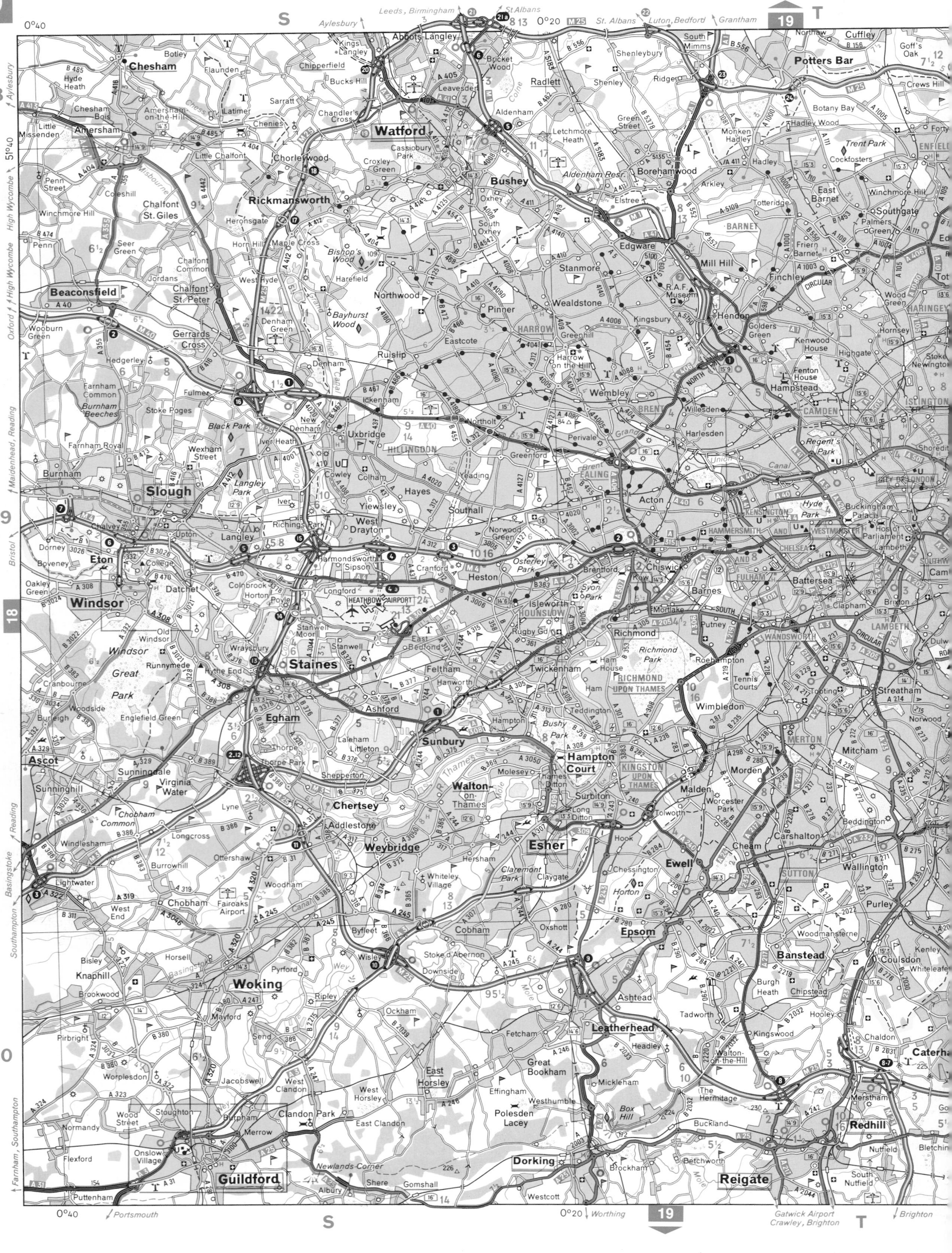

0°40 S Aylesbury 0°20 M25

Aylesbury

28

Chesham
Botley
Flaunden
Kings Langley
Abbots Langley
Chipperfield
Bucket Wood
Shenleybury
Shenley
Ridge
Northaw
Cuffley
Goff's Oak
Potters Bar
Crews Hill

Hyde Heath
Chesham Bois
Amersham-on-the-Hill
Latimer
Sarratt
Chandler's Cross
Leavesden
Radlett
Aldenham
Green Street
Letchmore Heath
Botany Bay
Hadley Wood
Trent Park

51°40
Little Missenden
Amersham
Chenies
Watford
Cassiobury Park
Croxley Green
Borehamwood
Elstree
Monken Hadley
Cockfosters

Penn Street
Coleshill
Chalfont St. Giles
Chorleywood
Rickmansworth
Bushey
South Oxhey
Aldenham Resr.
Arkley
East Barnet
Winchmore Hill
Southgate

Winchmore Hill
Heronsgate
Horn Hill
Maple Cross
Bishop's Wood
Edgware
R.A.F. Museum
BARNET
Friern Barnet
Palmers Green

Beaconsfield
Wooburn Green
Gerrards Cross
Chalfont St. Peter
West Hyde
Harefield
Northwood
Stanmore
Kingsbury
Hendon
Finchley
Golders Green
Highgate
Wood Green
Hornsey

Penn
Seer Green
Jordans
Chalfont Common
Denham Green
Bayhurst Wood
Pinner
Wealdstone
Greenhill
HARROW
Harrow on the Hill
Wembley
Kenwood House
Hampstead
Fenton House
Stoke Newington

Hedgerley
Farnham Common
Burnham Beeches
Denham
Ruislip
Eastcote
Northwood
Willesden
Harlesden
Regent's Park
CAMDEN
ISLINGTON

Burnham
Farnham Royal
Stoke Poges
Black Park
New Denham
Ickenham
Northolt
Perivale
BRENT
EALING
Acton

Slough
Langley Park
Iver
Cowley
Colham
Uxbridge
HILLINGDON
Yeading
Hayes
Southall
Greenford
Union Canal

29
Wexham Street
Iver Heath
West Drayton
Yiewsley
Norwood Green
HAMMERSMITH AND FULHAM
KENSINGTON
Hyde Park
Buckingham Palace
Parliament
WESTMINSTER

Eton
Datchet
Colnbrook
Horton
Longford
Harmondsworth
Sipson
Cranford
Heston
Brentford
Chiswick
Kew
Barnes
Battersea
Clapham
Brixton
LAMBETH

Windsor
Old Windsor
Wraysbury
HEATHROW AIRPORT
Stanwell Moor
Isleworth
HOUNSLOW
Syon Park
Richmond
Mortlake
Putney
WANDSWORTH

18
Windsor Great Park
Runnymede
Englefield Green
Hythe End
Staines
Stanwell
East Bedfont
Feltham
Twickenham
Ham
RICHMOND UPON THAMES
Richmond Park
Roehampton
Tooting
Streatham

Cranbourne
Woodside
Ascot
Sunningdale
Virginia Water
Egham
Thorpe
Thorpe Park
Ashford
Laleham
Littleton
Shepperton
Sunbury
Hampton
Bushy Park
Teddington
Hampton Court
Wimbledon
MERTON
Mitcham

Sunninghill
Chobham Common
Lyne
Longcross
Chertsey
Addlestone
Walton-on-Thames
Molesey
Thames Ditton
Surbiton
KINGSTON UPON THAMES
Malden
Worcester Park
Morden
Carshalton
Wallington

Windlesham
Burrowhill
Ottershaw
Weybridge
Hersham
Claremont Park
Claygate
Long Ditton
Hook
Tolworth
Esher
Cheam
SUTTON
Beddington
Purley

Lightwater
West End
Chobham
Fairoaks Airport
Woodham
Whiteley Village
Downside
Chessington
Horton
Ewell
Epsom
Banstead
Coulsdon
Whiteleafe

Bisley
Knaphill
Horsell
Pyrford
Wisley
Stoke d'Abernon
Cobham
Oxshott
Ashtead
Burgh Heath
Chipstead
Kingswood

Brookwood
Woking
Mayford
Ripley
Ockham
Fetcham
Leatherhead
Headley
Tadworth
Walton-on-the-Hill
Hooley
Chaldon

30
Pirbright
Send
East Horsley
Great Bookham
Mickleham
Box Hill
Kingswood
Caterham

Worplesdon
Stoughton
West Clandon
West Horsley
Effingham
Westhumble
Buckland
Merstham

Normandy
Wood Street
Merrow
Clandon Park
East Clandon
Polesden Lacey
The Hermitage
Betchworth
Nutfield
Redhill

Flexford
Onslow Village
Guildford
Newlands Corner
Shere
Gomshall
Albury
Dorking
Brockham
Reigate
South Nutfield

Key

BRENT   Borough
●——   Underground Station

Index to Greater London Boroughs

Barking and Dagenham	21 U 29	
Barnet	20 T 29	
Bexley	21 U 29	
Brent	20 T 29	
Bromley	21 U 29	
Camden	20 T 29	
City of London	20 T 29	
Croydon	20 T 29	
Ealing	20 T 29	
Enfield	20 T 29	
Greenwich	21 U 29	
Hackney	21 T 29	
Hammersmith and Fulham	20 T 29	
Haringey	20 T 29	
Harrow	20 S 29	
Havering	21 U 29	
Hillingdon	20 S 29	
Hounslow	20 S 29	
Islington	20 T 29	
Kensington and Chelsea	20 T 29	
Kingston-upon-Thames	20 T 29	
Lambeth	20 T 29	
Lewisham	21 T 29	
Merton	20 T 29	
Newham	21 U 29	
Redbridge	21 U 29	
Richmond-upon-Thames	20 T 29	
Southwark	20 T 29	
Sutton	20 T 29	
Tower Hamlets	21 T 29	
Waltham Forest	21 T 29	
Wandsworth	20 T 29	
Westminster	20 T 29	

GREATER LONDON

1/200 000

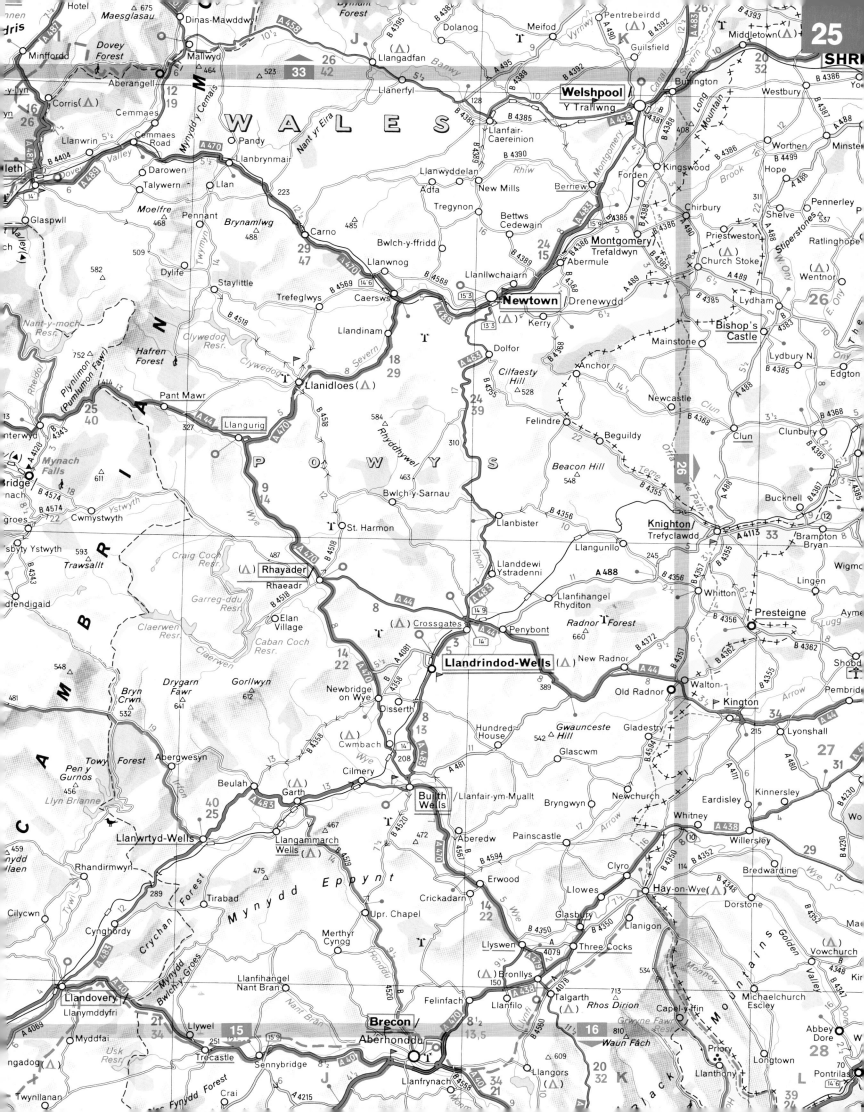

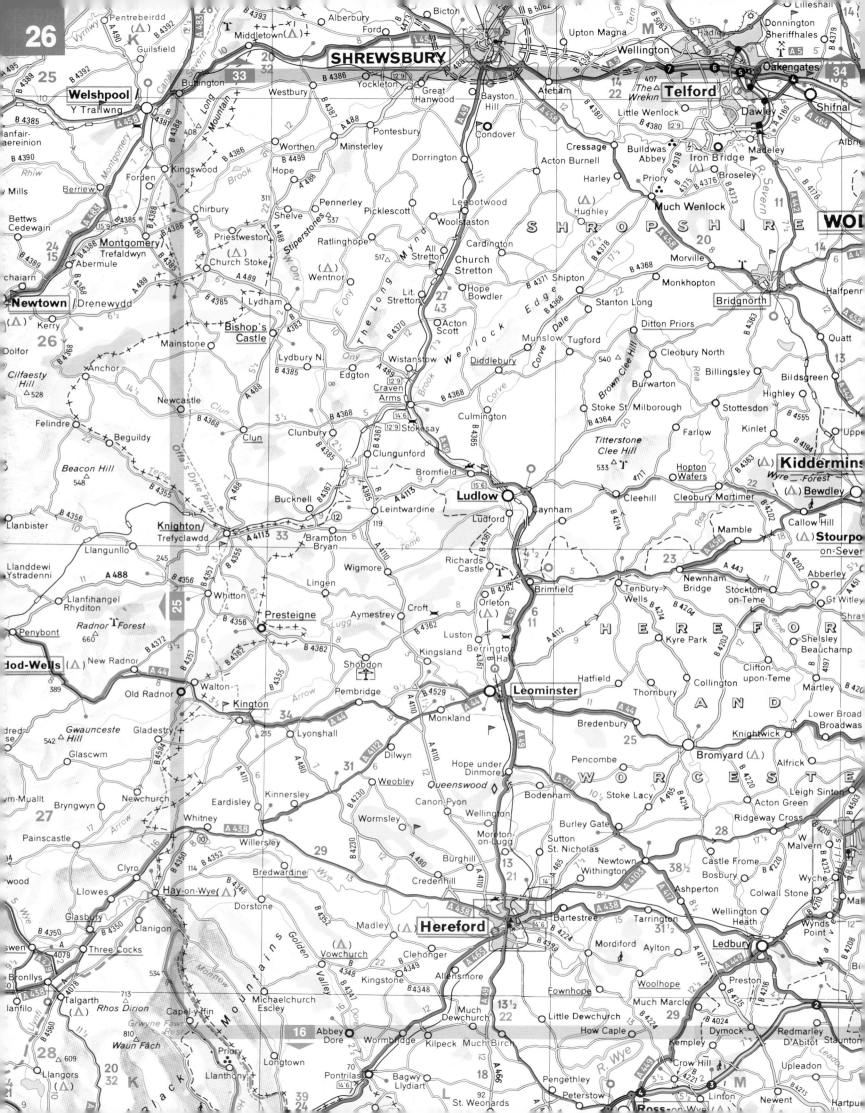

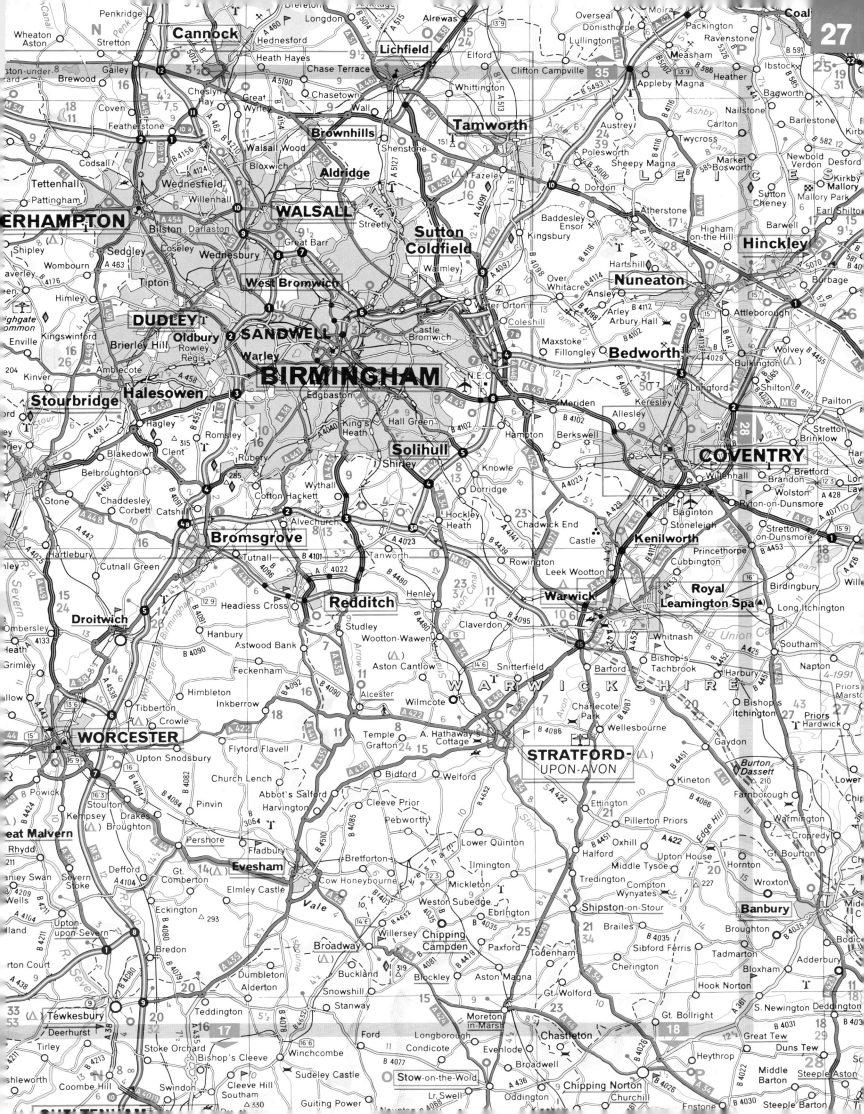

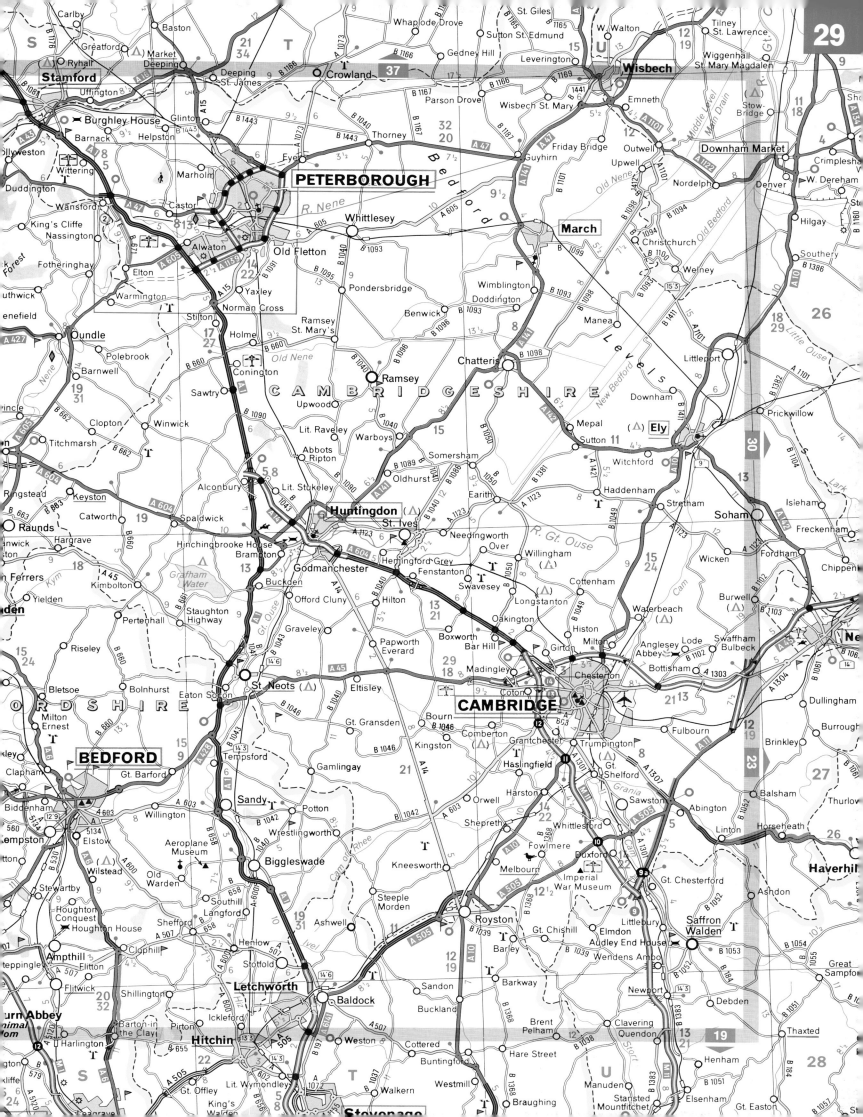

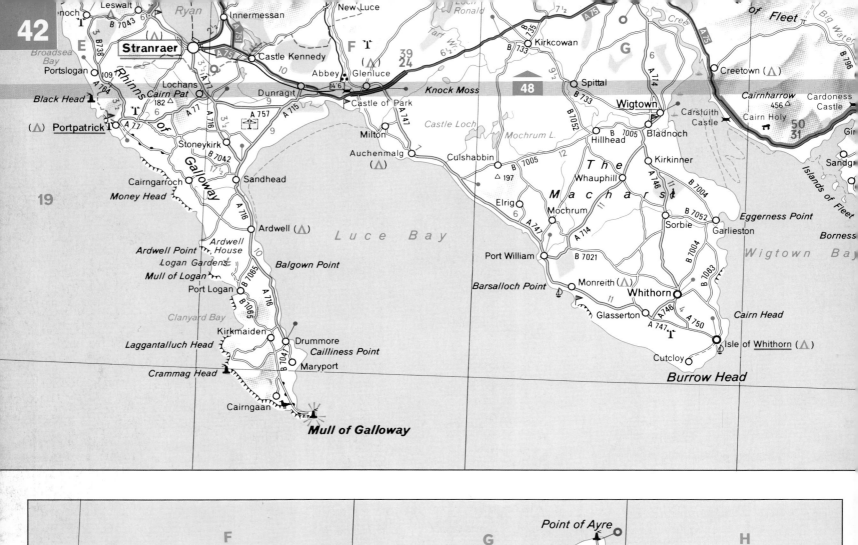

Ryan
Leswalt
noch
New Luce
of Fleet
Innermessan
B 7043
B738
E
Stranraer
Kirkcowan
Castle Kennedy
B 733
Creetown (Λ)
Broadsea
Bay
A75
Portslogan
Lochans
Abbey
Glenluce
39
24
Knock Moss
48
Spittal
A714
Cairn Pat
B 733
Wigtown
50
31
Black Head
Dunragit
Castle of Park
B 1052
Carsluith
Castle
Cairnharrow
Cardoness
Castle
(Λ) Portpatrick
A77
Milton
Castle Loch
B 7005
Hillhead
Bladnoch
Cairn Holy
Islands of Fleet
Stoneykirk
B 7042
Culshabbin
Mochrum L.
Kirkinner
A746
B 7004
Money Head
Cairngarroch
Sandhead
197
Whauphill
The
B 7052
Galloway
A716
Elrig
Machars
Eggerness Point
Luce Bay
Mochrum
A 747
Sorbie
Garlieston
Borness
Ardwell (Λ)
B 7021
Wigtown Bay
Ardwell
House
Port William
B 7004
Ardwell Point
Balgown Point
B 1063
Logan Gardens
Monreith (Λ)
Mull of Logan
Barsalloch Point
Whithorn
Port Logan
B 1065
A716
Glasserton
A 747
Cairn Head
Clanyard Bay
Kirkmaiden
A 750
Drummore
Laggantalluch Head
Caillness Point
Isle of Whithorn (Λ)
Crammag Head
Maryport
Cutcloy
Burrow Head
Cairngaan
Mull of Galloway

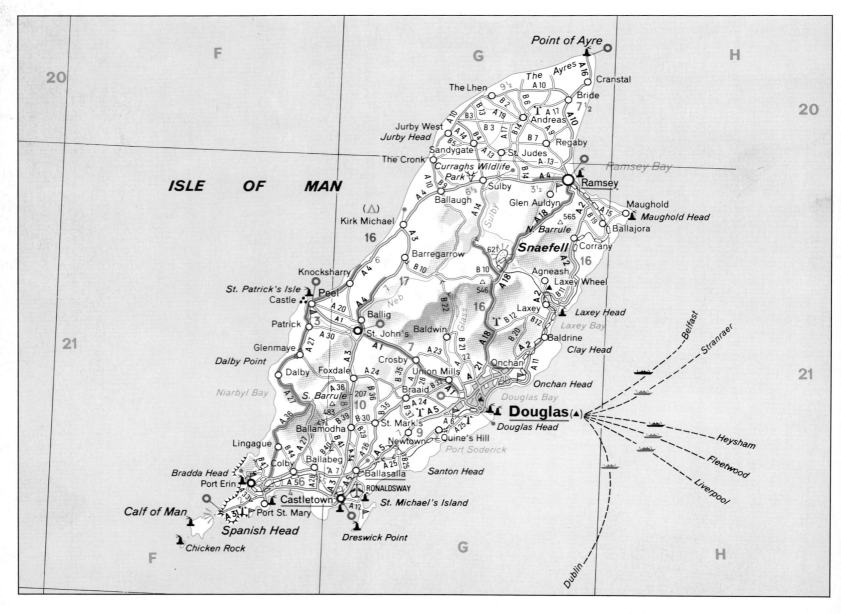

F
G
H
Point of Ayre
20
20
The Ayres
A16
The Lhen
A 10
Cranstal
ISLE OF MAN
B 13
B6
Bride
7½
Jurby West
A 19
A 17
Andreas
A 10
Jurby Head
B 14
Regaby
Sandygate
A 13
St. Judes
B 14
Ramsey
Ramsey Bay
The Cronk
Curraghs Wildlife
Park
A4
B9
Sulby
Maughold
Maughold Head
Kirk Michael (Λ)
A4
Ballaugh
A14
Glen Auldyn
N. Barrule
Ballajora
16
A18
565
B19
A15
Barregarrow
A3
621
Snaefell
Corrany
16
Knocksharry
B 10
Agneash
A18
Laxey Wheel
17
Peel
A4
546
Laxey
St. Patrick's Isle
Ballig
Baldwin
A2
Laxey Head
Castle
A 20
A1
B 12
Laxey Bay
Patrick
3
St. John's
A 18
B20
Baldrine
Glenmaye
A 27
A 30
Crosby
A 23
Clay Head
Dalby Point
A1
7
Union Mills
Onchan
Dalby
Foxdale
A 24
Braaid
A11
Niarbyl Bay
A 36
S. Barrule
207
Onchan Head
10
483
B 39
St. Mark's
Douglas
Ballamodha
9
Douglas Head
Lingague
A 27
Newtown
Quine's Hill
Belfast
Colby
Ballabeg
Santon Head
Port Soderick
Stranraer
Bradda Head
Ballasalla
21
Port Erin
A 56
RONALDSWAY
St. Michael's Island
21
Calf of Man
Castletown
Heysham
Port St. Mary
A 12
Fleetwood
Spanish Head
Dreswick Point
Liverpool
Chicken Rock
F
G
H
Dublin

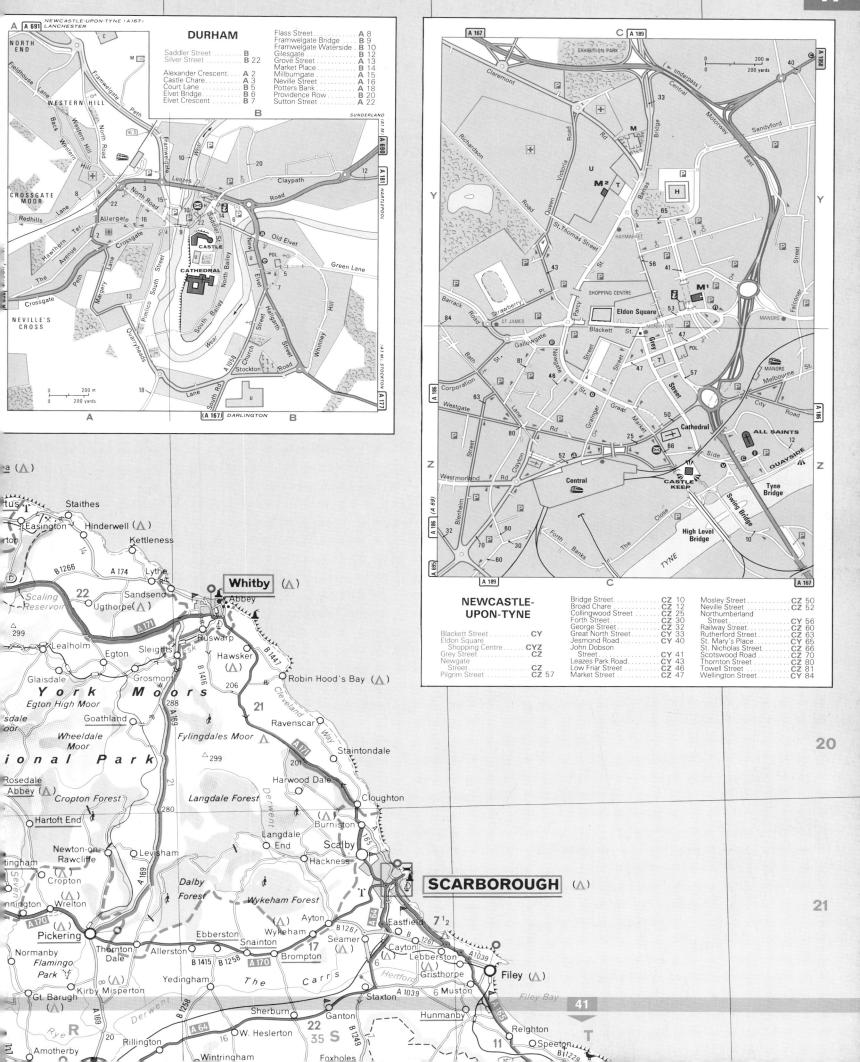

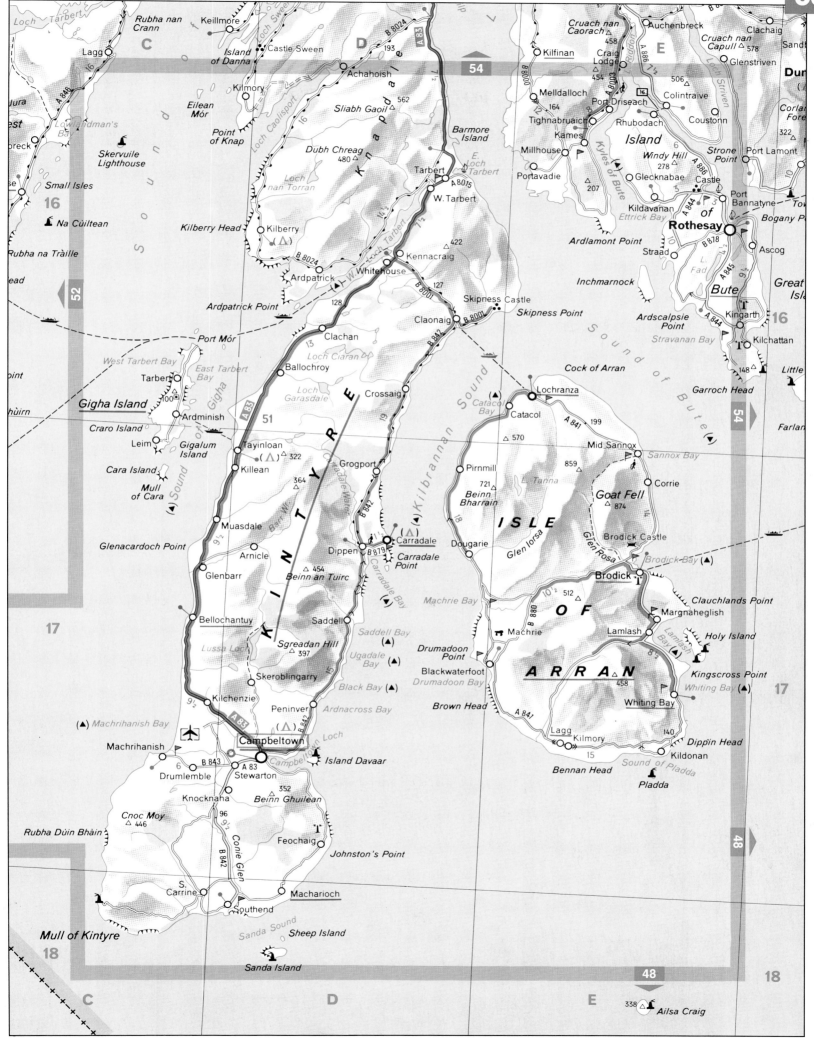

Loch Tarbert

Rubha nan Crann

Keillmore

Island of Danna

Castle Sween

B 8024

193

A 83

54

Cruach nan Caorach 458

Auchenbreck

Cruach nan Capull 578

Clachaig

Sandb

Lagg

C

Kilmory

Achahoish

Kilfinan

Craig Lodge 454

Glenstriven

Corlar Fore

Dun

Jura

Eilean Mór

Sliabh Gaoil 562

Melldalloch 164

Port Driseach

Colintraive

506

Lowlandman's Bay

Point of Knap

Barmore Island

Tighnabruaich

Kames

Rhubodach

Coustonn

322

reck

Skervuile Lighthouse

Dubh Chreag 480

Knapdale

E. Loch Tarbert

Millhouse

Portavadie

Island

Windy Hill 278

Strone Point

Port Lamont

16

Small Isles

Loch nan Torran

Tarbert

422

Glecknabae

207

Castle

Port Bannatyne

Tow

Na Cùiltean

W. Tarbert

A 8015

Ardlamont Point

Kildavanan

Ettrick Bay

of

Bogany P

Rubha na Tràille

Kilberry Head

Kilberry

(Λ)

Kennacraig

Straad

Rothesay

Ascog

52

Ardpatrick

Whitehouse

127

Inchmarnock

Bute

Great Isle

ead

B 8024

128

B 8001

Skipness Castle

Ardscalpsie Point

Kingarth

16

Ardpatrick Point

Claonaig

B 8001

Skipness Point

Stravanan Bay

A 844

Kilchattan

Port Mór

Clachan

13

B 842

Cock of Arran

Garroch Head

148

Little

West Tarbert Bay

East Tarbert Bay

Loch Ciaran

Ballochroy

Catacol Bay

Lochranza

Sound of Bute

point

Tarbert

100

Loch Garasdale

K

Crossaig

(Λ)

Catacol

A 841 199

54

Gigha Island

51

I

570

Mid Sannox

Sannox Bay

Craro Island

Ardminish

N

T

Grogport

Kilbrannan Sound

Pirnmill

859

Corrie

Farlan

hùirn

Leim

Gigalum Island

Tayinloan

(Λ) 322

364

Y

B 842

721

Beinn Bharrain

L. Tanna

Goat Fell 874

Cara Island

Killean

R

Carradale

Mull of Cara

Muasdale

454

Dippen

B 879

Carradale Point

Dougarie

Glen Iorsa

ISLE

Brodick Castle

Glen Rosa

Glenacardoch Point

Arnicle

E

Beinn an Tuirc

Carradale Bay

OF

Brodick

Brodick Bay (Λ)

17

Glenbarr

Saddell

Machrie Bay

512

Clauchlands Point

Bellochantuy

Barr Water

Saddell Bay

(Λ)

880

10½

Margnaheglish

Lussa Loch

Sgreadan Hill 397

Ugadale Bay

(Λ)

Drumadoon Point

Machrie

Lamlash

Holy Island

ARRAN

Skeroblingarry

Black Bay (Λ)

Blackwaterfoot

Drumadoon Bay

458

Kingscross Point

Kilchenzie

Peninver

(Λ)

B 842

Ardnacross Bay

Whiting Bay (Λ)

17

(Λ) Machrihanish Bay

A 83

Whiting Bay

Campbeltown

Brown Head

A 841

Machrihanish

B 843

A 83

Island Davaar

Lagg

140

Dippin Head

Drumlemble

Stewarton

352

Kilmory

15

Kildonan

Knocknaha

Beinn Ghuilean

Bennan Head

Sound of Pladda

Cnoc Moy 446

96

Pladda

Rubha Dùin Bhàin

Conie Glen

Feochaig

B 842

Johnston's Point

48

S. Carrine

Macharioch

Southend

Mull of Kintyre

18

Sanda Sound

Sheep Island

Sanda Island

48

18

C

D

E

338

Ailsa Craig

15

r Brigs

e Ness

Isle of May

16

tle

ne
uth

Dunbar (△)

A 1 13

Barns Ness

9

Spott

Thorntonloch

Innerwick

Cockburnspath

Pease Bay

Oldhamstocks

397

Fast Castle

St. Abb's Head

H i l l s

391

245

206

Heart Law

A 1167

B 6438

St. Abbs

Grantshouse

11

234

32 52

Coldingham (△)

B 6438

A 1107

B 6355

Eye Wr.

15½

A 1

Eyemouth (△)

hiteadder
Resr.

Cranshaws

6

Auchencrow

Reston

8

Burnmouth

m m e r m u i r

B 6438

Ayton

B 6355

8

B 6355

Preston

Chirnside

B 6355

398

B 6365

5½

Longformacus

A 6112

6½

Foulden

8½

Whiteadder Wr.

A 6105

A 6105

Manderston

Allanton

A 6105

Paxton

Berwick-upon-Tweed (▲△)

Duns

B 6437

Hutton

B 6461

B 6460

Tweedmouth

Spittal

235

B 6456

A 6105

6

B 6460

Whitsome

11½

7½

16

A 698

B 6461

Polwarth

7

A 6112

B 6461

Horncliffe

B 6354

229

Blackadder Wr.

Ladykirk Castle

A 1

Cheswick

26

Swinton

B 6470

Norham

15

Ancroft

Goswick

Road submerged at high tide
Chaussée submersible

Greenlaw
(△)

A 697

Leitholm

M e r s e

B 6461

6

B 6431

Beal

Holy Island

Gordon

B 6364

5

R. Tweed

Holy Island

Hume
Castle

B 6461

Duddo

B 6525

Holy
Island Sands

Coldstream

51

lerstain

Stichill

Eccles

Birgham

Cornhill-
on-Tweed

Etal

B 6353

Lowick

Fenwick

Ross

Farne Islands (▲)

Ednam

9

Wark

Crookham

Ford

143

126

B 6352

17

M

A 6089

Sprouston

N

O

Belford

Bamburgh
Castle

P

Floors
Castle

Kelso

B 6397

B 6396

20

Till

147

Milfield

5½

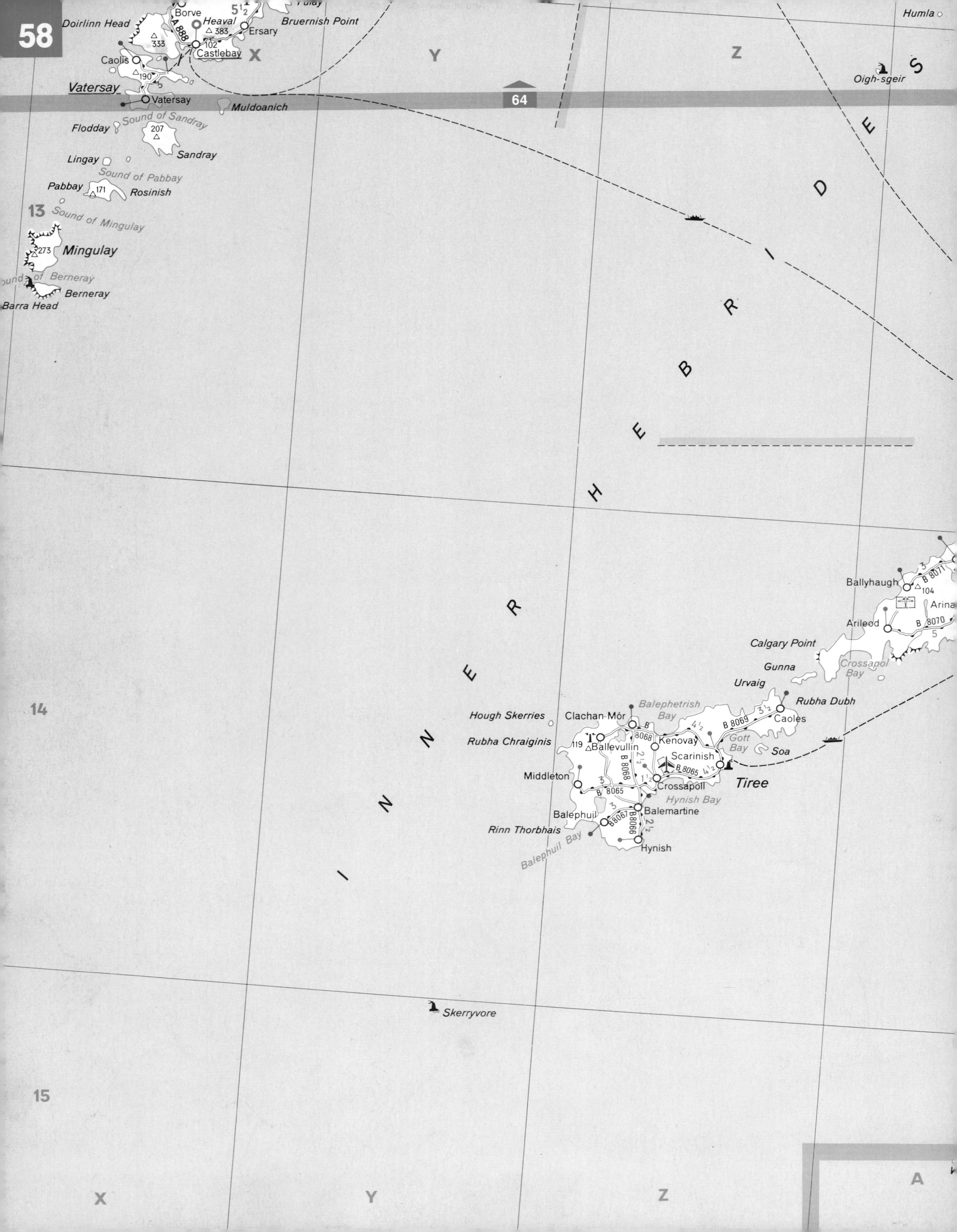

Humla

Doirlinn Head
Borve
Heaval
△ 383
Bruernish Point
△ 8888
△ 333
102
Ersary
Caolis
Castlebay
X
Y
Z
Oigh-sgeir
△ 190

Vatersay
a
Vatersay
Muldoanich
64

H
E
B
R
I
D
E
S

Flodday
Sound of Sandray
207
△

Lingay
Sandray

Sound of Pabbay

Pabbay △ 171
Rosinish

13
Sound of Mingulay

Sound of Berneray
△ 273
Mingulay

Berneray

Barra Head

14

I
N
N
E
R

H
E
B
R
I
D
E
S

Ballyhaugh
3
B 8071

△ 104

Arina

Arileod
B 8070

5

Calgary Point

Gunna

Crossapol
Bay

Urvaig

Rubha Dubh

Hough Skerries
Clachan Mór
Balephetrish
Bay

Caoles

Rubha Chraiginis
B 8068
3½
B 8069

119
Ballevullin
Kenovay
Gott
Bay
Soa

Scarinish
2½

Middleton
B 8068
1
B 8065
4½

3
Crossapoll
Tiree

B 8065
Hynish Bay

Balephuil
3
Balemartine

Rinn Thorbhais
B 8067 B 8066
2½

Hynish

Balephuil Bay

15

Skerryvore

X
Y
Z
A

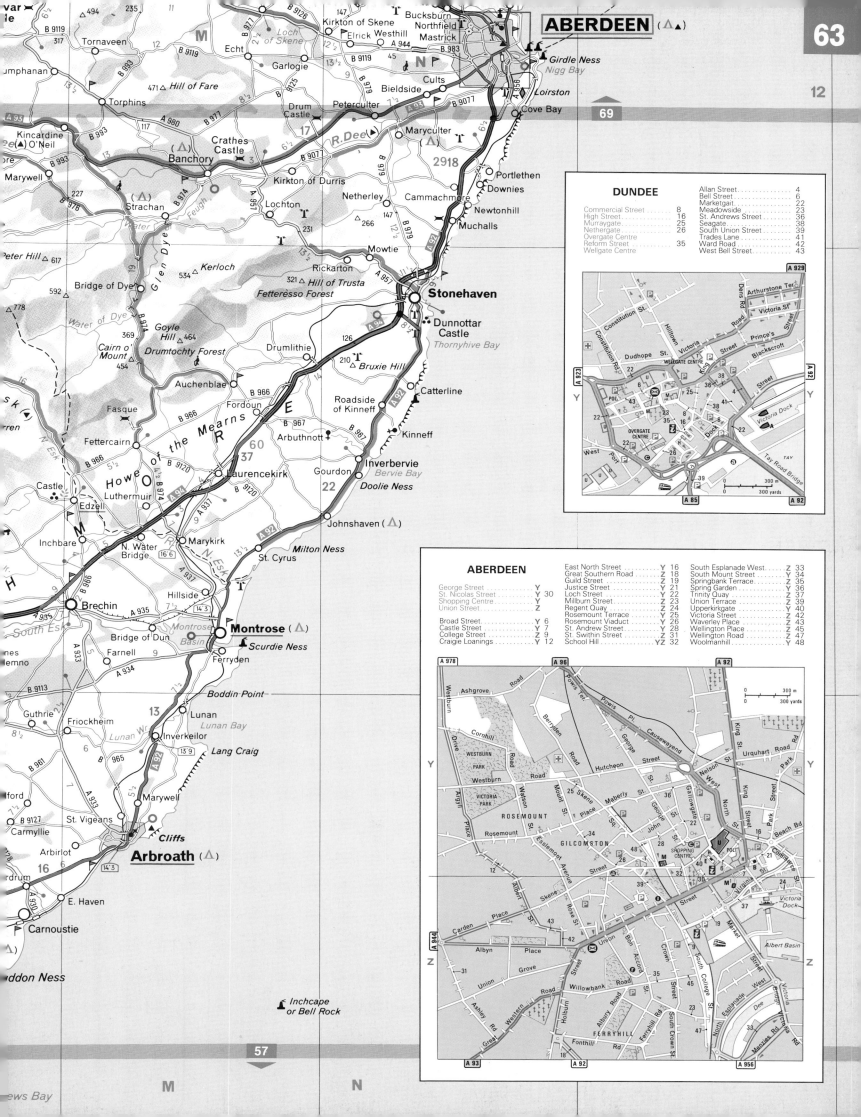

12

DUNDEE

Commercial Street	8	
High Street	16	
Murraygate	25	
Nethergate	26	
Overgate Centre		
Reform Street	35	
Wellgate Centre		

Allan Street	4	
Bell Street	6	
Marketgait	22	
Meadowside	23	
St. Andrews Street	36	
Seagate	38	
South Union Street	39	
Trades Lane	41	
Ward Road	42	
West Bell Street	43	

ABERDEEN

George Street	Y	30
St. Nicolas Street	Y	
Shopping Centre	Y	
Union Street	Z	
Broad Street	Y	6
Castle Street	Y	7
College Street	Z	9
Craigie Loanings	Y	12

East North Street	Y	16
Great Southern Road	Z	18
Guild Street	Z	19
Justice Street	Y	21
Loch Street	Y	22
Millburn Street	Z	23
Regent Quay	Y	24
Rosemount Terrace	Y	25
Rosemount Viaduct	Y	26
St. Andrew Street	Y	28
St. Swithin Street	Z	31
School Hill	YZ	32

South Esplanade West	Z	33
South Mount Street	Y	34
Springbank Terrace	Z	35
Spring Garden	Y	36
Trinity Quay	Z	37
Union Terrace	Y	39
Upperkirkgate	Y	40
Victoria Street	Z	42
Waverley Place	Z	43
Wellington Place	Z	45
Wellington Road	Z	47
Woolmanhill	Y	48

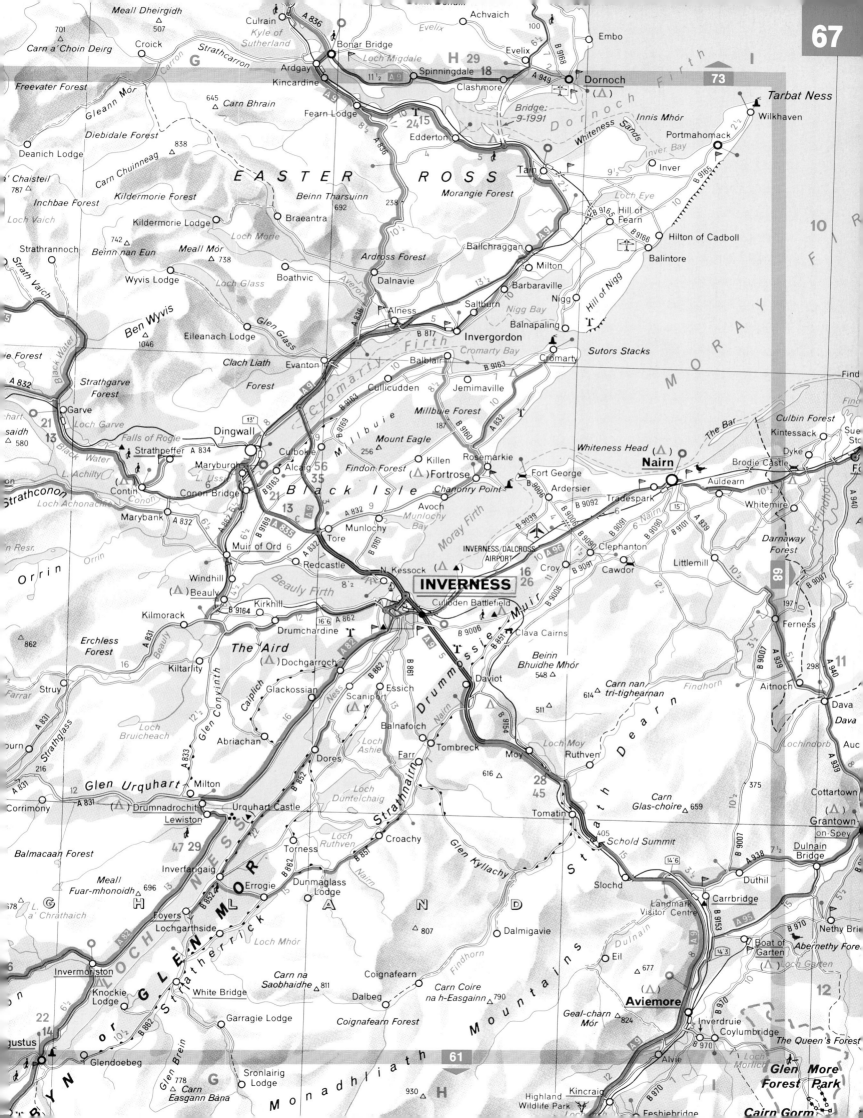

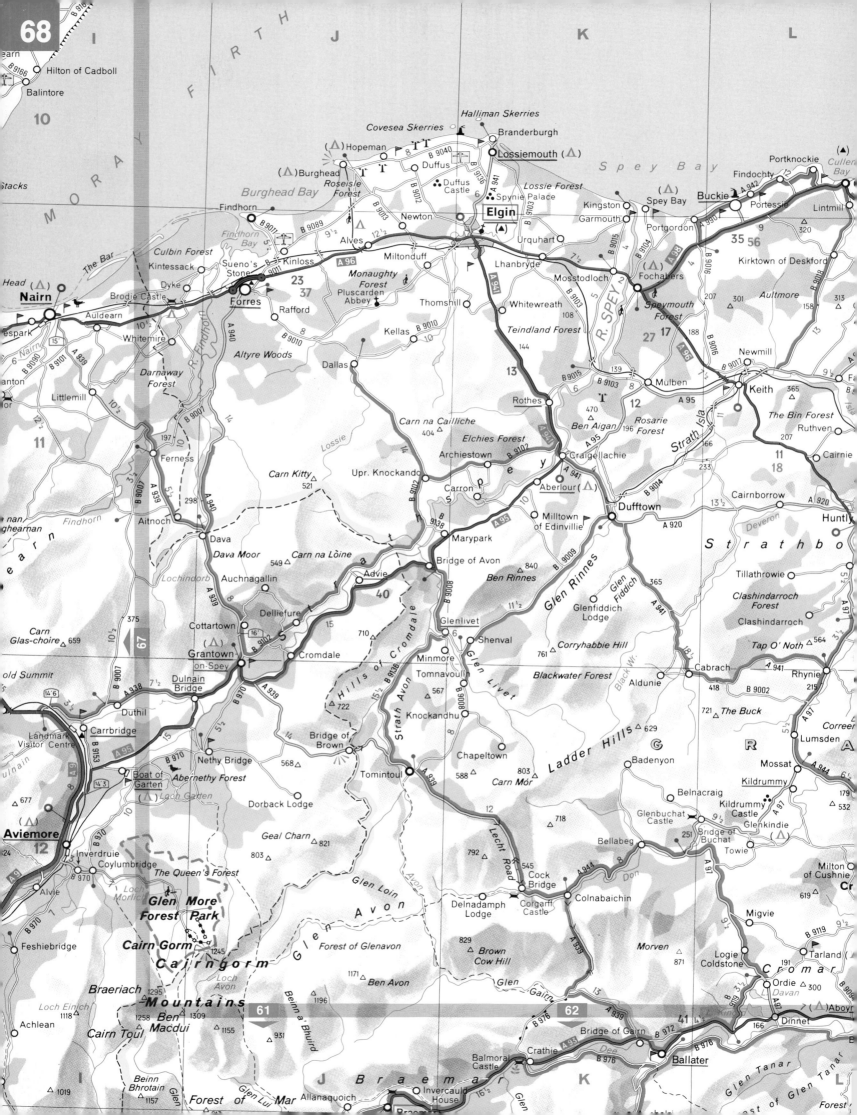

Butt of Lewis

B

Port of Ness

Skigersta

Cross

Ness

Cellar Head

Tolsta

Tolsta Head

C

T H E   M I N C H

D

Balchrick

E

Eilean an Ròin Mór

Kinloc

8

Ardmore Point

Fanagmore

△ 123

Handa Island

(△)

Scourie

Upr. Badcall

34

Portnaguran

Tiumpan Head

A 866

Garrabost

Bayble

Eye Peninsula

hicken Head

ay

Point of Stoer

72

Eddrachillis

Bay

Meall Mór

Calbha Beag

Calbha

Culkein

Eilean
Chrona

Drumbeg

Loch Chàir

Clashnessie

33½

Loch Poll

Stoer

Clachtoll

L. Cròcach

B 869

Lochass

12½

Achmelvich

19

A 837

Baddidarach

Inver Valley (▲)

Lo

Soyea Island

L. Inver

Lochinver

9

Glencanisp Forest

A' Chleit

Kirkaig
Point

Inverkirkaig

731 △

Suilven

Rubha Còigeach

Eilean Mór

11½

Fionn L.

L. Veyatie

Rubha Mór

Enard Bay

Loch Sionascaig

849 △

Reiff

Brae of Achnahaird

6

Badnagyle

Stac Pollaidh

Cul Mór

Eilean
Mullagrach

Altandhu

L.
Osgaig

613 △

Linneraineach

769 △

Cul Beag

Isle Ristol

Polbain

L. Bad a' Ghaill

Glas-leac Mór

Tanera
Mór

Achiltibuie

Loch Lurgainn

8

Tanera Beg

Badenscallie

Drumrunie

Summer Is.

Horse I.

Culnacraig

Ben Mór Coigach

125

Eilean Dubh

Achduart

△ 743

Coigach

Priest Island

Strathkanaird

Bottle I.

Càrn nan Sgeir

I. Martin

Strath Kanaird

10

Greenstone Point

Cailleach Head

Loch

Opinan

Rubha Beag

Scoraig

Annat Bay

Ardmair

Mellon Udrigle

Stattic Point

Badluarach

Beinn Ghòbhlach

Gob a' Gheodha

Gruinard
Island

Mungasdale

△ 635

Allt na h-Airbhe

Ullapool

Achgarve

Mellon
Charles

Laide

Coast

A 832

Badcaul

Badrallach

A 835

Blarnalearoch

Le

Rubha Réidh

Eilean Furadh Mór

Cove

Camusnagaul

(▲)

An Cuaidh

△ 296

B 8057

Aultbea

L. a' Bhaid-
Luachraich

△ 767

Dundonnell

Letters

Melvaig

I. of Ewe

B 8021

Inverasdale

Midtown

9

L. Fada

66

An Teallach

10

Loch Ewe

Inverewe Gardens

Tournaig

Fisherfield Forest

Loch na Sealga

△ 1062

29

Dundonnell Forest

B

N. Erradale

C

Poolewe

6

D

Fionn Loch

△ 908

E

Auchindrea

Falls of Meas

Gruinard
Bay

(▲)

D   E   F   G

Cape Wrath
163

Faraid Head

Inshore
The Parbh   457   Achiemore   **Durness** (△)   *Whiten Head*
Fashven   Leirinmore   Eilean Hoan
Am Balg   Kyle of   Keoldale   Ben Hutig △   408
Durness   W. Strathan
Sandwood   A 838   422   Meall Meadhonach   A 838   Talm
Loch   485   A' Mhòine   177
Balchrick   *Creag Riabhach*   13   Laid   31   Hope   212   A 838   10
Oldshoremore   *Dìonard*   Achuvoldrach
Eilean an Ròin Mór   Gualin House   *Cranstackie*   Eilean   21   Eriboll
Kinlochbervie   B 801   Achriesgill   800   Choraidh   Loch Hope   Kinloch Lodge
472   180   20   Polla   521
Ardmore Point   Rhiconich   *Foinaven*   908   *Ben Hope*   927
Fanagmore   Strath Dìonard   Strath More   Loch an Dherue
Foindle   5   757   465   Alltnacaillich
Handa Island   123   7   Laxford Bridge   *Arkle*   Allnabad
(△)   A 894   A 838   Lochstack Lodge   *Sàbhal Beag*   21   Loch Meadie   40
Scourie   Ben Stack   729 △
Upr. Badcall   *Loch Stack*   721   *Reay Forest*   801
Eddrachillis   34   Achfary   Loch an   Merkland   873   Altnaharra
Bay   *Meall Mór*   Leathaid Bhuain   Loch More   Ben Hee
Calbha Beag   Calbha Mór   Kylestrome   Loch Glendhu   144   Kinloch   36
Culkein   Oldany Island   *Loch a'*   Unapool   792   Merkland   473
Eilean   *Chàirn-Bhàin*   Loch Glencoul   Lodge   Strath Vagas
Chrona   33½   B 869   *Quinag*   20½   Loch   266   Crask Inn
Clashnessie   *Loch Poll*   808   A 894   261   Merkland   Loch Fiag   A 836
Stoer   Lochassynt Lodge   776   Gorm Loch Mór   Glen Flag   200
Clachtoll   B 869   Inver Valley (▲)   −80   Overscaig   19½
Achmelvich   12½   Loch Assynt   Ardvreck Castle   39   Strath
19   A 837   Fionn Loch Mór   998   Tirry
Baddidarach   731   Inchnadamph   Ben More Assynt   Loch Shin
Soyea Island   846   Stronchrubie   162   Duchally   Arscaig   Shinness
A' Chleit   Kirkaig   **Lochinver**   *Glencanisp Forest*   Canisp   ⁹   715   800   Beinn Sgeireach   476   Col
Rubha Còigeach   Point   Inverkirkaig   *Suilven*   △   △   Benmore   Sallachy
Enard Bay   11½   Cam L.   Lodge   Glen Cassley   Cnoc a' Choire
Rubha Mór   Fionn L.   849   A 837   Claonel
Reiff   Loch Sionascaig   Ledmore   L. Ailsh   402
Eilean   Brae of Achnahaird   L. Veyatie   Cul Mór   Altnacealgach   Glen Oykel   Invercassley   A 839   27
Mullagrach   Altandhu   6   613 △   Elphin   Loch Urigill   176   19   Lubcroy   Altass   31   A 837
Isle Ristol   Osgaig   Linneraineach   A 835   Oykel   Doune
Glas-leac Mór   Polbain   L. Bad a' Ghaill   769   Cul Beag   516   Meall an Fhuarain   Oykel Bridge   Strath Oykel   Achnahanat
Tanera   **Achiltibuie**   Loch Lurgainn   8   578   Glen Einig
Mór   Badenscallie   Stac Pollaidh   8½   Drumrunie   18   Cromalt Hills   *Rhidorroch Forest*   701   Meall Dheirgidh   Culrain
Summer Is.   Horse I.   Ben Mór Coigach   125   Rappach   Carn a' Choin Deirg   507   Croick   Strathcarron
Eilean Dubh   Achduart   *Coigach*   Strathkanaird   E. Rhidorroch   Kyle of
Bottle I.   Càrn nan Sgeir   I. Martin   Strath Kanaird   Lodge   Sutherland
Cailleach Head   A 835   10   *Glen Achall*
Rubha Beag   *Annat Bay*   Loch Achall   △
Stattic Point   Ardmair   Rhidorroch   Carron
(▲) *Gruinard*   Scoraig   Beinn Ghobhlach   **Ullapool**   66   Lodge   L-an Daimh   Glen Achall
Bay   Badluarach   635 △   Allt na h-Airbhe   Glen Achall
Mungasdale   Badrallach   A 835   *Strath Mulzie*
Coast   D   Badcaul   E   Blarnalearoch   F   G
A 832   Camusnagaul   Leckmelm

ORKNEY ISLANDS

Hoy

360
B 9047
Lyness
Fara
Scapa
Call of Flotta
Flotta
Water Sound
Burray
Causeway
St. Margaret's Hope
B 4043
Grim Ness
Herston
B 9042
Bow
Switha
Sound of Hoxa
B 9044
Wateringhouse
Hurliness
Cantick Head
118
South
Ronaldsay
Tor Ness
South Walls
Cleat
Burwick
Swona
Old Head
B 9041
Brough Ness

P e n t l a n d   F i r t h

Stromness

Langaton Point
Island of Stroma
Nethertown
Pentland Skerries
Uppertown
51

Dunnet Head
St. John's Point

Holborn Head
Thurso Bay
Scarfskerry
Brough
St. John's Loch
20
A 836
Mey
Gills
11½
Duncansby Head
John o' Groats (△)
Dunnet Bay
(▲)
A 836
Dunnet
Barrock
Canisbay
124
Skirza
Skirza Head
Thurso (△)
Castletown
B 876
Loch Heilen
13½
Freswick
Freswick Bay
A 836
5½
141
B 876
7½
Slickly
A 9
6
A 882
B 874
Roadside
B 874
Bower
Lyth
Sortat
Auckengill
Halkirk
(△)
Myrelandhorn
Keiss
8½
17
B 874
B 876
8
L. Scarmclate
Olgrinmore
Banniskirk
Loch Watten
A 882
B 870
Reiss
Sinclair's Bay
A 9
Spittal
5½
Watten
B 870
Reiss
B 874
Noss Head
A 395
Mybster
B 870
Bilbster
Wick
8
Girnigoe and Sinclair Castles
Staxigoe
21
34
Wick
(△)
North Head
Badlipster
South Head
Tannach
13
A 9
Grey Cairns of Camster
Thrumster
Loch Hempriggs
44
Achavanich
212
Sarclet
211
Ulbster
A 395
287
60
37
Hill o' Many Stanes
Houstry
Lybster
W. Clyth
4½
Latheron
Forse
Janetstown
A 9
Dunbeath (△)
20
73
Børgue
Berriedale

J
K
L

Inset map

4°20
3°

J
K
L

5
Sule Skerry
Mull Head
59°
Stack Skerry
Bow Head
Papa Westra
Noup Head
Pierowall
3°20
Westray
169
B 9066
The No Sound
Midbea
Rapness
Galfsound
3 3°20

6
Rousay
Wasbister
Egilsay
101
(▲) Brough of Birsay
250
Wyre
Eday
Brough Head
Birsay
B 9064
Brinyan
Stronsay
Twatt
Gurness Broch
Gairsay
Kitchener Memorial
Georth
B 9057
B 9058
Dounby
221
Skara Brae
L. of Harray
Balfour
Sandgarth
Yesnaby
Maes Howe
Finstown
A 965
Rennibister
Shapir
59°
Ring of Brodgar
Stenness
Wideford Hill Cairn
Kirkwall
Mainland
268
A 960
(△) Stromness
A 964
Graemsay
Orphir
St. Mary's
Old Man of Hoy
Monéss
479
Cava
Lamb Holm
Rose Ne
Rora Head
Rackwick
Fara
Causeway
Burray
Hoy
Lyness
Flotta
Causeway
B 9047
St. Margaret's Hope
7
Aberdeen
Tor Ness
South Walls
A 961
118
South Rona
Burwick
Old Head
P e n t l a n d   F i r t h
Dunnet Head
Stroma
Pentland Skerr
58°40
Scarfskerry
Scrabster
B 855
Gills
Duncansby Head
(△) Dunnet
A 836
John o' Groats (△)
Thurso
Castletown
5½
A 9

J
K
L

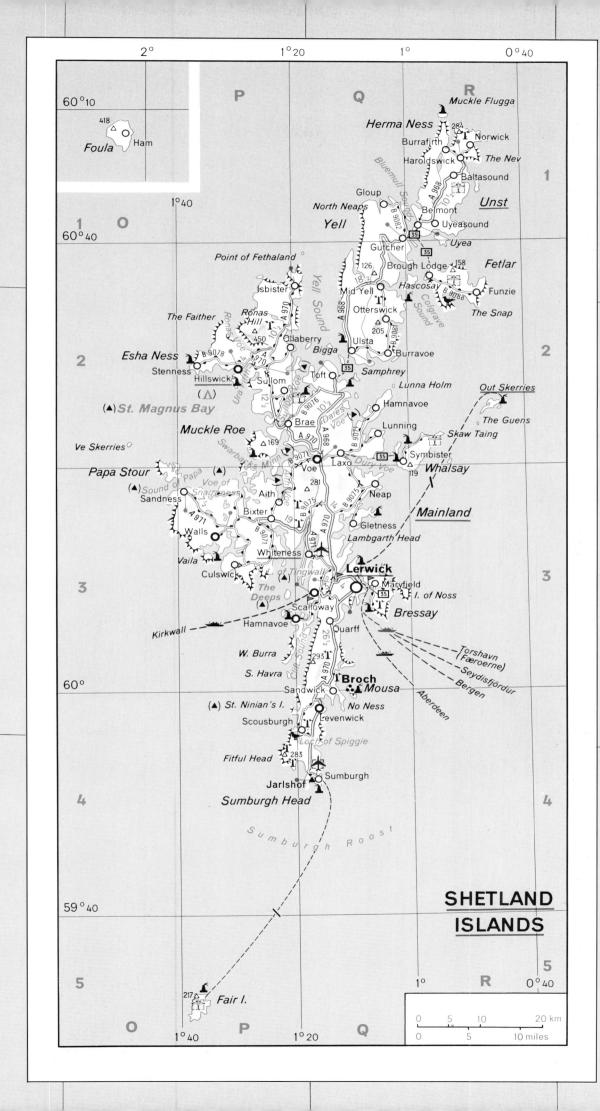

SHETLAND ISLANDS

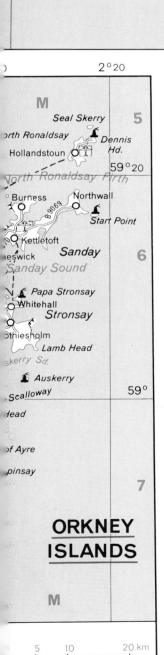

ORKNEY ISLANDS

Clonmel / Cluain Meala

Carrick-on-Suir / **Cárraig na Siúire** • Carrybeg

Kilbeheny
Gurtcourt
Inchnamuck
Tubbrid
Ardfinnan
Ballybeg
Laghtnafrankee
Glendalough
Rathgormuck
Curraghmore Gardens
Portlaw

Mitchelstown Caves
Clogheen
Newcastle
Knockanaffrin
Clonea
Mothel

Glenduff
Knockmealdown
The Gap
Knockmealdown
Ballymacarbry
Nier
Comeragh Mountains
R 678

Kilworth Mountains
Knockshanahullion
Mt. Melleray Monastery
Ballynamult
Ballynaguilkee
Monavullagh Mountains
Coumfea
Seefin
Furraleigh
Kilmacthomas
Kilmea
Newtown

Kilworth Camp
Araglin
Feagarrid
Knockboy
Millstreet
Kilbrien
Fews
Faha
Kill
Dunhill

Ballinvoher
Lyrenaglogh
Ballyduff
Cappoquin / Ceapach Choinn
Modelligo
Kilgobnet
The Pike
Lemybrien
Ballylaneen
Annestown

Clondulane
Tallowbridge
Lismore / Lios Mór
Ballinaspick
Whitechurch
The Pike
Stradbally
Bunmahon

Fermoy / Mainistir Fhear Maí
Currabeha
Knockmourne
Villierstown
Keereen
Dungarvan / Dún Garbhán
Ballyvoyle Head
Clonea Bay
Dunabratti Head

Abbey
Aghern
Conna
Curraglass
Tallow
Aglish
Drum Hills
Ballynacourty
Dungarvan Harbour

Bridebridge
Britway
Ballynoe
The Pike
Boola
Cross
Gorteen
Ballynagaul
Helvick Head

Ardglass
Clonmult
Mount Uniacke
Inch
Clashmore
Grange
Ringville / An Rinn
Loskeran
Muggort's Bay

Lisgoold
Walshtown
Dungourney
Dangan
Kinsalebeg
Kiely's Cross Roads
Reanaclogheen
Mine Head

Midleton / Mainistir na Corann
Killeagh
Mogeely
Youghal / Eochaill
Moord
Curragh
Ardmore / Aird Mhór
Ram Head

Ballynacorra
Castlemartyr
Gortaroo
Ballymadog
Knockadoon Head
Youghal Bay

East Ferry
Ladysbridge
Kilcredan
Ballymacoda
Ballymakeagh
Garryvoe

Saleen
Cloyne
Shanagarry
Rostellan
Churchtown
Ballycotton
Ballycotton Bay

Power Head

Le Havre
Roscoff

CORK/CORGAICH

Oliver Plunkett Street . . . . Z
St. Patrick's Street . . . . YZ

Camden Place . . . . Y 5
Coburg Street . . . . Y 10

Corn Market
  Street . . . . Y 14
Dominick Street . . . . Y 15
Emmet Place . . . . Y 18
Infirmary Road . . . . Z 23
John Redmond
  Street . . . . Y 24
Lancaster Quay . . . . Z 25

Langford Row . . . . Z 26
Merchant's Quay . . . . Y 30
Newsom's Quay . . . . Y 32
Parnell Place . . . . Y 33
Proby's Quay . . . . Z 34
Roman Street . . . . Y 36
St. Patrick's
  Quay . . . . Y 37

0   400 m
0   400 yards

B

LIMERICK/ LUIMNEACH

O'Connell Street .... Z 28
Patrick Street .... Z
Roches Street .... Z

Sarsfield Street .... Z 33
William Street .... Z

Baal's Bridge .... Y 2
Bank Place .... Y 3
Barrington Street .... Z 5
Bridge Street .... Y 6
Broad Street .... Y 7
Castle Street .... Y 8
Cathedral Place .... Z 9
Charlotte's Quay .... Y 12
Crescent (The) .... Z 13
Gerald Griffen Street .... Z 14
High Street .... Z 15
John Square .... Z 16
Lock Quay .... Y 17

Lord Edward Street .... Z 18
Lower Cecil Street .... Z 19
Lower Mallow
  Street .... Z 21
Mathew Bridge .... Y 22
Michael Street .... YZ 23
Mount Kenneth .... Z 24
Newtown Mahon .... Z 25
O'Dwyer Bridge .... Y 27
Rutland Street .... Y 29
St. Gerard Street .... Z 30
Sarsfield Bridge .... Y 32
Shannon Bridge .... Z 34
Shannon Street .... Z 35
Thomond Bridge .... Y 36
Wickham Street .... Z 38

Tullig Point

Feeard

Moneen

Kilbaha

Loop Head

Kilbaha Bay

Kilcloh

MOUTH OF

THE SHANNON

Dreenagh

Ballynaskreena

Kerry Head

Glenderry

(Δ) Ballyheige

Cause

Ballyheige Bay

Akeragh Lou

Lerrig

Banna

Banna Strand

Ardfert

The Seven Hogs or Magharee Islands

Illauntannig

Rough Point

Brandon Point

Fahamore

Kilshannig

Brandon Head

Brandon Bay

Brandon / Cé Bhréanainn

Ballyquin

Killmey

Castlegregory

Tralee Bay

Barrow Harbour

Chapeltown

Fenit Spa

Tralee
Trá Li

Ballydavid Head

Tiduff

Brandon Mountain
Δ 951

Kilcummin

Lough Gill

Kilmalkedar

Feohanagh

Cloghane

Stradbally

Aughacasla

Derrymore I.

Smerwick

Smerwick Harbour

Ballydavid

Ballinloghig

Feohanagh

Ballyduff

Beenoskee
Δ 825

Camp

Blennerville

Derrymore

Sybil Head

Murreagh

Ballyferriter
Baile an Fheirtéaraigh

Kilmalkedar

Gallarus Oratory Δ 623

D   I   N   G   L   E

850 Baurtregaum
Δ

Caherconree
Δ 825

Slieve Mish Mounta

L. Slat

OWENMORE

456 Δ   Δ 616

594

Owenascaul

Clogher Head

Ballineanig

Ballynana

R 559

Connor Pass

Lougher

White Gate Cross Roads

Boolter

Inishtooskert

Dunquin
Dún Chaoin

Ventry

Milltown

Dingle / An Daingean

Lispole / Lios Póil

Anascaul

Aughils
R 561

Castlema

Blasket Islands / Na Blascaodaí

516 Δ Mount Eagle

Fahan

Ventry Harbour

Dingle Harb

Doonmanagh

Inch

Castlemaine Harbour

Milltown

Great Blasket Island

Parkmore Pt.

Bull's Head

Minard Head

Cromane

Knockaunnaglashy

Killorglin
Cill Orglan

Tearaght Island

Slea Head

Illaunstookagh

Tullig

Inishnabro

Inishvickillane

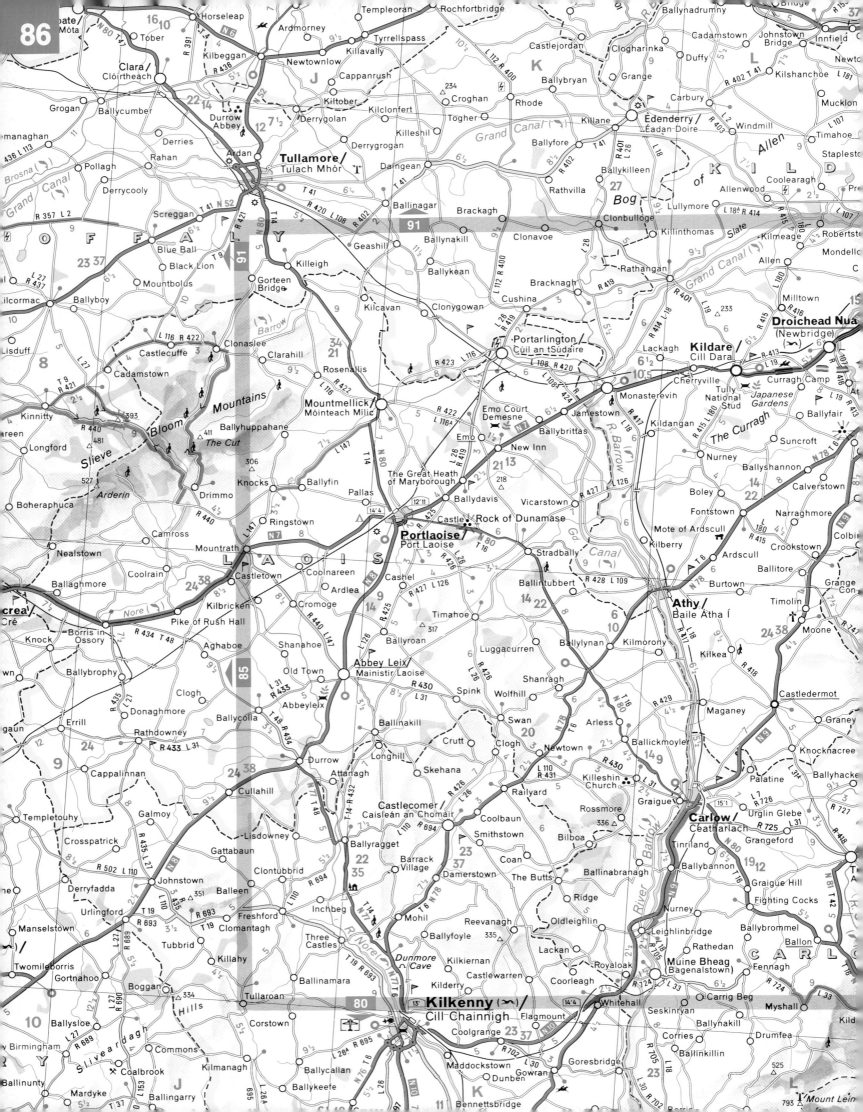

Ballynare · R 158 · R 125 · L 125 · R 158 · L 4 · R 156

Kilcock · Dunboyne · Clonee · St. Margaret's · Ward · Kinsaley · Portmarnock · Malahide (⚓)/ Mullach Íde · N

Maynooth / Maigh Nuad · Mulhuddart · St. Doolagh's · Santry · Baldoyle · Ireland's Eye

Laragh · Clonsilla · Blanchardstown · Finglas · Artane · Clontarf · Nose of Howth

Donadea · Leixlip · Lucan · Castleknock · Phoenix Park · Abbey · Howth / Binn Éadair · Douglas (I. of Man) · 7

Castletown House · Celbridge · Milltown · Rathmines · Holyhead

Mainham · Straffan · Newcastle · Clondalkin · Terenure · Blackrock · DUBLIN / BAILE ÁTHA CLIATH

Clane · Rathcoole · Saggart · Tallaght · Dundrum · Stillorgan · Dún Laoghaire (⚓) · Holyhead · Liverpool · 93

Sallins · Kill · Johnstown · Kilteel · Brittas · Killakee · Sandyford · Dalkey (▲)

Naas / An Nás · Furness · Three Rock Mt. · Stepaside · Ballybrack · Killiney (△) · Killiney Bay (▲)

Punchestown · Kilbride · Glencullen · Kilternan · Shankill

Blessington · Glencree · Powerscourt Demesne · Enniskerry · Little Bray · Bray (▲)/ Bré

Ballymore Eustace · Russborough House · Kippure · Powerscourt · Bray Head

Ballymore · Lackan · Liffey · Sally Gap · Killough · Killruddery

Brannockstown · Poulaphouca Reservoir · Dargle Waterfall · Great Sugar Loaf · Kilmacanoge

Valleymount · Mullaghcleevaun · Greystones / Na Clocha Liatha · 8

Hollywood · Ballyknockan · Lough Tay · Carriggower · Delgany

Glenbridge Lodge · Newtown Mt. Kennedy · Kilpedder · Kilcoole

Dunlavin · Granabeg · Wicklow Gap · Glenmacnass · Lough Dan · Roundwood · Sraghmore · Leamore Strand

Donard · Table Mountain · Vartry Reservoir · Newcastle

Toberbeg · WICKLOW MOUNTAINS · Tomdarragh · Killiskey

Davidstown · Glendalough · Laragh · Annamoe · Ashford · Mount Usher Gardens

Ballinclea · Upper Lake Valley · Ballycullen · Ballinalea · Rathnew

WICKLOW · Lugnaquillia Mountain · Clara · Glenealy · Wicklow (▲)/ Cill Mhantáin

Baltinglass / Bealach Conglais · Glenmalur · Vale of Clara · Wicklow Head

Talbotstown · Drumgoft · Ballinderry · Rathdrum / Ráth Droma · Kilmacurragh

Rathdangan · Aghavannagh · Greenan · Kilbride

Kilmurry · Kiltegan · Sheeanamore · Ballinaclash · Avondale Forest Park · Ballinacor · Ardmore Point

Rathvilly · Moyne · Askanagap · Meeting of the Waters · Kilmacoo

Lisnavagh · Hacketstown · Craffield · Aughrim · Avoca · Redcross (△) · Brittas Bay

Knockananna · Woodenbridge · Ardanairy

Clonmore · Bridgeland · Croghan Mountain · Mizen Head

Rathgall Stone Fort · Tinahely · Johnstown

Kilquiggin · Ferrybank

Aghowle Church · Coolboy · Johnstown · Arklow (▲)/ An tInbhear Mór

Ballard · Shillelagh · Crosspatrick · Clogga

Coolattin · Monaseed · Hollyfort · Coolgreany · Scarnagh · Kilmichael Point

Carnew · Knockbrandon · Killinierin · Inch · Castletown

Watch Ho·Village · Brideswell · Ballylacy

Graigue More · Craanford · Gorey / Guaire · 81

Askamore · R 725

Ballyroebuck · Clohamon · Courtown (△) · Clogh · Ballyduff

Inishbofin

Inishshark

Bofin

High Island

Aughrus More
Claddaghduff

Omey Island

Kingstown

Talbot Island

Errislannan

Doonloughan

Slyne Head

Croaghnakeela Island

St. Macdara's Island

Mweenish Island

B

Rinvyle Point
Rinvyle Castle
Cashleen

Ardnagreevagh
Rinvyle

Cleggan Bay
Ballynakill Harbour
356
Gowlaun
Tully Cross
Dawros
Cleggan /
An Cloigeann

Moyard
Letterfrack
Connemara
National Park

Streamstown B.
Streamstown

294

Clifden /
An Clochán

Derrylea

Tonakeera Point

Crump Island
94

Mweelrea Mountains

Delphi

Kinnadoohy

Glenkeen Br.
Doo Lough
Pass

Doo
Lough

Owenmore Bridge
Sheeffry
Hills
761

817

700 △ Ben Gorm
6
Salrock
Aasleagh
N 594
R 335
Leenane

Culfin
600 △ Lough
Garraun
Kylemore Abbey

Kylemore
Lough
R 344

Benbaun
728 △

The Twelve Pins
Benbreen
692
Bencorr
710

Carrowkennedy

Croaghrimbeg

D

393

Errif Bridge
66 41

Maumtrasna
671 △

Devilsmother
648 △

Glennagevlagh

Finny / Fionnaithe

Cloghbrack

Clonbur /
416 △ An Fhairche

Cornamona

Caggan

Partry Mountains

Tou
Tuar

Trean

LOU
MASK

Inishm
Island

LO

Inishdoorus

Joyce Country

Lough Nafooey
Bennacunneen
578
Drishaghaun

Kilmeelickin

Maum

Teernakill

274 △ Curraun
612

612

C

Owenglin
R 344

CONNEMARA

Ballynahinch
Lake

Ballinaboy

Ballyconneely

Callow

Errisbeg
300 △
Roundstone

Inishnee

Mannin
Bay

Maumeen Lough

Ballyconneely
Bay

Moyrus

Mace
Head
Ard

Carna

Ballinafad
Toombeola

Cashel / An Caiseal

Bunnahown

Gowla

Glinsk / Glinsce

Lough
Bola

L. Skannive

Lettermullan
Leitir Meallain

Derryneen

Recess /
Sraith Salach

Derryclare Lough

(▲) Leckavrea
Mountain

667

701

Maumturk Mountains

Kilbrickan

Rosmuck

Lettermore
Island

Lettercallow

Teeranea

Casheen Bay

Gorumna

Island

Golam Head

Maam Cross / An Teach Dóite

Oorid Lough

358

Lough Curreel

Gortmore /
An Gort Mór
R 340

Derryrush

Kylesa
Bay

Kilkieran /
Cill Chiaráin

Bealadangan

Camus Bay

Inishbarra

Lettermore

Costelloe / Casla

Rossaveel
R 343

Carraroe /
An Cheathrú Rua

Keeraunnagark

Ballynahown

Greatman's Bay

Cashla Bay

Raigh

Oughterard /
Uachtar Ard
49 79

Lough
Bofin

Glentrasna

346

Derryerglinna

Shannawona

Screeb /
Scriob

Lettermore

290 △

237

Lough Formoyle

Glenicmurrin Lough

Loughanillaunmore

Lough
Ugga Beg

Spiddle /
An Spidéal

Inver /
Indreabhán

Lettercraffroe
Lough

Owenriff

Killar

Owenboliska

Bolis
Loug

L 100

North Sound

GALWAY BA

8

Rock Island

Brannock
Islands
Dún Aengus Fort

Onaght

Kilmurvy
Oghil

Oatquarter
Fort

(▲) Inishmore /
Inis Mór

Killeany

Kilronan /
Cill Rónáin

Gregory's
Sound

Inishmaan /
Inis Meáin

Foul
Sound

Inisheer /
Inis Oírr
Fardurris Point

South Sound

Black Head

Murrough

Fanore

Derreen

Formoy

345 △
Slieve Elva

Cork

Th

ARAN ISLANDS /
Oileáin Árainn

9

B

C

83

D

O'Brien's Tower

Cliffs of Moher
Visitor Centre
(▲) Cliffs
of Moher
Hags Head

Derreen

Liscannor
Liscannor Bay

(▲) Lahinch /
An Leacht

Rinneen

Kilshanny

R 479
Toomaghera

Lisdoon
Lios Dú

Roadford
L 54 R 478

Doolin

Burren
Display Cen

Derreen

St. Fachtn

R 47

Ennistimor

N 85

N 67

Burren

R 481 L 53

T 69

R 478

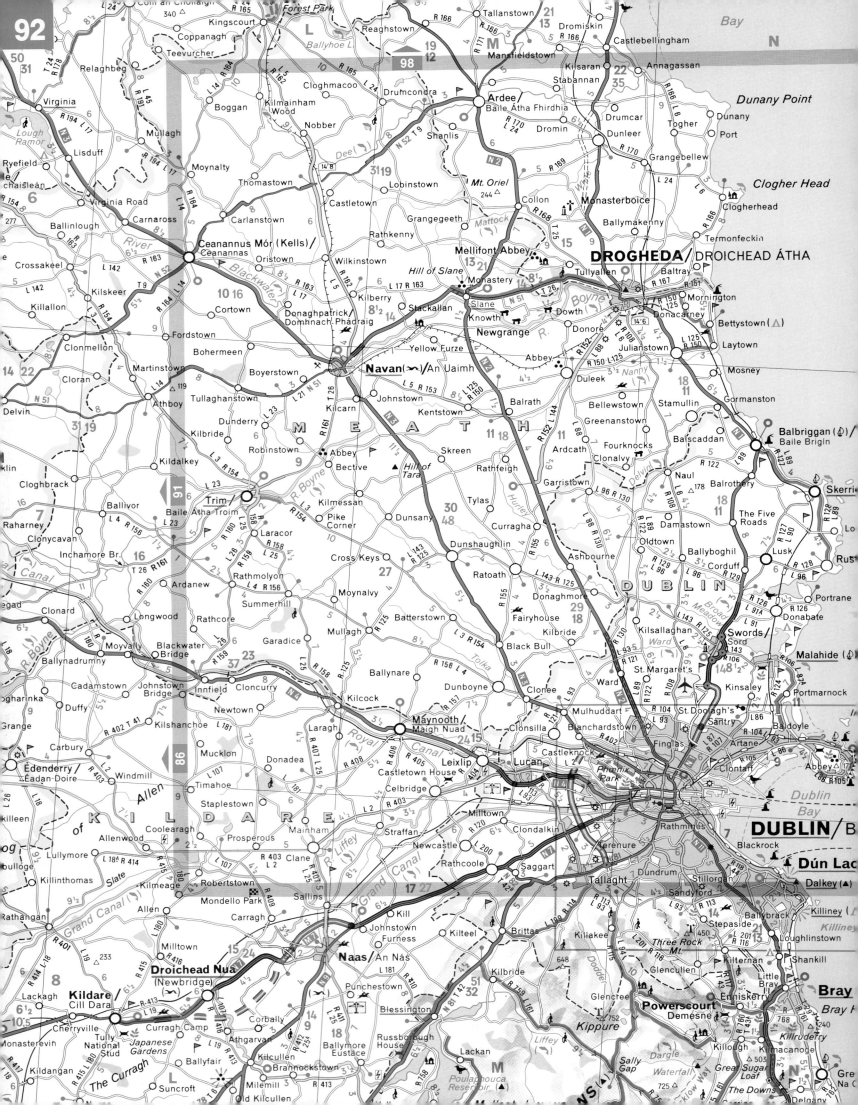

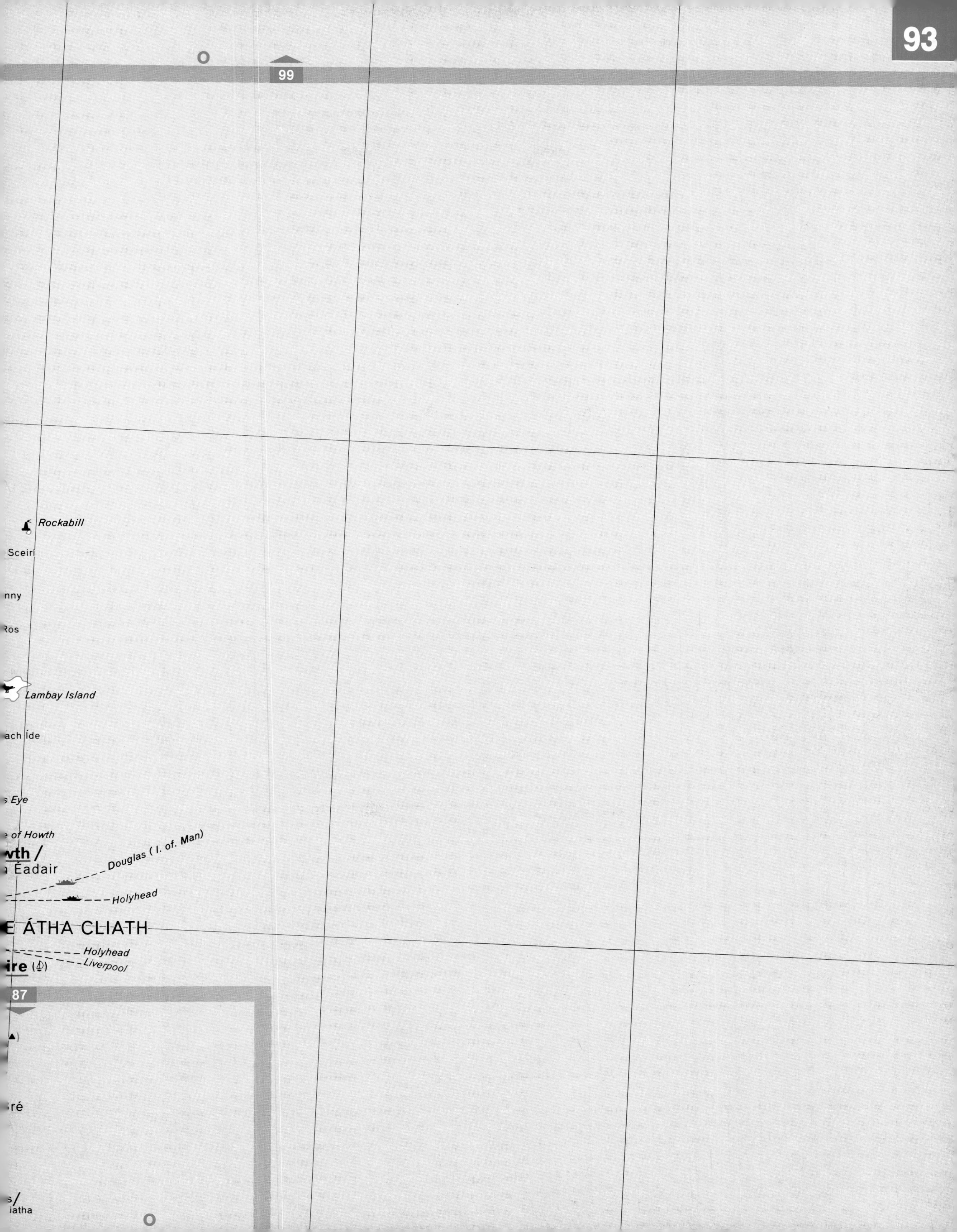

99

Rockabill

Sceirí

nny

Ros

Lambay Island

ach Íde

s Eye

e of Howth

wth /
Éadair   Douglas (I. of Man)

────── Holyhead

É ÁTHA CLIATH

─ ─ ─ Holyhead
─ ─ Liverpool

ire (⚓)

87

▲)

ré

s/
iatha

Carrickfergus

Douglas (I. of Man)

Greenisland
Belfast Lough
hiteabbey
B 90
Grey
Point
Helen's
Bay
15
Craigavad
Light House
Island
Mew Island
ouse
olywood
Crawfordsburn
B 20
Bangor
Groomsport
P
Copeland Island
7
The Ulster
Folk Museum
A 2
B 21
21
Conlig
A 48
Donaghadee
103
15
Craigantlet
Stormont
Parliament House
B 170
B 170
Six Road
Ends
Ballyvester
3½
Dundonald
A 20
Newtownards
Millisle (△)
9
15
Scrabo Hill
B 172
B 172
7
23
Comber
Carrowdore
Ballyferis Point
oneyreagh B 178
A 21
Gunningburn
Cardy
A 2
3½
nbreda
Mount Stewart
Gardens
Temple of the Winds
B 5
3½
Ballywalter (△)
yduff
Ballygowan
Lisbane
Greyabbey
Abbey
Ards Peninsula
(▲)
A 23
11½
Ardmillan
Mahee
Island
Nuns
Quarter
A 20
Baligган
Balloo
Cross Roads
B 6
Killinchy
Kircubbin
Ballyhalbert
A 2
Saintfield
A 25
Glastry
Burr Point
35
22
Raffrey
8½
Islandmore
Rubane
B 173
Strangford
Lough
Kirkistown
Derryboye
B 6
Portavogie
tooder
Ardkeen
Ringboy
Crossgar
B 7
Killyleagh
Cloghy
Cloghy Bay
A 2
Kilmore
rumaness
B 2
Annacloy
A 7
Audley's Castle
Castleward
House
(△)
Portaferry
Kearney
Kearney Point
land
Quoile
A 25
Churchtown
Strangford
A 2
adorn
Inch
Abbey
Saul
Kilclief
Downpatrick
Ballyalton
Ballyquintin Point
A 25
Bishops
Court
Killard Point
Clough
6
Church
Ballee
Ballynoe
B 176
Ballyhornan
Ballykinler
10½
Minerstown
Chapeltown
rum
Tyrella
A 2
Ardglass
Rossglass
Killough
(△)
Ringfad Point
Dundrum Bay
St. John's Point
tle (▲ △)

P

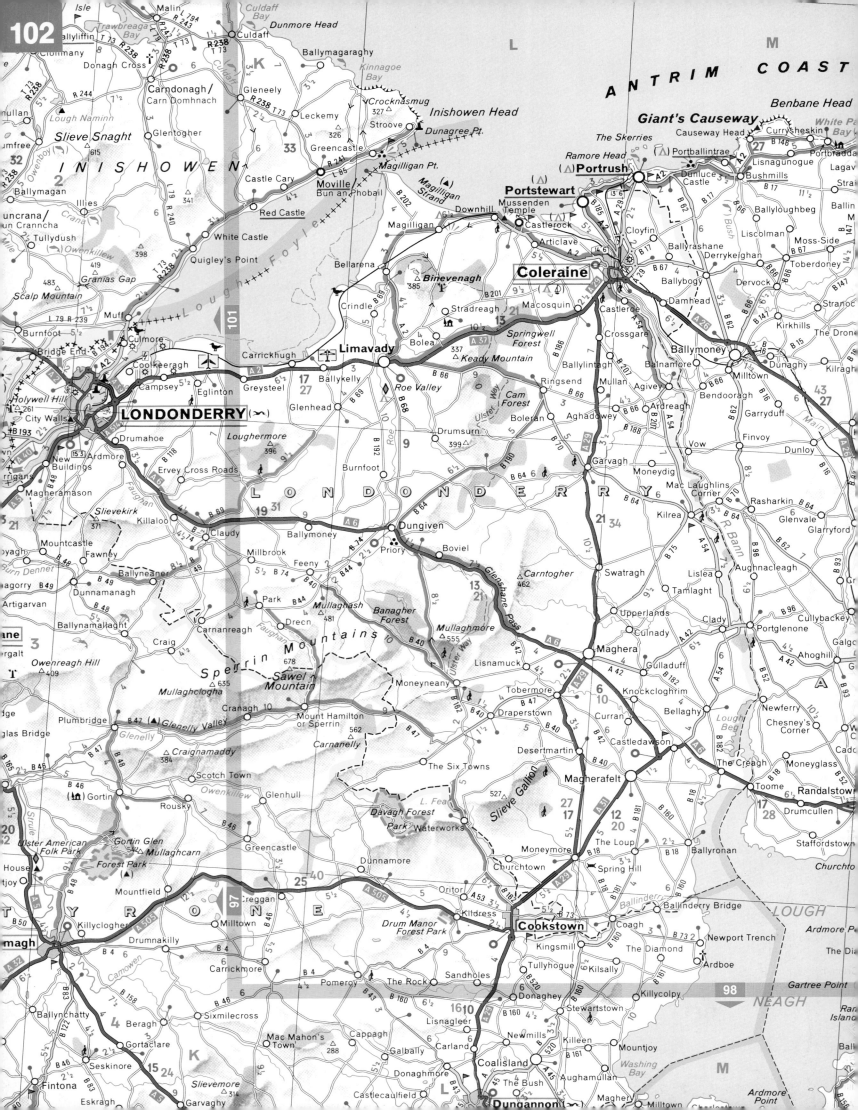

How to use
this index

Stonehaven   63 N13

Page number

Map co-ordinate common
to all Michelin publications

County
abbreviations

ENGLAND

Avon .... Avon
Bedfordshire .... Beds.
Berkshire .... Berks.
Buckinghamshire .... Bucks.
Cambridgeshire .... Cambs.
Cheshire................ Cheshire
Cleveland.............. Cleveland
Cornwall .... Cornwall
Cumbria .... Cumbria
Derbyshire .... Derbs.
Devon.................... Devon
Dorset .... Dorset
Durham .... Durham
East Sussex .... East Sussex
Essex .... Essex
Gloucestershire .... Glos.
Greater Manchester..... Gtr. Man.
Hampshire .... Hants.
Hereford and
    Worcester.... Heref. and Worc.
Hertfordshire............. Herts.
Humberside .... Humberside
Isle of Wight .... I. O. W.
Kent .... Kent
Lancashire............... Lancs.
Leicestershire .... Leics.
Lincolnshire .... Lincs.
Merseyside .... Merseyside
Norfolk .... Norfolk
Northamptonshire ..... Northants.
Northumberland....... Northumb.
North Yorkshire ..... North Yorks.
Nottinghamshire.......... Notts.
Oxfordshire .... Oxon.
Shropshire .... Salop
Somerset.............. Somerset
South Yorkshire .... South Yorks.
Staffordshire............ Staffs.
Suffolk.................. Suffolk
Surrey.................. Surrey
Tyne and Wear ... Tyne and Wear
Warwickshire .... Warw.
West Midlands.... West Midlands
West Sussex .... West Sussex
West Yorkshire ..... West Yorks.
Wiltshire................. Wilts.

WALES

Clwyd .... Clwyd
Dyfed.................... Dyfed
Gwent .... Gwent
Gwynedd............... Gwynedd
Mid Glamorgan .... Mid Glam.
Powys .... Powys
South Glamorgan .... South Glam.
West Glamorgan ..... West Glam.

Symbols
on townplans

Roads

Motorway, dual carriageway
Major throughroutes
Street: Unsuitable for traffic - Pedestrian
Shopping street - Car park
Car ferry - Lever bridge

Sights - Hotels - Restaurants
(See Michelin Red Guide)

Place of interest and its main entrance
Cathedral - Church or chapel
Reference letter locating a sight
Reference letter locating a hotel or a restaurant

Various signs

Tourist information centre - Hospital
Cathedral - Church - Cemetery
Garden, park, wood - Stadium
Golf course: visitors unrestricted - restricted
Public building located by letter:
Local government Offices - Town Hall
Police (Headquarters) - Museum
Theatre - University, polytechnics
Main post office with poste restante, telephone
Underground station

London

Borough - Area   **BRENT** SOHO
Borough boundary - Area boundary
Underground station

Légende
des plans de ville

Voirie

Autoroute, route à chaussées séparées
Grandes voies de circulation - Sens unique
Rue impraticable - Rue piétonne
Rue commerçante - Parc de stationnement
Bac pour autos - Pont mobile

Curiosités - Hôtels - Restaurants
(Voir le Guide Rouge Michelin)

Bâtiment intéressant et entrée principale
Cathédrale - Église ou chapelle
Lettre identifiant une curiosité
Lettre identifiant un hôtel ou un restaurant

Signes divers

Information touristique - Hôpital
Cathédrale - Église - Cimetière
Espace vert - Stade
Golf : Ouvert à tous - Réservé
Bâtiment public repéré par une lettre :
Administration du comté - Hôtel de Ville
Police (commissariat central) - Musée
Théâtre - Université, grande école
Bureau principal de poste restante, téléphone
Station de métro

Londres

Nom d'arrondissement - de quartier
Limite d'arrondissement - de quartier
Station de métro

Comnarthaí
ar phleanna bailte

Bóithre

Mótarbhealach, carrbhealach dúbailte
Priomh-thrébhealach - Bóthar aonslí
Sráid : neamhoiriúnach do thrácht - coisithe
Sráid siopadóireacha - Carrchlós
Bád fartha feithiclí - Droichead starrmhaidí

Ionaid inspéise - Óstáin - Bialanna
(Féach Eolaí Dearg Michelin)

Ionad inspéise agus an priomhbhealach isteach
Ardeaglais - Eaglais nó séipéal
Ionad inspéise curtha in iúl le litir thagartha
Óstán nó bialann curtha in iúl le litir thagartha

Comharthaí Éagsúla

Ionad eolais turasóireachta - Ospidéal
Ardeaglais - Eaglais - Reilig
Gairdín, páirc, coill - Staidiam
Galfchúrsa : gan bac ar chuairteoirí - cuairteoirí faoi theorannú
Foirgneamh poiblí curtha in iúl le litir thagartha :
Oifigí rialtais áitiúil - Halla baile
Póitíní (ceanncheathrú) - Músaem
Amharclann - Ollscoil, polaiteicnicí
Príomhoifig phoist le poste restante, teileafón
Stáisiún traenach faoi thalamh

Londain

Buirg - Limistéar   **BRENT** SOHO
Teorainn bhuirge - Teorainn limistéir
Stáisiún traenach faoi thalamh

Symbolau
ar gynlluniau'r trefi

Ffyrdd

Traffordd, ffordd ddeuol
Prif ffordd drwodd - Unffordd
Stryd : Anaddas i draffig - Cerddwr
Stryd siopa - Parc ceir
Fferi geir - Pont liferi

Golygfeydd - Gwestai - Tai bwyta
(Gweler Llyfr Coch Michelin)

Man diddorol a'i brif fynedfa
Eglwys Gadeiriol - Eglwys neu gapel
Llythyren gyfeirio sy'n dynodi golygfa
Llythyren gyfeirio sy'n dynodi gwesty neu dŷ bwyta

Arwyddion amrywiol

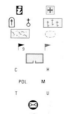

Canolfan croeso - Ysbyty
Eglwys Gadeiriol - Eglwys - Mynwent
Gardd, parc, coedwig - Staidwm
Cwrs golff : dim cyfyngiad ar ymwelwyr - cyfyngiad ar ymwelwyr
Adeilad cyhoeddus a ddynodir gan lythyren :
Swyddfeydd llywodraeth leol - Neuadd y Dref
Yr Heddlu (pencadlys) - Amgueddfa
Theatr - Prifysgol, Colegau Politechnig
Prif swyddfa bost gyda poste restante, ffôn
Gorsaf danddaearol

Llundain

Bwrdeistref - Ardal
Ffin Bwrdeistref - Ffin yr Ardal
Gorsaf danddaearol

Great Britain

A

Abbas Combe 8 M 30
Abbey 13 X 30
Abbey Dore 26 L 28
Abbey Town 44 K 19
Abbeydale 35 P 23
Abbeystead 38 L 22
Abbots Bromley 35 O 25
Abbots Langley 20 S 28
Abbotsbury 8 M 32
Abbotsford House 50 L 17
Abbotskerswell 4 J 32
Aber 32 H 24
Aberaeron 24 H 27
Aberaman 16 J 28
Aberangell 25 I 25
Abercarn 16 K 29
Aberchirder 69 M 11
Abercynon 16 J 29
Aberdare/Aberdâr 15 J 28
Aberdaron 32 F 25
Aberdaugleddau/Milford Haven 14 E 28
Aberdeen 69 N 12
Aberdour 56 K 15
Aberdour Bay 69 N 10
Aberdovey/Aberdyfi 24 H 26
Abereiddy 14 E 28
Aberfeldy 61 I 14
Aberffraw 32 G 24
Aberford 40 P 22
Aberfoyle 55 G 15
Abergavenny/Y-Fenni 16 L 28
Abergele 33 J 24
Abergwaun/Fishguard 14 F 28
Abergwesyn 25 I 27
Abergynolwyn 24 I 26
Aberhonddu/Brecon 25 J 28
Aberlady 56 L 15
Aberlour 68 K 11
Abermaw/Barmouth 32 H 25
Abernethy 56 K 15
Aberpennar/Mountain Ash 16 J 28
Aberporth 24 G 27
Abersoch 32 G 25
Abersychan 16 K 28
Abertawe/Swansea 15 I 29
Aberteifi/Cardigan 24 G 27
Abertillery 16 K 28
Aberuthven 55 J 15
Aberystwyth 24 H 26
Abingdon 18 Q 28
Abinger Common 19 S 30
Abington (Cambs.) 29 U 27
Abington (Strathclyde) 49 I 17
Aboyne 62 L 12
Abridge 21 U 29
Accrington 39 M 22
Achallader 60 F 14
Achanalt 66 F 11
Achaphubuil 60 E 13
Acharn 61 H 14
Achavanich 73 J 8
Achiltibuie 72 D 9
Achmelvich 72 E 9
Achmore 66 D 11
Achnasheen 66 E 11
Achnashellach Forest 66 E 11
Achray (Loch) 55 G 15
Achriesgill 72 F 8
Acklington 51 P 18
Ackworth 40 P 23
Acle 31 Y 26
Acomb 51 N 19
Acrise Place 13 X 30
Acton Turville 17 N 29
Adderbury 28 Q 27
Addingham 39 O 22
Addlestone 20 S 29
Adlington 38 M 23
Adlington Hall 35 N 24
Adwick-le-Street 40 Q 23
Ae (Forest of) 49 J 18
Affric (Glen) 66 F 12
Afon Dyfrdwy/Dee (River) 33 K 24
Ailort (Loch) 59 C 13
Ailsa Craig 48 E 18
Ainort (Loch) 65 B 12
Ainsdale 38 K 23
Ainwick 51 O 17
Aird (The) 67 G 11
Airdrie 55 I 16
Airidhbhruach 70 Z 9
Airigh na h-Airde (Loch) 70 Z 9
A La Ronde 4 J 32
Albourne 11 T 31
Albrighton 27 N 26
Albyn or Mor (Glen) 60 F 12
Alcester 27 O 27
Alconbury 29 T 26
Aldbourne 18 P 29
Aldbrough 41 T 22
Aldbury 19 S 28
Alde (River) 23 Y 27
Aldeburgh 23 Y 27
Aldenham 20 S 28
Alderley Edge 34 N 24
Alderney (Channel I.) 5
Aldershot 18 R 30
Aldridge 27 O 26
Aldringham 23 Y 27
Aldwick 10 R 31
Alexandria 55 G 16
Alfold Crossways 11 S 30
Alford (Grampian) 69 L 12
Alford (Lincs.) 37 U 24
Alfreton 35 P 24
Alfrick 26 M 27
Alfriston 12 U 31
Aline (Loch) 59 C 14
Alkborough 40 S 22
Alkham 13 X 30
Allendale Town 45 N 19
Allerston 47 S 21
Alligin Shuas 66 D 11
Alloa 55 I 15
Alloway 48 G 17
All Stretton 26 L 26
Alltan Fhèarna (Loch an) 73 H 9
Almond (Glen) 61 I 14
Almondbank 62 J 14
Almondsbury 17 M 29
Alness 67 H 10
Alnmouth 51 P 17
Alnwick 51 O 17
Alpheton 22 W 27
Alphington 4 J 31
Alpraham 34 M 24
Alrewas 35 O 25
Alsager 34 N 24
Alsh (Loch) 66 D 12
Alston 45 M 19
Alswear 6 I 31
Altarnun 3 G 32
Altnacealgach 72 F 9
Altnaharra 72 G 9
Alton (Hants.) 10 R 30
Alton (Staffs.) 35 O 25
Alton Towers 35 O 25
Altrincham 34 N 23
Alum Bay 9 P 31
Alva 55 I 15
Alvechurch 27 O 26
Alvediston 8 N 30
Alves 68 J 11
Alvie 67 I 12
Alyth 62 K 14
Amberley 11 S 31
Amble 51 P 18
Amblecote 27 N 26
Ambleside 44 L 20
Amersham 19 S 28
Amesbury 9 O 30
Amlwch 32 G 23
Ammanford/Rhydaman 15 I 28
Ampleforth 46 Q 21
Ampthill 29 S 27
Amroth 14 G 28
An Riabhachan 66 E 11
An Socach 62 J 13
An Teallach 66 E 10
Ancroft 57 O 16
Andover 18 P 30
Andoversford 17 O 28
Andreas 42 G 20
Angle 14 E 28
Anglesey (Isle of) 32 F 24
Anglesey Abbey 29 U 27
Angmering 11 S 31
Annan 50 K 19
Annan (River) 49 J 17
Annat 66 D 11
Annat Bay 72 E 10
Annbank Station 48 G 17
Anne Hathaway's Cottage 27 O 27
Annfield Plain 46 O 19
Anstey 28 Q 25
Anston 36 Q 23
Anstruther 56 L 15
Antony House 3 H 32
Appin 60 E 14
Appleby 45 M 20
Appleby Magna 27 P 25
Appledore (Devon) 6 H 30
Appledore (Kent) 12 W 30
Appleford 18 Q 29
Aran Fawddwy 33 I 25
Arberth/Narberth 14 F 28
Arbirlot 63 M 14
Arbroath 63 M 14
Arbury Hall 27 P 26
Archiestown 68 K 11
Ard (Loch) 55 G 15
Ardarroch 66 D 11
Ardcharnich 66 E 10
Ardechive 60 E 13
Ardeonaig 61 H 14
Ardersier 67 H 11
Ardfern 54 D 15
Ardgay 67 G 10
Ardgour 60 D 13
Ardingly 11 T 30
Ardivachar 64 X 11
Ardleigh 23 W 28
Ardlui 54 F 15
Ardlussa 52 C 15
Ardmore Point 64 A 11
Ardnamurchan 59 B 13
Ardnave Point 52 B 16
Ardrishaig 54 D 15
Ardrossan 54 F 17
Ardvasar 65 C 12
Ardverikie Forest 61 G 13
Argyll 54 D 15
Argyll Forest Park 54 F 15
Arienas (Loch) 59 C 14
Arinagour 59 A 14
Arisaig 59 C 13
Arkaig (Loch) 60 E 13
Arkengarthdale 45 O 20
Arklet (Loch) 55 G 15
Arlingham 17 M 28
Arlington Court 6 I 30
Armadale Bay 65 C 12
Armadale (Highland) 73 H 8
Armadale (Lothian) 55 I 16
Armitage 35 O 25
Armthorpe 40 Q 23
Arncliffe 39 N 21
Arncott 18 Q 28
Arnesby 28 Q 26
Arnisdale 66 D 12
Arnol 70 A 8
Arnold 36 Q 25
Arnside 44 L 21
Aros 59 B 14
Arran (Isle of) 53 E 17
Arrochar 54 F 15
Arun 11 S 31
Arundel 11 S 31
Ascot 20 R 29
Ascott House 18 R 28
Ascrib Islands 65 A 11
Asfordby 36 R 25
Ash (Kent) 13 X 30
Ash (Surrey) 18 R 30
Ash Mill 7 I 31
Ashbourne 35 O 24
Ashburton 4 I 32
Ashbury 17 P 29
Ashby de la Zouch 35 P 25
Ashcott 8 L 30
Ashford (Derbs.) 35 O 24
Ashford (Kent) 12 W 30
Ashford (Surrey) 20 S 29
Ashie (Loch) 67 H 11
Ashingdon 22 W 29
Ashington (Northumb.) 51 P 18
Ashington (West Sussex) 11 S 31
Ashover 35 P 24
Ashperton 26 M 27
Ashtead 21 T 30
Ashton-in-Makerfield 38 M 23
Ashton Keynes 17 O 29
Ashton-under-Lyne 39 N 23
Ashton-upon-Mersey 39 M 23
Ashwell 29 T 27
Askam in Furness 44 K 21
Askern 40 Q 23
Askernish 64 X 12
Askerswell 8 L 31
Askham 44 L 20
Askrigg 45 N 21
Aspatria 44 K 19
Aspley Guise 28 S 27
Assynt (Loch) 72 E 9
Aston Clinton 18 R 28
Aston Rowant 18 R 28
Aston Tirrold 18 Q 29
Astwood Bank 27 O 27
Atcham 26 L 25
Athelhampton Hall 8 N 31
Athelney 7 L 30
Atherington 6 H 31
Atherstone 27 P 26
Atherton 38 M 23
Atholl (Forest of) 61 H 13
Attleborough 30 X 26
Auchenblae 63 M 13
Auchencairn 43 I 19
Auchinleck 49 H 17
Auchleven 69 M 12
Auchnagatt 69 N 11
Auchterarder 55 I 15
Auchterderran 56 K 15
Auchterhouse 62 K 14
Auchtermuchty 56 K 15
Auchtertyre 66 D 12
Auckengill 74 K 8
Audenshaw 39 N 23
Audlem 34 M 25
Audley 34 N 24
Audley End House 29 U 27
Aughton (Lancs.) 38 L 23
Aughton (South Yorks.) 40 Q 23
Auldearn 67 I 11
Auldhouse 55 H 16
Aultbea 66 D 10
Aust 16 M 29
Austwick 39 M 21
Avebury 17 O 29
Aveley 21 U 29
Avening 17 N 28
Aveton Gifford 4 I 33
Aviemore 67 I 12
Avoch 67 H 11
Avon (County) 16 M 29
Avon (Glen) 62 J 12
Avon (River) 9 O 31
Avon (River) (R. Severn) 27 N 27
Avonbridge 55 I 16
Avonmouth 16 L 29
Awe (Loch) 54 E 15
Awliscombe 7 K 31
Awre 17 M 28
Axbridge 16 L 30
Axminster 8 L 31
Axmouth 5 K 31
Aylesbury 18 R 28
Aylesford 12 V 30
Aylesham 13 X 30
Aylsham 31 X 25
Aymestrey 26 L 27
Aynho 28 Q 28
Ayr 48 G 17
Aysgarth 45 O 21
Ayton 47 S 21

B

Bà (Loch) 59 C 14
Babbacombe Bay 4 J 32
Backaland 74 L 6
Backwater Reservoir 62 K 13
Baconsthorpe 30 X 25
Bacton 31 Y 25
Bacup 39 N 22
Bad a' Ghaill (Loch) 72 E 9
Bad an Sgalaig (Loch) 66 D 10
Badachro 66 C 10
Badanloch (Loch) 73 H 9
Badcaul 66 D 10
Baddidarach 72 E 9
Badenoch 61 H 13
Badluarach 72 D 10
Badminton 17 N 29
Badrallach 66 E 10
Bae Colwyn/Colwyn Bay 33 I 24
Bagh nam Faoileann 64 Y 11
Bagillt 33 K 24
Bagshot 19 R 29
Baile Mór 59 A 15
Bainbridge 45 N 21
Bainton 41 S 22
Bakewell 35 O 24
Bala 33 J 25
Balallan 70 A 9
Balbeggie 62 J 14
Balblair 67 H 10
Balcary Point 43 I 19
Balchrick 72 E 8
Balcombe 11 T 30
Balderton 36 R 24
Baldock 29 T 28
Balemartine 58 Z 14
Balephetrish Bay 58 Z 14
Balephuil Bay 58 Z 14
Baleshare 64 X 11
Balfour 74 L 6
Balfron 55 H 15
Balintore 67 I 10
Balivanich 64 X 11
Ballabeg 42 F 21
Ballachulish 60 E 13
Ballasalla 42 G 21
Ballater 62 K 12
Ballaugh 42 G 21
Ballingry 56 K 15
Balmaha 55 G 15
Balmedie 69 N 12
Balmoral Castle 62 K 12
Balmullo 56 L 14
Balnakeil Bay 72 F 8
Balvicar 54 D 15
Bamburgh Castle 51 O 17
Bampton (Cumbria) 44 L 20
Bampton (Devon) 7 J 31

BATH

Gay Street AV
Green Street BV 21
Milsom Street BV
New Bond Street BV 31

Ambury BX 2
Argyle Street BV 3
Bennett Street AV 4
Bridge Street BVX 6
Broad Quay BX 7
Chapel Row AVX 9
Charles Street AX 10
Charlotte Street AV 12
Cheap Street BX 13
Churchill Bridge BX 14
Circus Place AV 16
Grand Parade BX 17
Great Stanhope Street AV 18
Guinea Lane BV 23
Henry Street BX 24
Lower Borough Walls BX 26
Monmouth Place AVX 28
Monmouth Street AX 30
New Orchard Street BX 32
Nile Street AV 34
Northgate Street BVX 35
Old Bond Street BX 36
Orange Grove BX 38
Pierrepont Street BX 39
Quiet Street BV 41
Russell Street AV 42
Southgate Street BX 43
Stanley Road BX 45
Terrace Walk BX 46
Upper Borough Walls BX 48
Westgate Buildings AX 49
Westgate Street ABX 50
Wood Street AV 52
York Street BX 53

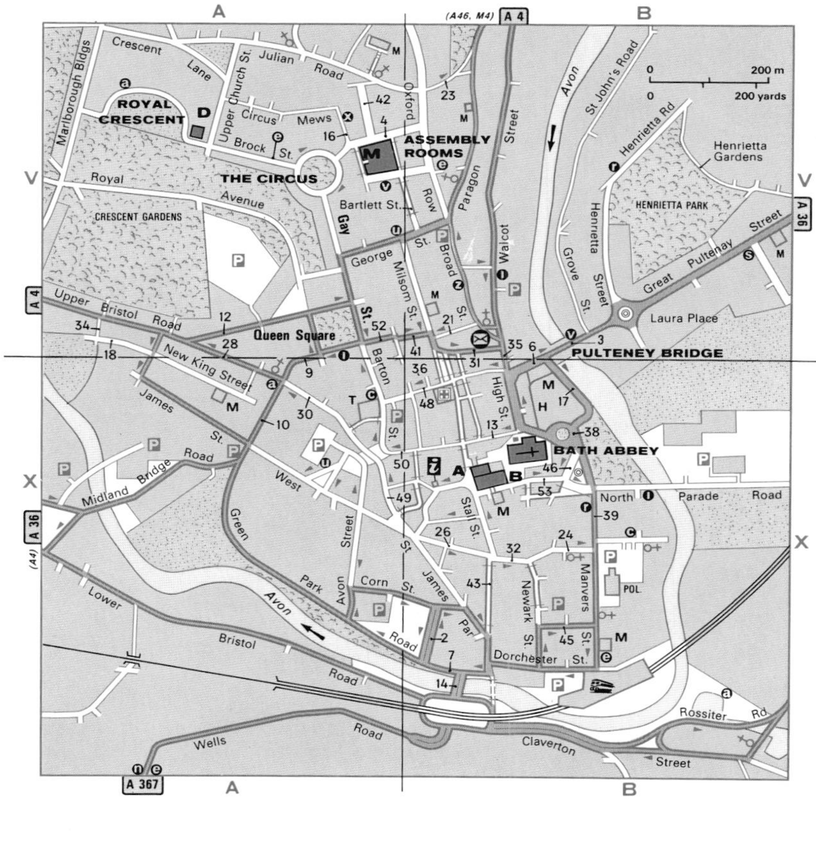

Bampton (Oxon.)	18 P 28	Bardsea	38 K 21	Barnard Castle	45 O 20	Barrhill	48 F 18	Barton (Staffs.)	35 O 25	Bath	17 M 29	Bearsted	12 V 30
Banavie	60 E 13	Bardsey Island	32 F 25	Barnby Dun	40 Q 23	Barri/Barry	16 K 29	Barton in the Clay	29 S 28	Bathgate	55 J 16	Beattock	49 J 18
Banbury	27 P 27	Barfreston	13 X 30	Barnby Moor (Humberside)	41 R 22	Barrington Court	8 L 31	Barton Mills	30 V 26	Batley	39 P 22	Beauchief	35 P 24
Banchory	63 M 12	Bargoed	16 K 28			Barrisdale Bay	60 D 12			Battle	12 V 31	Beaulieu	9 P 31
Banff	69 M 10	Barham	13 X 30	Barnby Moor (Notts.)	36 Q 23	Barrow	22 V 27	Barton-on-Sea	9 P 31	Baumber	37 T 24	Beauly	67 G 11
Bangor	32 H 24	Barking and Dagenham (London Borough)		Barnet (London Borough)	20 T 29	Barrow-in-Furness	38 K 21	Barton-upon-Humber	41 S 22	Bawdeswell	30 X 25	Beauly Firth	67 G 11
Bankfoot	62 J 14									Bawdsey	23 Y 27	Beaumaris	32 H 24
Bankhead	69 N 12			Barnetby-le-Wold	41 S 23	Barrow-upon-Humber	41 S 22	Barvas	70 A 8	Bawtry	36 Q 23	Beaupré Castle	16 J 29
Banks	38 L 22		21 U 29	Barnhill	68 J 11	Barrow-upon-Soar	36 Q 25	Barwell	27 P 26	Bayble	71 B 9	Bebington	34 L 23
Bannockburn	55 I 15	Barkston	36 S 25	Barnoldswick	39 N 22			Barwick-in-Elmet	40 P 22	Bayhead	64 X 11	Beccles	31 Y 26
Banstead	20 T 30	Barkway	22 U 28	Barnsley	40 P 23	Barrowby	36 R 25	Baschurch	34 L 25	Beachy Head	12 U 31	Beckingham	36 R 23
Banwell	16 L 30	Barlaston	35 N 25	Barnstaple	6 H 30	Barrowford	39 N 22	Basildon (Berks.)	18 Q 29	Beacon (The)	2 E 33	Beckington	17 N 30
Bapchild	12 W 30	Barlborough	36 Q 24	Barr	48 F 18	Barry/Barri (South Glam.)	16 K 29	Basildon (Essex)	22 V 29	Beaconsfield	20 S 29	Beckton	21 U 29
Bar Hill	29 U 27	Barley	29 U 27	Barra	64 X 13			Basingstoke	18 Q 30	Beadnell Bay	51 P 17	Bedale	46 P 21
Barbaraville	67 H 10	Barmouth/ Abermaw	32 H 25	Barra (Sound of)	64 X 12	Barry (Tayside)	63 L 14	Baslow	35 P 24	Beaford	6 H 31	Beddgelert	32 H 24
Barbon	45 M 21			Barra Head	58 X 13	Bartestree	26 M 27	Bass Rock	56 M 15	Beaminster	8 L 31	Beddingham	11 U 31
Barcombe Cross	11 U 31	Barmouth Bay	32 H 25	Barrhead	55 G 16	Barton (Lancs.)	38 L 22	Bassenthwaite	44 K 19	Beamish Hall	46 P 19	Bedford	29 S 27
Bardney	37 T 24	Barmston	41 T 21					Bassingham	36 S 24	Bearsden	55 G 16	Bedford Levels	29 T 26

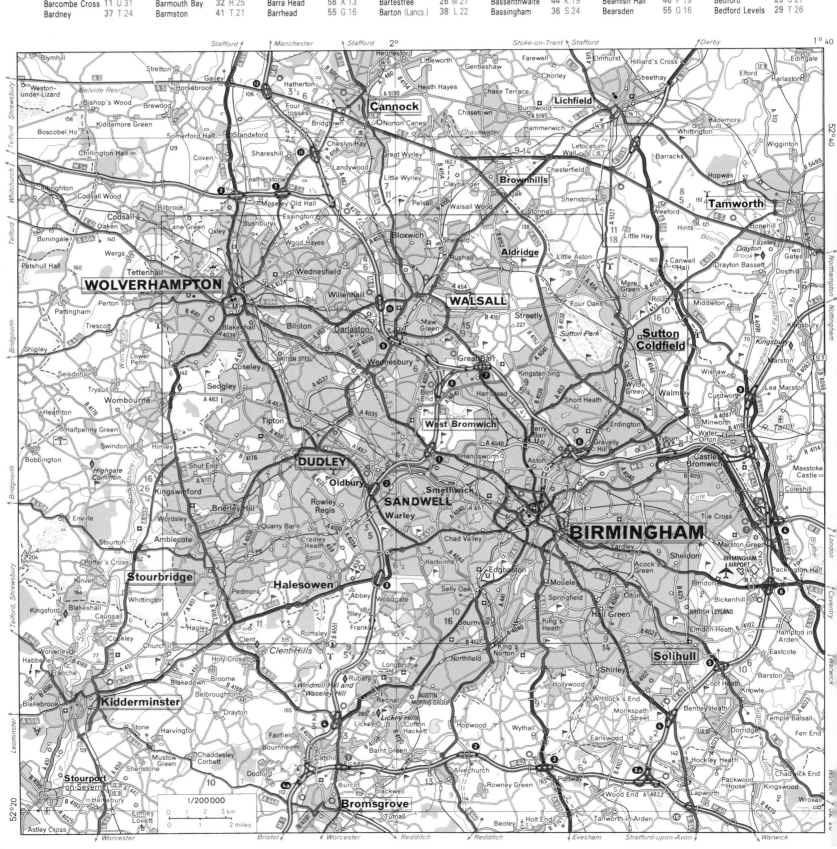

BIRMINGHAM

Bull Ring Centre	**KZ**	Holloway Circus	**JZ** 32	Priory Queensway	**KY** 57
Corporation Street	**KY**	James Watt		St Chads Circus	**JKY** 62
New Street	**JZ**	Queensway	**KY** 35	St Chads Ringway	**KY** 63
		Jennen's Road	**KY** 36	St Martin's Circus	**KZ** 64
Albert Street	**KZ** 2	Lancaster Circus	**KY** 39	Severn Street	**JZ** 69
Bull Street	**KY** 13	Lancaster Street	**KY** 41	Shadwell Street	**KY** 70
Dale End	**KZ** 21	Masshouse Circus	**KY** 43	Smallbrook Queensway	**KZ** 71
Hall Street	**JY** 29	Moor Street		Snow Hill Queensway	**KY** 73
		Queensway	**KZ** 46	Summer Row	**JY** 77
		Navigation Street	**KZ** 49	Temple Row	**KZ** 80
		Newton Street	**KY** 52	Waterloo Street	**JZ** 84

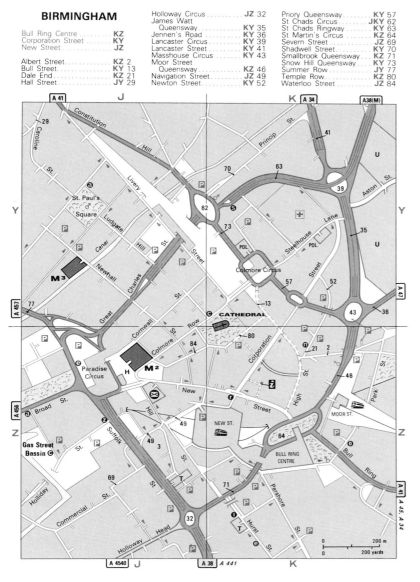

Bedfordshire
(County) ..... 29 S 27
Bedgebury
Pinetum ..... 12 V 30
Bedlington ..... 51 P 18
Bedwas ..... 16 K 29
Bedworth ..... 27 P 26
Bee (Loch) ..... 64 X 11
Beer ..... 5 K 31
Beeston ..... 36 Q 25
Beeswing ..... 49 I 18
Beinn a' Ghlò ..... 61 I 13
Beinn a'
Mheadhoin ..... 66 F 12
Beinn Dearg
(Highland) ..... 66 F 10
Beinn Dearg
(Tayside) ..... 61 I 13
Beinn
Heasgarnich ..... 60 G 14
Beinn Ime ..... 54 F 15
Beith ..... 55 G 16
Belbroughton ..... 27 N 26
Belford ..... 51 O 17
Bellingham ..... 51 N 18
Bellshill ..... 55 H 16
Belmont ..... 75 R 1
Belnahua ..... 52 C 15
Belper ..... 35 P 24
Belsay ..... 51 O 18
Belton
(Humberside) ..... 41 R 23
Belton (Norfolk) ..... 31 Y 26
Belvoir ..... 36 R 25
Bembridge ..... 10 Q 31
Bempton ..... 41 T 21
Ben Alder ..... 61 G 13
Ben Armine
Forest ..... 73 H 9
Ben Chonzie ..... 61 I 14
Ben Cruachan ..... 60 E 14

Ben-damph
Forest ..... 66 D 11
Ben Hope ..... 72 G 8
Ben Klibreck ..... 73 G 9
Ben Lawers ..... 61 H 14
Ben Ledi ..... 55 H 15
Ben Lomond ..... 55 G 15
Ben Loyal ..... 73 G 8
Ben Macdui ..... 61 I 12
Ben More Assynt 72 F 9
Ben More
(Central) ..... 60 G 14
Ben More
(Strathclyde) ..... 59 C 14
Ben Nevis ..... 60 E 13
Ben Starav ..... 60 E 14
Ben Vorlich ..... 55 H 14
Ben Wyvis ..... 67 G 10
Benbecula ..... 64 X 11
Benderloch ..... 60 E 14
Benenden ..... 12 V 30
Benington ..... 37 U 25
Benllech ..... 32 H 24
Benmore Lodge ..... 72 F 9
Benson ..... 18 Q 29
Bentley ..... 40 Q 23
Benwick ..... 29 T 26
Beoraid (Loch) ..... 60 D 13
Bere Alston ..... 3 H 32
Bere Regis ..... 8 N 31
Berkeley ..... 17 M 28
Berkhamsted ..... 19 S 28
Berkshire
(County) ..... 18 P 29
Berneray
(near Barra) ..... 58 X 13
Berneray
(near North Uist) 64 Y 10
Bernisdale ..... 65 B 11
Berriew ..... 25 K 26

Berrington Hall ..... 26 L 27
Berrow ..... 7 K 30
Berry Head ..... 4 J 32
Berry Hill ..... 16 M 28
Berrynarbor ..... 6 H 30
Bervie Bay ..... 63 N 13
Berwick-
upon-Tweed ..... 57 O 16
Berwyn ..... 33 J 25
Bethersden ..... 12 W 30
Bethesda ..... 32 H 24
Bettyhill ..... 73 H 8
Betws-y-Coed ..... 33 I 24
Beverley ..... 41 S 22
Bewcastle ..... 50 L 18
Bewdley ..... 26 N 26
Bexhill ..... 12 V 31
Bexley (London
Borough) ..... 21 U 29
Beyton ..... 22 W 27
Bhaid-Luachraich
(Loch) ..... 66 D 10
Bhealaich
(Loch a') ..... 72 G 9
Bhraoin (Loch a') 66 E 10
Bhrollum (Loch) ..... 70 A 10
Bibury ..... 17 O 28
Bicester ..... 18 Q 28
Bickington ..... 4 I 32
Bickleigh ..... 7 J 31
Bicton gardens ..... 4 K 31
Biddenden ..... 12 V 30
Biddestone ..... 17 N 29
Biddulph ..... 35 N 24
Bideau nam Bian 60 E 14
Bideford ..... 6 H 30
Bidford ..... 27 O 27
Bieldside ..... 69 N 12
Bierton ..... 18 R 28
Bigbury ..... 4 I 33
Bigbury-on-Sea ..... 4 I 33

Biggar ..... 56 J 17
Biggleswade ..... 29 T 27
Bignor ..... 11 S 31
Bildeston ..... 23 W 27
Bill of Portland ..... 8 M 32
Billericay ..... 22 V 29

Billesdon ..... 35 R 26
Billingborough ..... 37 S 25
Billinge ..... 38 L 23
Billingham ..... 46 Q 20
Billinghay ..... 37 T 24
Billingshurst ..... 11 S 30
Bilsington ..... 12 W 30
Bilsthorpe ..... 36 Q 24
Bilston ..... 27 N 26
Binbrook ..... 41 T 23
Binfield ..... 18 R 29
Bingham ..... 36 R 25
Bingley ..... 39 O 22
Binham ..... 30 W 25
Binns (The) ..... 56 J 16
Birchington ..... 13 X 29
Birdham ..... 10 R 31
Birdworld ..... 18 R 30
Birkenhead ..... 34 K 23
Birling Gap ..... 12 U 31
Birmingham ..... 27 O 26
Birnam ..... 62 J 14
Birsay ..... 74 K 6
Birsemore ..... 62 L 12
Birstall ..... 28 Q 25
Birtley ..... 46 P 19
Birtsmorton
Court ..... 26 N 27
Bishop Auckland 46 P 20
Bishop Monkton 40 P 21
Bishop's Castle ..... 26 L 26
Bishop's Caundle 8 M 31
Bishop's Cleeve ..... 27 N 28
Bishop's
Nympton ..... 6 I 31
Bishop's Palace
(near
St. David's) ..... 14 E 28
Bishop's Palace
(near Tenby) ..... 14 F 28
Bishop's
Stortford ..... 22 U 28
Bishop's Tawton ..... 6 H 30
Bishop's
Waltham ..... 10 Q 31
Bishops Lydeard 7 K 30
Bishopsteignton ..... 4 J 32
Bishopstocke ..... 9 P 31
Bishopston ..... 15 I 28
Bishopstone ..... 17 P 29
Bishopthorpe ..... 40 Q 22
Bishopton ..... 55 G 16
Bix ..... 18 R 29
Blaby ..... 28 Q 26
Black Bay ..... 53 D 17
Black Down
Hills ..... 7 K 31
Black Isle ..... 67 G 11
Black Mount ..... 60 F 14
Black Mountain ..... 15 I 28
Black Mountains 26 L 27
Black Water
Valley ..... 66 F 11

Blackburn
(Grampian) ..... 69 N 12
Blackburn
(Lancs.) ..... 38 M 22
Blackfield ..... 9 P 31
Blackford ..... 55 I 15
Blacklunans ..... 62 J 13
Blackmoor Gate ..... 6 I 30
Blackness Castle 56 J 15
Blackpool ..... 38 K 22
Blackridge ..... 55 I 16
Blackthorn ..... 18 Q 28
Blackwater
(River) ..... 23 W 28
Blackwater
Reservoir ..... 60 F 13
Blackwaterfoot ..... 53 D 17
Blackwood ..... 16 K 29
Bladnoch ..... 48 G 19
Bladon ..... 18 P 28
Blaenau
Ffestiniog ..... 32 I 25
Blaenavon ..... 16 K 28
Blaengarw ..... 15 J 29
Blagdon ..... 16 L 30
Blaich ..... 60 E 13
Blaina ..... 16 K 28
Blair Atholl ..... 61 I 13
Blair Castle ..... 61 I 13
Blairgowrie ..... 62 J 14
Blakeney (Glos.) 17 M 28
Blakeney
(Norfolk) ..... 30 X 25
Blakesley ..... 28 Q 27
Blandford Forum ..... 8 N 31
Blarnalearoch ..... 66 E 10
Blaydon ..... 51 O 19
Bleaklow Hill ..... 39 O 23
Blean ..... 13 X 30
Blenheim Palace 18 P 28
Bletchley ..... 28 R 27
Blewbury ..... 18 Q 29
Blickling Hall ..... 30 X 25
Blidworth ..... 36 Q 24
Blindley Heath ..... 19 T 30
Blisland ..... 3 F 32
Blisworth ..... 28 R 27
Blithe ..... 35 O 25
Blithfield Hall ..... 35 O 25
Blithfield
Reservoir ..... 35 O 25
Blockley ..... 27 O 27
Blofield ..... 31 Y 26
Bloxham ..... 27 P 27
Bluemull Sound ..... 75 Q 1
Blyth
(Northumb.) ..... 51 P 18
Blyth (Notts.) ..... 36 Q 23
Blythburgh ..... 31 Y 27
Blyton ..... 41 R 23
Bo' Ness ..... 55 J 15

Boarhills ..... 56 L 15
Boat of Garten ..... 67 I 12
Bocking ..... 22 V 28
Boddam ..... 69 O 11
Bodenham ..... 26 L 27
Bodiam Castle ..... 12 V 30
Bodmin ..... 3 F 32
Bodmin Moor ..... 3 G 32
Bodnant Gardens 33 I 24
Bognor Regis ..... 10 R 31
Boisdale (Loch) ..... 64 Y 12
Boldon ..... 51 P 19
Bollin (River) ..... 35 N 23
Bollington ..... 35 N 24
Bolney ..... 11 T 31
Bolsover ..... 36 Q 24
Boltby ..... 46 Q 21
Bolton ..... 39 M 23
Bolton Abbey ..... 39 O 22
Bolton-le-Sands 38 L 21
Bolton-upon-
Dearne ..... 40 Q 23
Bonar Bridge ..... 67 G 10
Bonawe Quarries 60 E 14
Boncath ..... 24 G 27
Bonhill ..... 55 G 16
Bonnybridge ..... 55 I 16
Bonnyrigg ..... 56 K 16
Bont-faen/
Cowbridge ..... 16 J 29
Boosbeck ..... 47 R 20
Bootle (Cumbria) 43 J 21
Bootle
(Merseyside) ..... 38 K 23
Border Forest
Park (The) ..... 57 M 18
Borders (Region) 50 K 17
Bordon Camp ..... 10 R 30
Boreham ..... 22 V 28
Boreham Street ..... 12 V 31
Borehamwood ..... 20 T 29
Borgue ..... 43 H 19
Borness ..... 43 H 19
Borough Green ..... 21 U 30
Boroughbridge ..... 40 P 21
Borrobol Forest ..... 73 H 9
Borrowash ..... 35 P 25
Borth ..... 24 H 26
Borve
(Barra Isle) ..... 64 X 13
Borve
(Isle of Lewis) ..... 70 A 8
Bosbury ..... 26 M 27
Boscastle ..... 3 F 31
Boscombe ..... 9 O 31
Bosham ..... 10 R 31
Bosherston ..... 14 F 29
Boston ..... 37 T 25
Boston Spa ..... 40 P 22
Botesdale ..... 30 W 26
Bothel ..... 44 K 19
Bothwell ..... 55 H 16
Botley ..... 10 Q 31

BOURNEMOUTH

Old Christchurch Road ... **DY**		Fir Vale Road	**DY** 18
Square (The)	**CY** 60	Gervis Place	**DY** 20
Westover Road	**DZ** 73	Hinton Road	**DZ** 25
		Lansdowne (The)	**DY** 26
Branksome Wood Road	**CY** 10	Lansdowne Road	**DY** 27
Commercial Road	**CY** 13	Madeira Road	**DY** 32
Durley Road	**CZ** 15	Manor Road	**EY**
Exeter Road	**CDZ** 17	Meyrick Road	**EYZ** 35
		Post Office Road	**CY** 41
		Priory Road	**CZ** 43
		Richmond Hill	**CY** 45
Russell Cotes Road	**DZ** 47
St. Michael's Road	**CZ** 48
St. Paul's Road	**EY** 49
St. Peter's Road	**DY** 50
St. Stephen's Road	**CY** 51
St. Swithuns Road
South	**EY** 52
Suffolk Road	**CY** 61
Triangle (The)	**CY** 63
Upper Hinton Road	**DZ** 64
West Cliff Promenade	**CZ** 67

BRADFORD

Bank Street	AZ 4
Broadway	BZ 8
Charles Street	BZ 13
Market Street	BZ 28
Canal Road	BZ 10
Cheapside	BZ 14
Darley Street	AZ 18
Drewton Road	AZ 19
Harris Street	BZ 23
Ivegate	AZ 25
Kirkgate	AZ 26
Otley Road	BZ 31
Peckover Street	BZ 32
Prince's Way	AZ 33
School Street	BZ 35
Stott Hill	BZ 39

Bottesford	36 R 25	Bowland	
Bottisham	29 U 27	(Forest of)	38 M 22
Boughton	36 Q 24	Bowmore	52 B 16
Boughton Street	12 W 30	Bowness	44 L 20
Boultham	36 S 24	Bowness-on-	
Bourne	37 S 25	Solway	44 K 19
Bournemouth	9 O 31	Bowood House	17 N 29
Bourton	8 N 30	Box	17 N 29
Bourton-		Box Hill	20 T 30
on-the-Water	17 O 28	Boxford	23 W 27
Bovey Tracey	4 I 32	Boxworth	29 T 27
Bovingdon	19 S 28	Brabourne Lees	13 W 30
Bowerchalke	9 O 30	Bracadale (Loch)	65 A 12
Bowes	45 N 20	Bracebridge	
Bowhill	50 L 17	Heath	36 S 24
Brackley	28 Q 27		
Bracknell	18 R 29		
Braco	55 I 15		
Bradan Resr			
(Loch)	48 G 18		
Bradfield	18 Q 29		
Bradford	39 O 22		
Bradford Abbas	8 M 31		
Bradford-			
on-Avon	17 N 29		
Brading	10 Q 31		
Bradwell	35 O 24		
Bradwell-on-Sea	23 W 28		
Bradworthy	6 G 31		
Brae	75 P 2		

Brae Roy Lodge	60 F 13
Braemar	62 J 12
Braeriach	61 I 12
Braich y Pwll	32 F 25
Bràigh Mór	70 Y 9
Brailes	27 P 27
Brailsford	35 P 25
Braintree	22 V 28
Braishfield	9 P 30
Braithwell	40 Q 23
Bramcote	36 Q 25
Bramfield	31 Y 27
Bramford	23 X 27
Bramhall	35 N 23
Bramham	40 P 22
Bramhope	39 P 22
Bramley (South Yorks.)	36 Q 23
Bramley (Surrey)	19 S 30
Brampton (Cambs.)	29 T 27
Brampton (Cumbria)	50 L 19
Brampton (South Yorks.)	40 P 23
Brampton (Suffolk)	31 Y 26
Brancaster	30 V 25
Branderburgh	68 K 10
Brandesburton	41 T 22
Brandon (Durham)	46 P 19
Brandon (Suffolk)	30 V 26
Branscombe	5 K 31
Bransgore	9 O 31
Branston	36 S 24
Bratton Fleming	6 I 30
Braughing	22 U 28
Braunston	28 R 26
Braunstone	28 Q 26
Braunton	6 H 30
Bray-on-Thames	18 R 29
Bray Shop	3 G 32
Brayton	40 Q 22
Breadalbane	61 G 14
Bream	16 M 28
Breamore House	9 O 31
Breasclete	70 Z 9
Breaston	36 Q 25
Brechin	63 M 13
Breckland	30 V 26
Brecon/ Aberhonddu	25 J 28
Brecon Beacons National Park	15 J 28
Bredbury	39 N 23
Brede	12 V 31
Bredenbury	26 M 27
Bredon	27 N 27
Bredwardine	26 L 27
Brendon Hills	7 J 30
Brenig Reservoir	33 J 24
Brent (London Borough)	20 T 29
Brent Knoll	16 L 30
Brent Pelham	22 U 28
Brentwood	21 U 29
Brenzett	12 W 30
Bressay	75 Q 3
Bretherton	38 L 22
Brewlands Bridge	62 K 13
Brewood	27 N 25
Bride	42 G 20
Bridestowe	3 H 31
Bridge	13 X 30
Bridge of Allan	55 I 15
Bridge of Avon	68 J 11
Bridge of Craigisla	62 K 13
Bridge of Don	69 N 12
Bridge of Earn	56 J 14
Bridge of Forss	73 J 8
Bridge of Gairn	62 K 12
Bridge of Orchy	60 F 14
Bridgemary	10 Q 31
Bridgend (Islay)	52 B 16
Bridgend/ Pen-y-bont (Mid Glam.)	15 J 29
Bridgend (Tayside)	62 J 14
Bridgend of Lintrathen	62 K 13
Bridgnorth	26 M 26
Bridgwater	7 L 30
Bridlington	41 T 21
Bridport	8 L 31
Brierfield	39 N 22
Brierley Hill	27 N 26
Brigg	41 S 23
Brighouse	39 O 22
Brighstone	9 P 32
Brightlingsea	23 X 28
Brighton	11 T 31
Brightwell	18 Q 29
Brigstock	28 S 26
Brill	18 Q 28
Brimfield	26 L 27
Brimham Rocks	39 O 21
Brimington	35 P 24
Brinkburn Priory	51 O 18
Brinklow	27 P 26
Brinkworth	17 O 29
Brinyan	74 L 6
Brisley	30 W 25
Bristol	16 M 29
Briston	30 X 25
Briton Ferry	15 I 29
Brittle (Loch)	65 B 12
Brixham	4 J 32
Brixworth	28 R 27
Brize Norton	18 P 28
Broad Bay	70 B 9
Broad Blunsdon	17 O 29
Broad Chalke	9 O 30
Broad Law	49 J 17
Broadclyst	4 J 31
Broadford	65 C 12
Broadmayne	8 M 31
Broads (The)	31 Y 25
Broadstairs	13 Y 29
Broadstone	9 O 31
Broadwas	26 M 27
Broadway	27 O 27
Broadwey	8 M 32
Broadwindsor	8 L 31
Broch of Gurness	49 J 17
Brock	38 L 22
Brockenhurst	9 P 31
Brockley	16 L 29
Brockworth	17 N 28
Brodick	53 E 17
Brodick Castle	53 E 17
Brodick Bay	53 E 17
Brodie Castle	67 I 11
Brolass	59 B 14
Bromborough	34 L 24
Brome	30 X 26
Bromfield	26 L 26
Bromham	17 N 29
Bromley (London Borough)	21 U 29
Brompton (Kent)	12 V 29
Brompton (near Northallerton)	46 P 20
Brompton (Near Scarborough)	47 S 21
Brompton on Swale	45 O 20
Brompton Regis	7 J 30
Bromsgrove	27 N 26
Bromyard	26 M 27
Bronllys	25 K 27
Brooke	31 Y 26
Brookland	12 W 30
Brookmans Park	19 T 28
Broom (Loch)	66 E 10
Broomfield	7 K 30
Broomhaugh	51 O 19
Brora	73 H 9
Brotherton	40 Q 22
Brotton	47 R 20
Brough	45 N 20
Brough Head	74 J 6
Brough Lodge	75 R 2
Brough of Birsay	74 J 6
Broughton (Hants.)	9 P 30
Broughton (Humberside)	41 S 23
Broughton (Lancs.)	38 L 22
Broughton (Northants.)	28 R 26
Broughton (Oxon.)	27 P 27
Broughton-in-Furness	38 K 21
Broughty Ferry	62 L 14
Brownhills	27 O 26
Brownsea Island	9 O 31
Broxbourne	19 T 28
Broxburn	56 J 16
Bruichladdich	52 A 16
Brundall	31 Y 26
Brushford	7 J 30
Bruton	8 M 30
Brymbo	33 K 24
Brympton d'Evercy	8 L 31
Brynamman	15 I 28
Brynbuga/Usk	16 L 28
Bryncethin	15 J 29
Bryn-Henllan	14 F 27
Brynmawr	16 K 28
Bubwith	41 R 22
Buchlyvie	55 H 15
Buckden (Cambs.)	29 T 27
Buckden (North Yorks.)	45 N 21
Buckfast Abbey	4 I 32
Buckfastleigh	4 I 32
Buckhaven	56 K 15
Buckie	68 L 10
Buckingham	28 Q 27
Buckinghamshire (County)	18 R 28
Buckland (Herts.)	29 T 28
Buckland (Oxon.)	18 P 28
Buckland Abbey	3 H 32
Buckland Newton	8 M 31
Buckland St. Mary	7 K 31
Bucklers Hard	9 P 31
Buckley/Bwcle	33 K 24
Buckminster	36 R 25
Bucknell	26 L 26
Bucksburn	69 N 12
Bude	6 G 31
Budleigh Salterton	4 K 32
Bugle	3 F 32
Bugthorpe	40 R 21
Buildwas Abbey	26 M 26
Builth/Llanfair-ym-Muallt	25 J 27
Bulford	17 O 30
Bulkington	27 P 26
Bulwell	36 Q 24
Bunarkaig	60 F 13
Bunessan	59 B 15
Bungay	31 Y 26
Buntingford	29 T 28
Burbage (Leics.)	27 P 26
Burbage (Wilts.)	17 O 29
Bures	22 W 28
Burford	18 P 28
Burgess Hill	11 T 31
Burgh-by-Sands	44 K 19
Burgh-le-Marsh	37 U 24
Burghead	68 J 10
Burghley House	29 S 26
Burley	9 O 31
Burley-in-Wharfedale	39 O 22
Burneside	44 L 20
Burnham	20 S 29
Burnham Market	30 W 25
Burnham-on-Crouch	23 W 29
Burnham-on-Sea	7 L 30
Burnhaven	69 O 11
Burniston	47 S 21
Burnley	39 N 22
Burntisland	56 K 15
Burpham	20 S 30
Burravoe	75 Q 2
Burray	74 L 7
Burrelton	62 K 14
Burrow Head	42 G 19
Burry Port/ Porth Tywyn	15 H 28
Burscough	38 L 23
Burscough Bridge	38 L 23
Bursledon	10 Q 31
Burslem	34 N 24
Burton	44 L 21
Burton Agnes	41 T 21
Burton Bradstock	8 L 31
Burton Constable Hall	41 T 22
Burton in Lonsdale	38 M 21
Burton Joyce	36 Q 25
Burton Latimer	28 R 26
Burton Leonard	40 P 21
Burton Pidsea	41 T 22
Burton-upon-Stather	41 R 23
Burton-upon-Trent	35 O 25
Burwarton	26 M 26
Burwell (Cambs.)	29 U 27
Burwell (Lincs.)	37 U 24
Bury	39 N 23
Bury St. Edmunds	22 W 27
Busby	55 H 16
Buscot	17 P 28
Bushey	20 S 29
Bute (Kyles of)	54 E 16
Bute (Island of)	54 E 16
Bute (Sound of)	54 E 16
Butt of Lewis	71 B 8
Buttermere	44 K 20
Buxted	12 U 31
Buxton (Derbs.)	35 O 24
Buxton (Norfolk)	31 X 25
Bwcle/Buckley	33 K 24
Bwlch	16 K 28
Bwlch Oerddrws	33 I 25
Bwlch-y-Groes	15 I 28
Bwlch-y-Sarnau	25 J 26
Byfield	28 Q 27
Byfleet	20 S 30
Byland Abbey	46 Q 21

C

Cabrach	68 K 12
Cader Idris	32 I 25
Cadhay	5 K 31
Cadishead	34 M 23
Cadnam	9 P 31
Caerdydd/Cardiff	16 K 29
Caerffili/ Caerphilly	16 K 29
Caerfyrddin/ Carmarthen	15 H 28
Caergwrle	33 K 24
Caergybi/ Holyhead	32 G 24
Caerlaverock Castle	49 J 19
Caerleon	16 L 29
Caernarfon	32 H 24

BRISTOL CENTRE

Broadmead	DY
Fairfax Street	DY 35
Galleries' Shopping Centre (The)	DY
Horse Fair (The)	DY
Merchant Street	DY 47
Nelson Avenue	CY 51
Park Street	CY
Bedminster Parade	CZ 5
Bridgehead	CZ 9
Broad Quay	CYZ 13
Broad Street	CY 14
College Green	CZ 30
College Street	CZ 32
Colston Avenue	CY 33
Frog Lane	CY 37
Haymarket	DY 38
High Street	CDY 39
Lower Castle Street	CDY 43
Marlborough Street	CDY 46
Narrow Plain	DY 50
North Street	DY 52
Old Market Street	DY 54
Passage Street	DY 55
Quay Street	CY 58
Queen Charlotte Street	CZ 60
Redcliffe Mead Lane	DZ 61
St. Augustine's Parade	CY 66
Temple Gate	DZ 75
Trenchard Street	CY 77
Wine Street	DY 80

CAMBRIDGE

Grafton Centre . . . . . **Y**
Lion Yard Centre . . . . **Z**
Market Hill . . . . **Z** 18
Market Street . . . . . **Y** 19
Petty Cury . . . . **Z** 27
St. Andrew's St. . . . . **Z** 28
Sidney Street . . . . . **Y** 32
Trinity Street . . . . . **Y** 36

Bridge Street . . . . . **Y** 2
Corn Exchange St. . . **Z** 6
Downing Street . . . . **Z** 7
Free School Lane . . . **Z** 12
Hobson Street . . . . . **Y** 14

King's Parade . . . . . **Z** 15
Madingley Rd . . . . . **Y** 16
Magdalene St. . . . . . **Y** 17
Milton Road . . . . . . **Y** 20
Newmarket Road . . . **Y** 21
Northampton St. . . . **Y** 22
Parker Street . . . . . **Y** 23
Peas Hill . . . . **Z** 25
Pembroke Street . . . **Z** 26
St. John's Street . . . **Y** 29
Short Street . . . . . . **Y** 30
Tennis Court Road . . **Z** 35
Trumpington Road . . **Z** 37
Wheeler Street . . . . **Z** 39

COLLEGES
CHRIST'S . . . . **Y A**
CLARE . . . . **Z B**
CORPUS CHRISTI . . **Z D**
DARWIN . . . . **Z D**
DOWNING . . . . **Z E**
EMMANUEL . . . . . . **Z F**
GONVILLE
AND CAIUS . . . . . **Y G**
HARVEY COURT . . . **Z K**
HUGUES HALL . . . . **Z J**
JESUS . . . . **Y K**
KING'S . . . . **Z**

LUCY CAVENDISH **Y O**
MAGDALENE . . . . **Y N**
PEMBROKE . . . . . **Z O**
PETERHOUSE . . . . **Z O**
QUEENS' . . . . **Z**
RIDDLEY HALL . . . . **Z Q**
ST-CATHARINE'S . . **Z R**
ST-EDMUNDS
ST-JOHN'S . . . . . **Y U**
SIDNEY SUSSEX . . **Y P**
TRINITY . . . . **Y**
TRINITY HALL . . . . **Y V**
WESTMINSTER . . . **Y W**

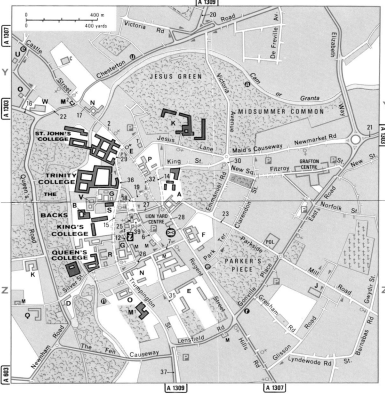

CANTERBURY
Burgate . . . . **Y**
Butchery Lane . . . . . **Y** 5
Guildhall Street . . . . **Y** 6
High Street . . . . **Y** 8
Mercery Lane . . . . . **Y** 12

Palace Street . . . . . **Y**
St. George's Street . . **Z** 17
St. Margaret's Street **YZ** 18
St. Peter's Street . . . **Y** 20

Beercart Lane . . . . . **YZ** 2
Borough (The) . . . . . **Y** 4
Lower Bridge Street . **Z** 9

Lower Chantry Lane . **Z** 10
Rhodaus Town . . . . . **Z** 13
Rosemary Lane . . . . **Z** 14
St. George's Place . . **Z** 16
St. Mary's Street . . . **Z** 19
St. Radigund's Street **Y** 21
Upper Bridge Street . **Z** 23
Watling Street . . . . . **Z** 25

CARDIFF
CAERDYDD
Duke Street . . . . **BZ** 26
High Street . . . . **BZ**
Queen Street . . . . . . **BZ**
St. David's
Centre . . . . **BZ**
St. Mary Street . . . . . **BZ**
Working Street . . . . . **BZ** 67

Castle Street . . . . . . **BZ** 9
Cathays Terrace . . . . **BY** 10
Central Square . . . . . **BZ** 12
Church Street . . . . . . **BZ** 14
City Hall Road . . . . . **BY** 15
College Road . . . . . . **BY** 20
Corbett Road . . . . . . **BY** 21
Customhouse Street . **BZ** 23
David Street . . . . **BZ** 25
Dumfries Place . . . . . **BY** 28
Greyfriars Road . . . . . **BZ** 29
Guilford Street . . . . . **BZ** 30

Hayes (The) . . . . **BZ** 32
King Edward VII Avenue **BY** 36
Mary Ann Street . . . . **BZ** 39
Moira Terrace . . . . . . **BZ** 42
Museum Avenue . . . . **BY** 43
Nantes (Boulevard de) **BY** 44
Newport Road . . . . . **BY** 46
Penarth Road . . . . . . **BZ** 49
St. Andrews Place . . . **BY** 56
St. John Street . . . . . **BZ** 58
Station Terrace . . . . . **BZ** 61
Stuttgart Street . . . . . **BY** 62

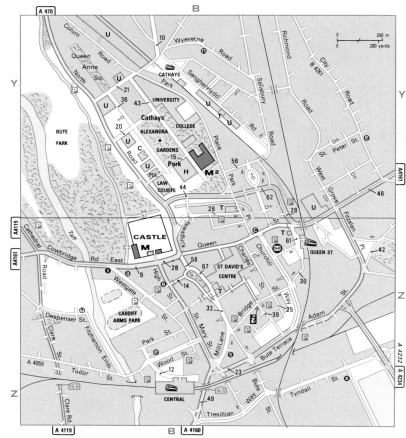

Caernarfon Bay . . . 32 G 24
Caerphilly/
Caerffili . . . . 16 K 29
Caersws . . . . 25 J 26
Caerwent . . . . 16 L 29
Cailliness Point . . . 42 F 19
Cairn Edward
Forest . . . . 49 H 18
Cairn Gorm . . . . . . 62 J 12
Cairn Table . . . . . . 49 H 17
Cairn Toul . . . . 61 I 12
Cairnborrow . . . . . 68 L 11
Cairndow . . . . 54 F 15
Cairnpapple Hill . . . 56 J 16
Cairnryan . . . . 48 E 19
Cairnsmore
of Carsphairn . . . 49 H 18
Cairnsmore of
Fleet . . . . 48 G 19
Cairraig Fhada . . . 52 B 17
Caister-on-Sea . . . 31 Z 26
Caistor . . . . 41 T 23
Calbourne . . . . 9 P 31
Caldbeck . . . . 44 K 19
Caldecott . . . . 28 R 26
Calder (Loch) . . . . 73 J 8
Calder Bridge . . . . 43 J 20
Caldercruix . . . . . . 55 I 16
Caldey Island . . . . 14 F 29
Calf of Man . . . . . . 42 F 21
Calfsound . . . . 74 L 6
Calgary Bay . . . . . 59 B 14
Caliach Point . . . . . 59 B 14
Callander . . . . 55 H 15
Callater (Glen) . . . 62 J 13
Callington . . . . 3 H 32
Calne . . . . 17 N 29
Calow . . . . 35 P 24
Calstock . . . . 3 H 32
Calvay . . . . 64 Y 12
Calvine . . . . 61 I 13
Cam . . . . 29 U 27
Cam Loch . . . . 72 E 9
Camas Chil
Mhalieu . . . . 60 D 14
Camber . . . . 12 W 31

Camberley . . . . . . 18 R 30
Camborne . . . . 2 E 33
Cambrian
Mountains . . . . . 25 I 27
Cambridge . . . . . . 29 U 27
Cambridgeshire
(County) . . . . . . 29 T 26
Cambusbarron . . . 55 I 15
Camden (London
Borough) . . . . . 20 T 29
Camelford . . . . 3 F 32
Cammachmore . . . 63 N 12
Campbeltown . . . . 53 D 17
Campsie Fells . . . . 55 H 15
Canewdon . . . . . . 22 W 29
Canisbay . . . . 74 K 8
Canna . . . . 65 A 12
Cannich . . . . 66 F 11
Cannich (Glen) . . . 66 F 11
Cannington . . . . . . 7 K 30
Cannock . . . . 27 N 25
Canonbie . . . . 50 L 18
Canterbury . . . . . . 13 X 30
Canvey Island . . . . 22 V 29
Caol . . . . 60 E 13
Caolas a'
Mhòrain . . . . 64 Y 10
Caolis . . . . 58 X 13
Caolisport (Loch) . . 53 D 16
Cape Cornwall . . . 2 C 33
Cape Wrath . . . . . 72 E 8
Capel . . . . 11 T 30
Capel Curig . . . . . . 32 I 24
Capel Garmon . . . 33 I 24
Capel Le Ferne . . . 13 X 30
Capel St. Mary . . . 23 X 27
Capesthorne Hall . 34 N 24
Capthorne . . . . . . 11 T 30
Caputh . . . . 62 J 14
Cara Island . . . . . . 53 C 17
Carbis Bay . . . . . . 2 D 33
Carbost . . . . 65 A 12
Cardiff/Caerdydd . . 16 K 29
Cardigan/
Aberteifi . . . . . . 24 G 27
Cardigan Bay . . . . 24 G 26

Cardinham . . . . . . 3 G 32
Cardross . . . . 54 G 16
Carew . . . . 14 F 28
Carhampton . . . . . 7 J 30
Carinish . . . . 64 Y 11
Carisbrooke . . . . . 10 Q 31
Cark . . . . 44 L 21
Carlisle . . . . 44 L 19
Carloway . . . . 70 Z 9
Carlton (Notts.) . . . 36 Q 25
Carlton
(South. Yorks.) . . 40 Q 22
Carlton Colville . . . 31 Z 26
Carlton in
Lindrick . . . . 36 Q 23
Carlton-on-Trent . . 36 R 24
Carluke . . . . 55 I 16
Carmarthen/
Caerfyrddin . . . . 15 H 28
Carmel Head . . . . 32 G 23
Carmunnock . . . . . 55 H 16
Carn Ban . . . . 61 H 12
Carn Coire
na h-Easgainn . . 67 H 12
Carn Eige . . . . 66 E 12
Carn Glas-choire . 67 I 11
Carn Mairg . . . . . . 61 H 14
Carnedd
Llewelyn . . . . . . 32 I 24
Carnforth . . . . 38 L 21
Carnoustie . . . . . . 63 L 14
Carnwath . . . . 56 J 16
Carradale . . . . 53 D 17
Carradale Bay . . . . 53 D 17
Carrbridge . . . . . . 67 I 12
Carrick . . . . 54 F 15
Carrick Roads . . . . 2 E 33
Carron (Loch) . . . . 66 C 11
Carse
of Gowrie . . . . . 62 K 14
Carsluith . . . . 42 G 19
Carsphairn . . . . . . 49 H 18
Carstairs . . . . 55 I 16
Cartmel . . . . 44 L 21
Cas-Gwent/
Chepstow . . . . . 16 M 29

CARLISLE

Botchergate .... **BZ**
Castle Street .... **BY 6**
English Street .... **BY 13**
Scotch Street .... **BY 19**

Annetwell Street .... **AY 2**

Bridge Street .... **AY 3**
Brunswick Street ...... **BZ 4**
Caldcotes .... **AY 5**
Charlotte Street ...... **AZ 7**
Chiswick Street .... **BY 8**
Church Street .... **AY 10**
Eden Bridge .... **BY 14**
Lonsdale Street .... **BY 15**
Lowther Street .... **BY**

Port Road .... **AY 16**
St. Aidan's Road ...... **BY 17**
St. Nicholas Street .... **BZ 18**
Spencer Street .... **BY 20**
Tait Street .... **BZ 21**
Victoria Viaduct ...... **ABZ 24**
West Tower Street .... **BY 26**
West Walls .... **ABY 27**
Wigton Road .... **AZ 29**

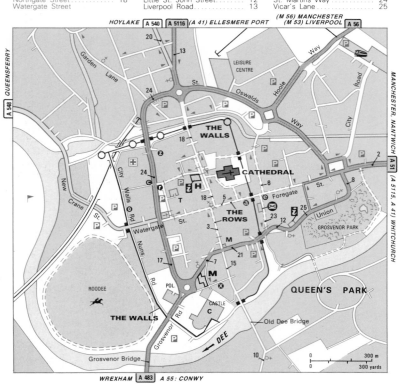

Casnewydd/
Newport 16 L 29
Cassley (Glen) 72 F 9
Castell-Nedd/
Neath 15 I 29
Castell Newydd
Emlyn/New-
castle Emlyn 24 G 27
Castle Acre 30 W 25
Castle Ashby 28 R 27
Castle Bolton 45 O 21
Castle Campbell 55 I 15
Castle Cary 8 M 30
Castle Combe 17 N 29
Castle Donington 35 P 25
Castle Douglas 49 I 19
Castle Drogo 4 I 31
Castle Fraser 69 M 12

Castle
Hedingham 22 V 28
Castle Howard 40 R 21
Castle Kennedy 42 F 19
Castle Lachlan 54 E 15
Castle Loch 42 F 19
Castlebay 64 X 13
Castleford 40 P 22
Castlemartin 14 F 29
Castlerigg 44 K 20
Castleton
(North Yorks.) 46 R 20
Castleton (Derbs.) 35 O 23
Castletown 73 J 8
Castletown 15 H 29
Catacol Bay 53 D 16
Caterham 20 T 30
Caterton 18 P 28

Catfield 31 Y 25
Catlodge 61 H 12
Caton 38 L 21
Catrine 49 H 17
Catteral 38 L 22
Catterick 46 P 20
Catterick
Garrison 45 O 20
Catworth 29 S 26
Cauldcleuch
Head 50 L 18
Cava 74 K 7
Cavendish 22 V 27
Cawdor 67 I 11
Cawood 40 Q 22
Caythorpe 36 S 24
Ceall (Loch nan) 59 C 13
Cefn Bryn 15 H 29

Cefn-Coed-
y-Cymer 16 J 28
Cefn-mawr 33 K 25
Ceinewydd/
New Quay 24 G 27
Ceiriog (Vale of) 33 K 25
Cemaes 32 G 23
Cemaes Head 24 F 27
Cemmaes 25 I 26
Cenarth 24 G 27
Central (Region) 55 G 15
Cerne Abbas 8 M 31
Cerrigydrudion 33 J 24
Chadderton 39 N 23
Chaddesden 35 P 25
Chadlington 18 P 28
Chadwell
St. Mary 21 V 29

Chagford 4 I 31
Chàirn Bhain
(Loch a') 72 E 9
Chalfont
St. Giles 20 S 29
Chalfont
St. Peter 20 S 29
Chalford 17 N 28
Chalgrove 18 Q 29
Challock 12 W 30
Chambercombe
Manor 6 H 30
Chandler's Ford 9 P 31
Channel Islands 5
Chapel-en-le-Frith 35 O 24
Chapel St.
Leonards 37 V 24
Chapelhall 55 I 16
Chapeltown 40 P 23
Chapmanslade 17 N 30
Chard 7 L 31
Charing 12 W 30
Charlbury 18 P 28
Charlecote Park 27 P 27
Charleston
Manor 12 U 31
Charlestown 3 F 33
Charlton Kings 17 N 28
Charlton Marshall 8 N 31
Charlwood 11 T 30
Charminster 8 M 31
Charmouth 7 L 31
Charsfield 23 X 27
Chartham 13 X 30
Chartwell 21 U 30
Chastleton 27 P 28
Chatburn 39 M 22
Chatham 12 V 29
Chatsworth
House 35 P 24
Chatteris 29 U 26
Chatton 51 O 17
Chawleigh 6 I 31
Cheadle
(Gtr. Mches.) 35 N 23
Cheadle (Staffs.) 35 O 25
Cheddar Gorge 16 L 30
Cheddington 19 S 28
Cheddleton 35 N 24
Chedworth 17 O 28
Chelford 34 N 24
Chellaston 35 P 25
Chelmsford 22 V 28
Cheltenham 17 N 28
Chelveston 29 S 27
Chepstow/
Cas-Gwent 16 M 29
Cheriton Bishop 4 I 31
Chertsey 20 S 29
Cherwell (River) 18 Q 28
Cheselbourne 8 M 31
Chesham 20 S 28
Chesham Bois 20 S 28
Cheshire (County) 34 M 24
Cheshunt 21 T 28
Chesil Beach 8 M 32
Cheslyn Hay 27 N 26
Chester 34 L 24
Chester-le-Street 46 P 19
Chesterfield 35 P 24
Chesters Fort 51 N 18
Chesterton 18 Q 28
Cheviot (The) 51 N 17
Cheviot Hills
(The) 50 M 17
Chew Magna 16 M 29
Chewton Mendip 16 M 30
Chichester 10 R 31
Chickerell 8 M 32
Chicklade 8 N 30
Chiddingfold 11 S 30
Chiddingstone 12 U 30
Chideock 8 L 31
Chigwell 21 U 29
Chilcompton 17 M 30
Chilham 13 W 30
Chilmark 8 N 30
Chiltern Hills 18 R 29
Chilton 18 Q 29
Chippenham 17 N 29
Chipping 38 M 22
Chipping
Campden 27 O 27
Chipping Norton 18 P 28
Chipping Ongar 21 U 28
Chipping
Sodbury 17 M 29
Chipping Warden 28 Q 27

Chirbury 25 K 26
Chirk Castle 33 K 25
Chirnside 57 N 16
Chiseldon 17 O 29
Chislet 13 X 30
Chitterne 8 N 30
Chittlehampton 6 I 30
Chobham 20 S 29
Choire (Loch) 73 H 9
Cholesbury 19 S 28
Cholsey 18 Q 29
Chon (Loch) 55 G 15
Chopwell 51 O 19
Chorley 38 M 23
Chorleywood 20 S 29
Christchurch 9 O 31
Chroisg (Loch a') 66 E 11
Chudleigh 4 J 32
Chulmleigh 6 I 31
Church 39 M 22
Church Eaton 34 N 25
Church Fenton 40 Q 22
Church Stoke 25 K 26
Church Stretton 26 L 26
Churchill (Avon) 16 L 29
Churchill (Oxon.) 18 P 28
Churnet 35 N 24
Churt 10 R 30
Cilcain 33 K 24
Cilgerran 24 G 27
Cilmery 25 J 27
Cinderford 17 M 28
Cirencester 17 O 28
City of London
(London
Borough) 20 T 29
Clach Leathad 60 F 14
Clachan 53 D 16
Clachan Mór 58 Z 14
Clachan
of Glendaruel 54 E 15
Clackavoid 62 J 13
Clackmannan 55 I 15
Clacton-on-Sea 23 X 28
Claggain Bay 52 B 16
Claidh (Loch) 70 A 10
Clandon Park 20 S 30
Clapham (Beds.) 29 S 27
Clapham
(North Yorks.) 39 M 21
Clàr (Loch nan) 73 H 9
Clare 22 V 27
Clashmore 67 H 10
Clashnessie 72 E 9
Clatteringshaws
(Loch) 49 H 18
Clauchlands
Point 53 E 17
Clavering 22 U 28
Claverley 26 N 26
Claverton Manor 17 N 29
Clawdd-newydd 33 J 24
Clawton 6 H 31
Claxton 40 R 21
Clay Cross 35 P 24
Claydon 23 X 27
Claydon House 18 R 28
Clayton 11 T 31
Clayton-le-Moors 39 M 22
Clayton West 39 P 23
Cleadale 59 B 13
Cleadon 51 P 19
Cleator Moor 43 J 20
Cleckheaton 39 O 22
Cleehill 26 M 26
Cleethorpes 41 U 23
Cleeve Abbey 7 J 30
Clehonger 26 L 27
Cleigh 60 D 14
Clent 27 N 26
Cleobury
Mortimer 26 M 26
Cleobury North 26 M 26
Clephanton 67 I 11
Clevedon 16 L 29
Cleveland
(County) 46 Q 20
Cleveland Hills 46 Q 20
Cleveleys 38 K 22
Cley Next the
Sea 30 X 25
Cliffe 12 V 29
Clifton Hampden 18 Q 29
Clisham 70 Z 10
Clitheroe 39 M 22
Cliveden House 19 R 29
Clocaenog Forest 33 J 24
Clola 69 O 11

Clophill 29 S 27
Clouds Hill 8 N 31
Cloughton 47 S 20
Clova (Glen) 62 K 13
Clovelly 6 G 31
Clovulin 60 E 13
Clowne 36 Q 24
Cluanie Loch 66 E 12
Clumber Park 36 Q 24
Clun 25 K 26
Clunbury 26 L 26
Clunes Forest 60 F 13
Clunie 62 J 14
Clutton 16 M 30
Clwyd (County) 33 J 24
Clwydian Range 33 K 24
Clydach 15 I 28
Clyde (Firth of) 48 F 17
Clyde (River) 55 I 16
Clydebank 55 G 16
Clydesdale 55 I 16
Clywedog Resr. 25 J 26
Coalville 35 P 25
Coatbridge 55 H 16
Cobham 20 S 30
Cock Bridge 68 K 12
Cockburnspath 57 M 16
Cockenzie
and Port Seton 56 L 16
Cockermouth 43 J 20
Cocking 10 R 31
Codford St. Mary 8 N 30
Codicote 19 T 28
Codnor 35 P 24
Codsall 27 N 26
Coe (Glen) 60 F 14
Coed y Brenin
Forest 32 I 25
Coedpoeth 33 K 24
Coggeshall 22 W 28
Coigach 72 E 10
Coignafearn
Forest 67 H 12
Colby 42 F 21
Colchester 23 W 28
Cold Fell 45 M 19
Coldbackie 72 G 8
Colden Common 10 Q 31
Coldingham 57 N 16
Coldstream 57 N 17
Coleford (Glos.) 16 M 28
Coleford
(Somerset) 17 M 30
Coleshill 27 O 26
Colgrave Sound 75 R 2
Coll 59 A 14
Collieston 69 O 11
Collin 49 J 18
Collingham
(Notts.) 36 R 24
Collingham
(West Yorks.) 40 P 22
Collyweston 29 S 26
Colmonell 48 F 18
Coln (River) 17 O 28
Colnabaichin 68 K 12
Colne 39 N 22
Colne (River) 23 X 28
Colonsay 52 B 15
Colpy 69 M 11
Colquhon Castle 69 N 11
Colsterworth 36 S 25
Coltishall 31 Y 25
Colwall Stone 26 M 27
Colwyn Bay/
Bae Colwyn 33 I 24
Colyton 5 K 31
Combe Florey 7 K 30
Combe Martin 6 H 30
Combwich 7 K 30
Compton (Berks.) 18 Q 29
Compton
(West Sussex) 10 R 31
Compton Castle 4 J 32
Compton
Wynyates 27 P 27
Comrie 61 I 14
Cona Glen 60 D 13
Condover 26 L 26
Congleton 34 N 24
Congresbury 16 L 29
Coningsby 37 T 24
Conisbrough 40 Q 23
Coniston 44 K 20
Connah's Quay 33 K 24
Connel 60 D 14
Conon Bridge 67 G 11
Consett 45 O 19

CHESTER

Bridge Street 3
Eastgate Street 5
Northgate Street 18
Watergate Street

Boughton 2
Frodsham Street 6
Grosvenor Street 7
Grosvenor Park Road .. 8
Handbridge 10
Little St. John Street ... 12
Liverpool Road 13

Lower Bridge Street ... 15
Nicholas Street 17
Parkgate Road 20
Pepper Street 21
St. John Street 23
St. Martins Way 24
Vicar's Lane 25

COVENTRY

Broadgate 6
Corporation Street
Shopping Precincts

Bayley Lane 3
Bishop Street 5
Burges 7
Earl Street 10
Fairfax Street 12

Far Gosford Street 13
Gosford Street 15
Greyfriars Lane 16
Hales Street 17
Hearsall Lane 21
High Street 22
Ironmonger Row 23
Jordan Well 26
Leicester Row 29
Light Lane 30
Little Park Street 31
Primrose Hill Street .. 34

Queen Victoria Road .. 35
St. Johns (Ringway) ... 38
St. Nicholas (Ringway) . 39
Swanswell (Ringway) .. 40
Trinity Street 41
Upper Well Street 43
Vecquaery Street 45
Victoria Street 46
Warwick Row 49
White Street 51
Windsor Street 52
White Friars (Ringway) . 54

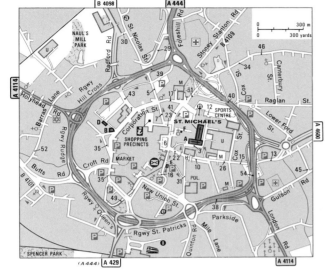

Constantine Bay	2 E 32	Cowal	54 E 15	Cringleford	31 X 26
Contin	67 G 11	Cowan Bridge	45 M 21	Crocketford	49 I 18
Convinth (Glen)	67 G 11	Cowbridge/		Crockham Hill	21 U 30
Conway Falls	33 I 24	Bont-faen	16 J 29	Croft	26 L 27
Conwy	33 I 24	Cowdenbeath	56 K 15	Croft-on-Tees	46 P 20
Conwy (River)	33 I 24	Cowdray House	10 R 31	Croggan	59 C 14
Conwy (Vale of)	33 I 24	Cowes	10 Q 31	Cromalt Hills	72 E 9
Cooden Beach	12 V 31	Cowfold	11 T 31	Cromar	68 L 12
Cookham	18 R 29	Cowplain	10 Q 31	Cromarty	67 H 10
Coolham	11 S 31	Coxheath	12 V 30	Cromarty Firth	67 H 11
Coombe Bissett	9 O 30	Coylton	48 G 17	Cromdale	68 J 11
Copdock	23 X 27	Cragside		Cromdale	
Copmanthorpe	40 Q 22	Gardens	51 O 18	(Hills of)	68 J 12
Copplestone	7 I 31	Craig	66 E 11	Cromer	31 X 25
Coquet (River)	51 N 17	Craig-y-nos	15 I 28	Cromford	35 P 24
Corbridge	51 N 19	Craigellachie	68 K 11	Crondall	18 R 30
Corby	28 R 26	Craighead	56 M 15	Crook	45 O 19
Corby Glen	36 S 25	Craighouse	53 C 16	Crook of Devon	56 J 15
Corfe Castle	8 N 32	Craigievar Castle	69 L 12	Crookham Village	18 R 30
Corhampton	10 Q 31	Craignish (Loch)	54 D 15	Cropwell Bishop	36 R 25
Cornhill	69 L 11	Craignure	59 C 14	Crosby	38 K 23
Cornhill-on-		Craigrothie	56 L 15	Crosby	
Tweed	57 N 17	Craik	50 K 17	Ravensworth	45 M 20
Cornwall		Crail	56 M 15	Croscombe	8 M 30
(County)	3 F 32	Cramlington	51 P 18	Cross	71 B 8
Cornwood	4 I 32	Cramond	56 K 16	Cross Fell	45 M 19
Corpach	60 E 13	Cranborne	9 O 31	Cross Hands	15 H 28
Corpusty	30 X 25	Cranbrook	12 V 30	Cross Inn	24 H 27
Corran	60 E 13	Cranfield	28 S 27	Crossapoll	58 Z 14
Corrie	53 E 17	Cranleigh	11 S 30	Crosshill (Fife)	56 K 15
Corrieshalloch		Crathes Castle	63 M 12	Crosshill	
Gorge	66 E 10	Crathie	62 K 12	(Strathclyde)	48 G 18
Corrimony	67 F 11	Crathorne	46 Q 20	Crosshouse	54 G 17
Corringham	22 V 29	Craven Arms	26 L 26	Crosskeys	16 K 29
Corryvreckan		Crawford	49 J 17	Crosskirk	73 J 8
(Gulf of)	52 C 15	Crawley (Hants.)	9 P 30	Crossmichael	49 I 19
Corscombe	8 L 31	Crawley		Crouch (River)	23 W 29
Corsham	17 N 29	(West Sussex)	11 T 30	Crowborough	12 U 30
Corsham Court	17 N 29	Crawley Down	11 T 30	Crowcombe	7 K 30
Corstopitum	51 N 19	Creag Meagaidh	60 G 13	Crow Hill	17 M 28
Corwen	33 J 25	Creagorry	64 Y 11	Crowhurst	12 V 31
Cosby	28 Q 26	Crediton	7 J 31	Crowland	29 T 25
Cosham	10 Q 31	Creetown	48 G 19	Crowle	41 R 23
Costessey	30 X 26	Creran (Loch)	60 D 14	Crowlin Island	66 C 11
Cotehele	3 H 32	Cressage	26 M 26	Crowthorne	18 R 29
Cotherstone	45 O 20	Creswell	36 Q 24	Croxley Green	20 S 29
Cothi (River)	15 H 28	Crewe	34 M 24	Croy	67 H 11
Cotswold Hills	17 N 29	Crewkerne	8 L 31	Croyde	6 H 30
Cotswold		Crianlarich	60 G 14	Croydon (London	
Wildlife Park	17 O 28	Criccieth	32 H 25	Borough)	20 T 29
Cottenham	29 U 27	Crich	35 P 24	Cruden Bay	69 O 11
Cottered	29 T 28	Crichton	56 L 16	Crudgington	34 M 25
Cottingham		Crick	28 Q 26	Crudwell	17 N 29
(Humberside)	41 S 22	Cricket		Crugybar	24 I 27
Cottingham		St. Thomas	8 L 31	Crulivig	70 Z 9
(Northants.)	28 R 26	Crickhowell	16 K 28	Crynant	15 I 28
Countesthorpe	28 Q 26	Cricklade	17 O 29	Cuckfield	11 T 31
Coupar Angus	62 K 14	Crieff	61 I 14	Cuckney	36 Q 24
Cove Bay	69 N 12	Crimond	69 O 11	Cuddington	34 M 24
Coventry	27 P 26	Crinan	54 D 15	Cudworth	40 P 23
Coverack	2 E 33	Crinan (Loch)	54 D 15	Cuffley	20 T 28

Cuillin Hills	65 B 12	Deben (River)	23 X 27
Cuillin Sound	65 B 12	Debenham	23 X 27
Culdrose	2 E 33	Deddington	28 Q 28
Cullen	68 L 10	Dedham	23 X 28
Cullen Bay	68 L 10	Dee (River)	
Cullen House	68 L 10	(Scotland)	69 N 12
Cullipool	54 D 15	Dee/Afon	
Cullompton	7 J 31	Dyfrdwy	
Culmington	26 L 26	(River) (Wales)	33 K 24
Culmstock	7 K 31	Deeping	
Culrain	72 G 10	St. Nicholas	37 T 25
Culross	56 J 15	Deeps (The)	75 P 3
Culter Fell	49 J 17	Defford	27 N 27
Cults	69 N 12	Delabole	3 F 32
Culzean Castle	48 F 17	Delamere Forest	34 L 24
Cumbernauld	55 I 16	Delph	39 N 23
Cumbria (County)	44 K 19	Denby Dale	39 P 23
Cumbrian		Denham	20 S 29
Moutains	44 K 20	Denholm	50 L 17
Cuminestown	69 N 11	Denmead	10 Q 31
Cummersdale	44 L 19	Dennington	31 Y 27
Cummertrees	49 J 19	Denny	55 I 15
Cumnock	49 H 17	Dent	45 M 21
Cumnor	18 P 28	Denton	39 N 23
Cunninghame	54 G 17	Derby	35 P 25
Cunninghamhead	54 G 17	Derbyshire	
Cupar	56 K 15	(County)	35 O 24
Curdridge	10 Q 31	Dersingham	30 V 25
Currie	56 K 16	Dervaig	59 B 14
Curry Rivel	8 L 30	Derwent (River)	
Cwm	16 K 28	(R. Ouse)	40 R 22
Cwm Bychan	32 H 25	Derwent (River)	
Cwmbrân	16 K 29	(R. Trent)	35 P 24
Cwmllynfell	15 I 28	Derwent (River)	
Cwmystwyth	25 I 26	(R. Tyne)	45 O 19
Cydweli/Kidwelly	15 H 28	Derwent Dale	39 O 23
Cymmer	16 J 29	Derwent	
Cymyran Bay	32 G 24	Reservoir	
		(Derbs.)	35 O 23

D

		Derwent	
		Reservoir	
		(Northumb.)	45 N 19
Dailly	48 F 18	Derwent Water	44 K 20
Daimh (Loch an)	61 G 14	Desborough	28 R 26
Dairsie or		Desford	28 Q 26
Osnaburgh	56 L 14	Detling	12 V 30
Dalavich	54 E 15	Deveron (River)	69 M 11
Dalbeattie	49 I 19	Devil's Beef Tub	49 J 17
Dalby	42 F 21	Devil's Bridge/	
Dale	14 E 28	Pontarfynach	25 I 26
Daliburgh	64 X 12	Devil's Elbow	62 J 13
Dalkeith	56 K 16	Devil's Punch	
Dallas	68 J 11	Bowl	10 R 30
Dallington	12 V 31	Devizes	17 O 29
Dalmally	60 F 14		
Dalmellington	48 G 18		
Dalmeny	56 J 16		
Dalnabreck	59 C 13		
Dalry (Dumfries			
and Galloway)	49 H 18		
Dalry			
(Strathclyde)	54 F 16		
Dalrymple	48 G 17		
Dalston	44 L 19		
Dalton (Dumfries			
and Galloway)	49 J 18		
Dalton			
(North Yorks.)	46 P 20		
Dalton			
(Strathclyde)	48 G 18		
Dalton in Furness	44 K 21		
Damh (Loch)	66 D 11		
Danbury	22 V 28		
Dane	35 N 24		
Darenth	21 U 29		
Darfield	40 P 23		
Darlington	46 P 20		
Darowen	25 I 26		
Dartford	21 U 29		
Dartford Tunnel	21 U 29		
Dartington	4 I 32		
Dartmeet	4 I 32		
Dartmoor			
National Park	4 I 32		
Dartmouth	4 J 32		
Darton	40 P 23		
Darvel	55 H 17		
Darwen	39 M 22		
Datchet	20 S 29		
Dava	68 J 11		
Daventry	28 Q 27		
Davidstow	3 G 32		
Daviot	67 H 11		
Dawley	26 M 26		
Dawlish	4 J 32		
Deal	13 Y 30		
Dean Forest Park	16 M 28		
Deanich Lodge	67 F 10		
Deanston	55 H 15		
Dearham	44 J 19		

Devon (County)	6 I 31	Donnington	
Devonport	3 H 32	(Berks.)	18 Q 29
Dewsbury	39 P 22	Donnington	
Dherue		(Salop)	34 M 25
(Loch an)	72 G 8	Donyatt	7 L 31
Didcot	18 Q 29	Doon (Loch)	48 G 18
Diddlebury	26 L 26	Dorchester	
Dighty Water	62 K 14	(Dorset)	8 M 31
Dilwyn	26 L 27	Dorchester	
Dinas Dinlle	32 G 24	(Oxon.)	18 Q 29
Dinas Head	14 F 27	Dordon	27 P 26
Dinbych/Denbigh	33 J 24	Dorking	19 T 30
Dinbych-		Dormans Land	11 U 30
y-pysgod/		Dormanstown	46 Q 20
Tenby	14 F 28	Dornie	66 D 12
Dingwall	67 G 11	Dornoch	67 H 10
Dinnet	62 L 12	Dornoch Firth	67 H 10
Dinnington	36 Q 23	Dorrington	26 L 26
Dinton	9 O 30	Dorset (County)	8 M 31
Dirleton	56 L 15	Dorstone	25 K 27
Dishforth	40 P 21	Douchary (Glen)	66 F 10
Diss	30 X 26	Douglas	
Distington	43 J 20	(Isle of Man)	42 G 21
Ditcheat	8 M 30	Douglas	
Ditchley Park	18 P 28	(Strathclyde)	49 I 17
Ditchling	11 T 31	Douglastown	62 L 14
Ditton Priors	26 M 26	Dounby	74 K 6
Doc Penfro/		Doune	55 H 15
Pembroke		Dove (River)	35 O 24
Dock	14 F 28	Dovedale	35 O 24
Docherty (Glen)	66 E 11	Dover	13 Y 30
Dochgarroch	67 H 11	Doveridge	35 O 25
Docking	30 V 25	Dovey/Dyfi	
Doddington		(River)	24 I 26
(Cambs.)	29 U 26	Downderry	3 G 32
Doddington		Downham	29 U 26
(Kent)	12 W 30	Downham	
Doddington		Market	30 V 26
(Lincs.)	36 S 24	Downies	63 N 12
Doddington		Downton	9 O 31
(Northumb.)	51 O 17	Draycott	35 P 25
Dodman Point	3 F 33	Draycott-	
Dodworth	40 P 23	in-the-Moors	35 N 25
Dolfor	25 K 26	Drayton (Norfolk)	31 X 25
Dolgellau	32 I 25	Drayton (Oxon.)	18 Q 29
Dolgoch Falls	24 I 26	Dreghorn	54 G 17
Dollar	55 I 15	Drenewydd/	
Dolton	6 H 31	Newtown	25 K 26
Don (River)	40 Q 23	Dreswick Point	42 G 21
Don (River)	68 K 12	Drigg	43 J 20
Doncaster	40 Q 23	Drimnin	59 C 14
Donington	37 T 25	Droitwich	27 N 27
Donington-on-		Dronfield	35 P 24
Bain	37 T 24	Drongan	48 G 17
Donisthorpe	35 P 25	Droylsden	39 N 23

DERBY

Corn Market .... Z 13
Iron Gate .... Y 22
Shopping Centre .... Z
Victoria Street .... Z 39

Albert Street .... Z 2
Babington Lane .... Z 3
Bold Lane .... Y 4
Bradshaw Way .... Z 5
Cathedral Road .... Y 7
Charnwood Street ...... Z 9
Corporation Street .... YZ 14
Duffield Road .... Y 17

East Street .... Z 18
Full Street .... Y 19
Jury Street .... Y 23
King Street .... Y 25
Leopold Street .... Z 26
Market Place .... YZ 27
Midland Road .... Z 28
Mount Street .... Z 29
Normanton Road ...... Z 31
Queen Street .... Y 32
St. Mary's Gate .... Z 33
St. Peter's Street ..... Z 34
Sacheverel
Street .... Z 36
Stafford Street .... Z 37
Wardwick .... Z 41

Druidibeg (Loch) 64 Y 12
Druim a' Chliabhain (Loch) 73 H 8
Drum Castle 69 M 12
Drumbeg 72 E 9
Drumclog 55 H 17
Drumlanrig Castle 49 I 18
Drumlithie 63 M 13
Drummond Castle 55 I 14
Drummore 42 F 19
Drummossie Muir 67 H 11
Drumnadrochit 67 G 11
Drumtochty Forest 63 M 13
Druridge Bay 51 P 18
Drybrook 16 M 28
Dryburgh Abbey 50 M 17
Drygarn Fawr 25 J 27
Drymen 55 G 15
Ducklington 18 P 28
Duddington 29 S 26
Dudley 27 N 26
Duff House 69 M 11
Duffield 35 P 25
Dufftown 68 K 11
Duffus 68 J 10
Duich (Loch) 66 D 12
Duirinish 65 C 12
Duke's Pass 55 G 15
Dukinfield 39 N 23
Dulnain Bridge 68 J 12
Duloe 3 G 32
Dulverton 7 J 30
Dumbarton 55 G 16
Dumfries 49 J 18
Dumfries and Galloway (Region) 49 H 18
Dun Carloway Broch 70 Z 9
Dunbar 57 M 15
Dunbeath 73 J 9
Dunblane 55 I 15
Duncansby Head 74 K 8
Dunchurch 28 Q 26
Duncton 11 S 31
Dundee 62 L 14
Dundonald 48 G 17
Dundrennan 43 I 19
Dunecht 69 M 12
Dunfermline 56 J 15
Dungeness 13 W 31
Dunholme 36 S 24
Dunkeld 62 J 14
Dunkery Beacon 7 J 30
Dunlop 55 G 16
Dunnet 73 J 8
Dunnet Bay 73 J 8
Dunnet Head 74 J 7
Dunning 56 J 15
Dunnottar Castle 63 N 13
Dunoon 54 F 16
Dunrobin Castle 73 I 10
Duns 57 M 16
Dunscore 49 I 18
Dunsfold 11 S 30
Dunsford 4 I 31
Dunsop Bridge 38 M 22
Dunstable 19 S 28
Dunstanburgh Castle 51 P 17
Dunster 7 J 30
Duntelchaig (Loch) 67 H 11
Dunure 48 F 17
Dunvegan 65 A 11
Dunvegan (Loch) 64 A 11
Dunvegan Castle 65 A 11
Dunvegan Head 64 Z 11
Dunwich 31 Y 27
Durdle Door 8 N 32
Durham 46 P 19
Durham (County) 45 N 19
Durlston Head 9 O 32
Durness 72 F 8
Durrington 17 O 30
Dursley 17 M 28
Dury Voe 75 Q 2
Duston 28 R 27
Duxford 29 U 27
Dyce 69 N 12
Dyfed (County) 14 F 28
Dyfi/Dovey (River) 24 I 26
Dykehead 62 K 13
Dykends 62 K 13
Dymchurch 13 W 30
Dymock 26 M 28
Dyrham 17 M 29
Dyrham Park 17 M 29
Dyserth 33 J 24

E

Eaglesham 55 H 16
Eakring 36 R 24
Ealing (London Borough) 20 T 29
Earba (Lochan na h-) 61 G 13
Earby 39 N 22
Eardisley 25 K 27
Earl Shilton 28 Q 26
Earl Soham 23 X 27
Earl Stonham 23 X 27
Earley Winnersh 18 R 29
Earls Barton 28 R 27
Earls Colne 22 W 28
Earlsferry 56 L 15
Earlston 56 L 17
Earn (Loch) 61 H 14
Earn (River) 61 H 14
Earn (River) 56 J 14
Easdale 54 D 15
Easebourne 10 R 31
Easington 46 P 19
Easington Lane 46 P 19
Easingwold 40 Q 21
East Bergholt 23 X 28
East Brent 16 L 30
East Budleigh 4 K 32
East Cowes 10 Q 31
East Dereham 30 W 25
East Glen (River) 37 S 25
East Grinstead 11 T 30
East Hagbourne 18 Q 29
East Hanney 18 P 29
East Harling 30 W 26
East Hendred 18 P 29
East Hoathly 12 U 31
East Horsley 20 S 30
East Huntspill 8 L 30
East Ilsley 18 Q 29
East Kilbride 55 H 16
East Knoyle 8 N 30
East Lambrook 8 L 31
East Leake 36 Q 25
East Linton 56 M 16
East Loch Roag 70 Z 9
East Loch Tarbet 70 Z 10
East Looe 3 G 32
East Lulworth 8 N 32
East Markham 36 R 24
East Meon 10 Q 31
East Midlands Airport 36 Q 25
East Moor 35 P 24
East Retford 36 R 24
East Rhidorroch Lodge 72 F 10
East Sussex (County) 12 U 30
East Wemyss 56 K 15
East Wittering 10 R 31
Eastbourne 12 U 31
Eastchurch 12 W 29
Eastdean 12 U 31
Easter Ross 67 G 10
Eastergate 10 S 31
Eastham 34 L 24
Eastleigh 9 P 31
Easton (Dorset) 8 M 32
Easton (Norfolk) 30 X 26
Easton-in-Gordano 16 L 29
Eastriggs 50 K 19
Eastry 13 X 30
Eastville 37 U 24
Eastwood 36 Q 24
Ebbw Vale/Glyn Ebwy 16 K 28
Ebchester 45 O 19
Ecclefechan 50 K 18
Eccles 39 M 23
Eccleshall 34 N 25
Echt 69 M 12
Eckington (Derbs.) 35 P 24
Eckington (Heref. and Worc.) 27 N 27
Edale 35 O 23
Eday 74 L 6
Edderton 67 H 10
Eddrachillis Bay 72 E 9
Edenbridge 12 U 30
Eden (River) 44 K 19
Edgmond 34 M 25
Edinburgh 56 K 16
Edington 17 N 30
Edlesborough 19 S 28
Edwinstowe 36 Q 24
Edzell 63 M 13
Eggerness Point 42 G 19

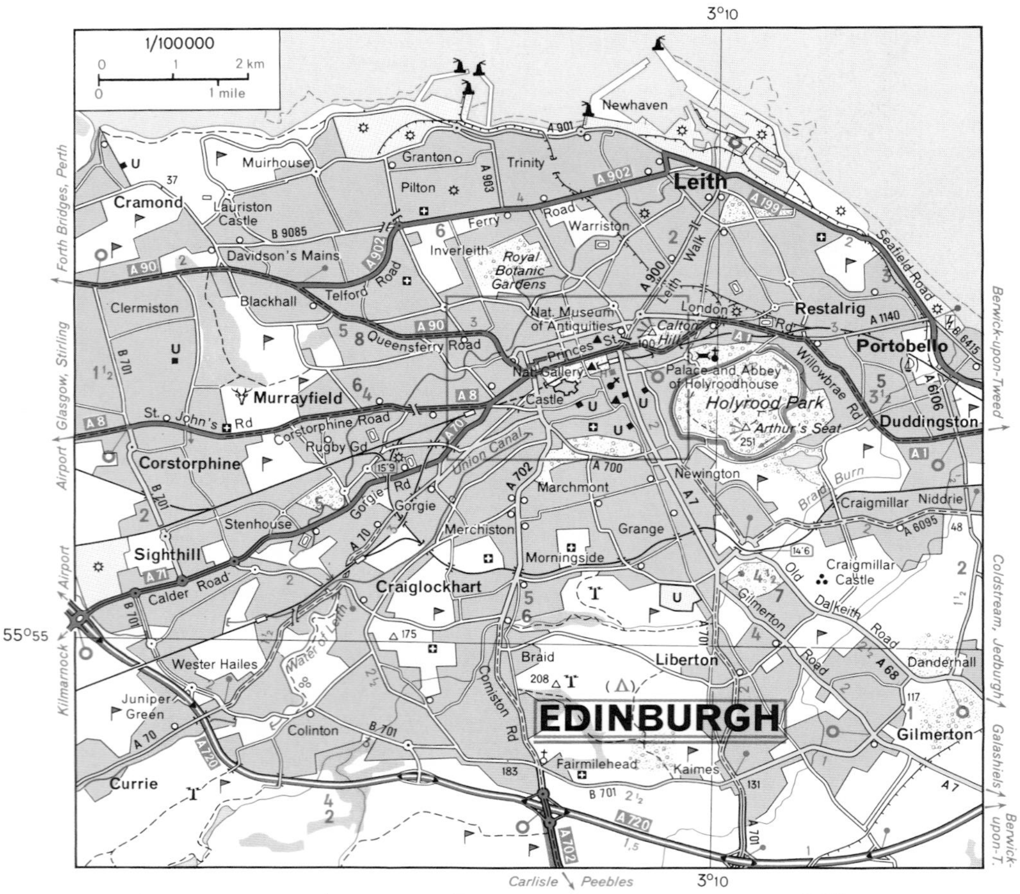

1/100000
0 1 2 km
0 1 mile
3°10
55°55
Newhaven
Leith
Granton
Trinity
Muirhouse
Cramond
Lauriston Castle
Pilton
Warriston
Inverleith
Royal Botanic Gardens
Davidson's Mains
Restalrig
Portobello
Clermiston
Blackhall
Nat. Museum of Antiquities
Calton Hill
Queensferry Road
Princes St.
Nat. Gallery
Castle
Palace and Abbey of Holyroodhouse
Holyrood Park
Arthur's Seat
Murrayfield
St. John's Rd
Corstorphine Road
Corstorphine
Rugby Gd
Union Canal
Duddingston
Marchmont
Newington
Craigmillar
Niddrie
Stenhouse
Gorgie
Merchiston
Grange
Sighthill
Calder Road
Craiglockhart
Morningside
Craigmillar Castle
Wester Hailes
Water of Leith
Braid
Liberton
Danderhall
Juniper Green
EDINBURGH
Colinton
Fairmilehead
Kaimes
Gilmerton
Currie
Comiston Rd
Forth Bridges, Perth
Glasgow, Stirling
Airport
Kilmarnock
Berwick-upon-Tweed
Coldstream, Jedburgh
Galashiels
Berwick-upon-T.
Carlisle
Peebles

EDINBURGH

Castle Street DY
Frederick Street DY
George Street DY
Hanover Street DY
High Street EYZ 37
Lawnmarket EYZ 46
Princes Street DY
St. James Centre EY
Waverley Market EY

Bernard Terrace EZ 3
Bread Street DZ 6
Bristo Place EZ 7
Candlemaker Row EZ 9
Castlehill DZ 10
Chambers Street EZ 12
Chapel Street EZ 13
Charlotte Square CY 14
Deanhaugh Street CY 23
Douglas Gardens CY 25
Drummond Street EZ 27
Forrest Road EZ 31
Gardner's Crescent CZ 32
George IV Bridge EZ 33
Grassmarket DZ 35
Home Street DZ 38
Hope Street CY 39
Johnston Terrace DZ 42
King's Bridge DZ 44
King's Stables Road DZ 45
Leith Street EY 47
Leven Street DZ 48
Lothian Street EZ 51
Mound (The) DY 55
North Bridge EY 61
North St. Andrew Street EY 66
Raeburn Place CY 69
Randolph Crescent CY 71
St. Andrew Square EY 73
St. Mary's Street EY 75
Shandwick Place CYZ 77
South Charlotte Street DY 78
South St. David Street DEY 79
Spittal Street DZ 83
Victoria Street EZ 84
Waterloo Place EY 87
Waverley Bridge EY 89
West Maitland Street CZ 92

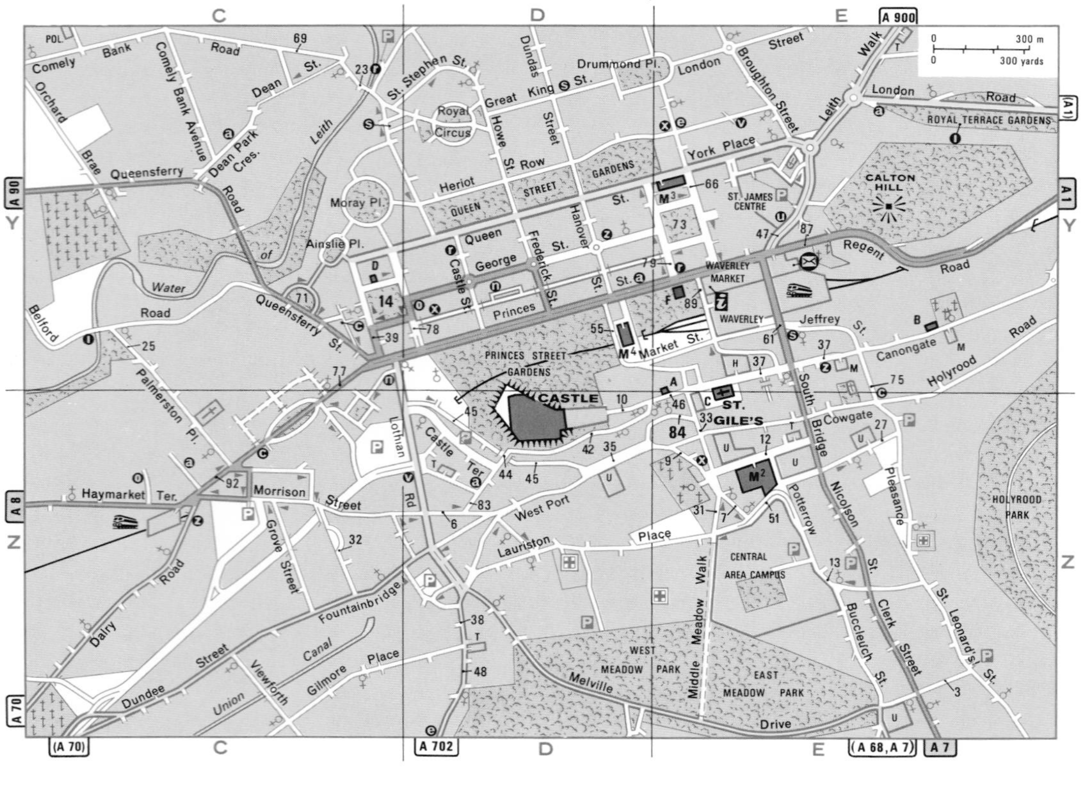

0 300 m
0 300 yards
Comely Bank
Orchard Brae
Queensferry Road
Dean Park Cres.
Comely Bank Avenue
Royal Circus
Great King St.
Drummond Pl.
London Road
Broughton Street
Leith Walk
York Place
ROYAL TERRACE GARDENS
CALTON HILL
Heriot Row
QUEEN STREET GARDENS
Moray Pl.
Ainslie Pl.
Queen St.
George St.
Princes St.
ST. JAMES CENTRE
WAVERLEY MARKET
WAVERLEY
Regent Road
Jeffrey St.
Canongate
Holyrood Road
Market St.
PRINCES STREET GARDENS
CASTLE
ST. GILE'S
Cowgate
Water of Leith
Belford Road
Palmerston Pl.
Lothian Rd
Haymarket Ter.
Morrison Street
West Port
Lauriston Place
Grove Street
Dalry Road
Fountainbridge
Dundee Street
Gilmore Place
Union Canal
Viewforth
CENTRAL AREA CAMPUS
Middle Meadow Walk
WEST MEADOW PARK
EAST MEADOW PARK
Melville Drive
Nicolson St.
South Bridge
Potterrow
Buccleuch St.
Clerk Street
Pleasance
St. Leonard's St.
HOLYROOD PARK
A 90
A 8
A 70
A 702
A 900
A 1
A 68, A 7
A 7

EXETER

Bedford Street	Y 6
Fore Street	Z
High Street	Y
Shopping Precinct	Y
Alphington Road	Z 2

Barnfield Road	Z 3
Bartholomew Road	Z 5
Castle Street	Y 13
Coombe Street	Z 14
Corwick Street	Z 15
Edmund Street	Z 18
King Street	Z 22
Mary Arches	Z 26
Mint (The)	Z 28

New Bridge Street	Z 31
Northernhay Street	Y 33
Palace Gate	Z 36
Paul Street	Y 37
Preston Street	Z 40
Princesshay	Y 44
Quay Hill	Z 45
Queen's Terrace	Y 46
St. Martin's Lane	Y 49

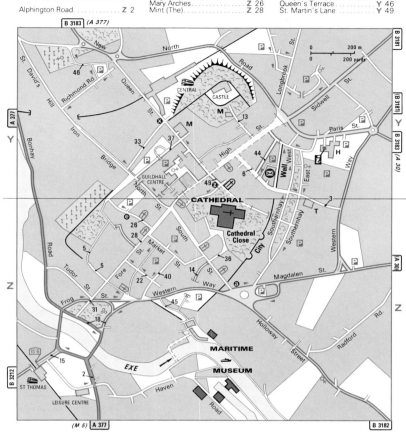

Eye (Cambs.)	29 T 26
Eye (Suffolk)	30 X 27
Eye Peninsula	71 B 9
Eyemouth	57 N 16
Eynort (Loch) (Highland)	65 A 12
Eynort (Loch) (Western Isles)	64 Y 12
Eynsford	21 U 29
Eynsham	18 P 28
Eyre Point	65 B 12
Eythorne	13 X 30

F

Fada	66 E 10
Fada (Loch)	64 Y 11
Failsworth	39 N 23
Fair Isle	75 P 5
Fair Oak	10 Q 31
Fairbourne	32 H 25
Fairford	17 O 28
Fairlie	54 F 16
Fairlight	12 V 31
Fakenham	30 W 25
Falfield	17 M 29
Falkirk	55 I 16
Falkland	56 K 15
Fallin	55 I 15
Falmouth	2 E 33
Fanagmore	72 E 8
Fannich (Loch)	66 E 11
Fara	74 K 7
Fareham	10 Q 31
Faringdon	18 P 29
Farleigh-Hungerford	17 N 30
Farley Mount	9 P 30
Farmborough	17 M 29
Farmtown	68 L 11
Farnborough (Hants.)	18 R 30
Farnborough (Warw.)	27 P 27
Farndon	36 R 24
Farne Islands	51 P 17
Farnham (Dorset)	8 N 31
Farnham (Surrey)	18 R 30
Farnham Royal	20 S 29
Farningham	21 U 29
Farnsfield	36 Q 24
Farnworth	39 M 23
Farrington Gurney	16 M 30
Farway	5 K 31
Fasnakyle Forest	66 F 11
Fasque	63 M 13
Fauldhouse	55 I 16
Faversham	12 W 30
Fawley	9 P 31
Fazeley	27 O 26
Fearnan	61 H 14
Fearnmore	66 C 11
Featherstone (Staffs.)	27 N 26
Featherstone (West Yorks.)	40 P 22
Feering	22 W 28
Felindre	25 K 26
Felixstowe	23 Y 28
Felling	51 P 19
Felpham	11 S 31
Felsted	22 V 28
Feltham	20 S 29
Felton	51 O 18
Feltwell	30 V 26
Fenstanton	29 T 27
Fenwick	57 O 17
Feochan (Loch)	60 D 14
Feolin Ferry	52 B 16

Ferndown	9 O 31
Ferness	67 I 11
Fernhurst	10 R 30
Ferryden	63 M 13
Ferryhill	46 P 19
Feshie (Glen)	61 I 12
Fetcham	20 S 30
Fetlar	75 R 2
Fetterangus	69 N 11
Fettercairn	63 M 13
Ffestiniog	32 I 25
Ffestiniog (Vale of)	32 H 25
Fflint/Flint	33 K 24
Fiaray	64 X 12
Fife (Region)	56 K 15
Filey	47 T 21
Filton	16 M 29
Finchampstead	18 R 29
Finchingfield	22 V 28
Findhorn	68 J 11
Findhorn (River)	67 H 12
Findhorn Bay	68 J 11
Findochty	68 L 10
Findon	11 S 31
Finedon	28 S 26
Fingest	18 R 29
Finningley	41 R 23
Finsbay	70 Z 10
Finstock	18 P 28
Finstown	74 K 6
Fintry	55 H 15
Fionn Loch	66 D 10
Fionn Loch Mór	72 F 9
Fionnphort	59 A 15
Fishbourne	10 Q 31
Fisherfield Forest	66 D 10
Fishguard/Abergwaun	14 F 28
Fittleworth	11 S 31
Flackwell Heath	18 R 29
Fladbury	27 N 27
Fladda-Chùain	65 A 10
Flamborough	41 T 21
Flamborough Head	41 T 21
Flamingo Park	47 R 21
Flamstead	19 S 28
Flash	35 O 24
Fleckney	28 Q 26
Fleet	18 R 30
Fleet (Islands of)	43 H 19
Fleet (Loch)	73 H 10
Fleetwood	38 K 22
Flimby	44 J 19
Flint/Fflint	33 K 24
Flitton	29 S 27
Flitwick	29 S 27
Flodday (near Hellisay)	64 X 13
Flodday (near Sandray)	58 X 13
Floors Castle	50 M 17
Flotta	74 K 7
Flowerdale Forest	66 D 11
Fochabers	68 K 11
Foinaven	72 F 8
Folkestone	13 X 30
Folkingham	37 S 25
Fontmell Magna	8 N 31
Ford	54 D 15
Forde Abbey	7 L 31
Fordham	30 V 27
Fordingbridge	9 O 31
Fordoun	63 M 13
Fordyce	69 L 11
Foreland	10 Q 31
Foreland Point	6 I 30
Foremark Reservoir	35 P 25

Forest Fawr	15 J 28
Forest Row	11 U 30
Forfar	62 L 14
Formby	38 K 23
Formby Point	38 K 23
Fornham All Saints	23 W 27
Forres	68 J 11
Fort Augustus	67 F 12
Fort George	67 H 11
Fort Victoria	9 P 31
Fort William	60 E 13
Forter	62 K 13
Forth	55 I 16
Forth (Firth of)	56 K 15
Forth (River)	55 G 15
Forth Bridges	56 J 15
Fortingall	61 H 14
Forton	34 M 25
Fortrose	67 H 11
Fortuneswell	8 M 32
Fosdyke	37 T 25
Fotheringhay	29 S 26
Foulness Point	23 W 29
Foulridge	39 N 22
Fountains Abbey	39 P 21
Four Crosses	33 K 25
Four Elms	21 U 30
Four Marks	10 Q 30
Foveran	69 N 12
Fowey	3 G 32
Fowlmere	29 U 27
Fownhope	26 M 27
Foxdale	42 G 21
Foxholes	41 S 21
Foyers	67 G 12
Fraddon	2 F 32
Framfield	12 U 31
Framlingham	23 Y 27
Frampton-on-Severn	17 M 28
Framwellgate Moor	46 P 19
Frant	12 U 30
Fraserburgh	69 O 10
Fraserburgh Bay	69 O 10
Freckenham	30 V 27
Freckleton	38 L 22
Freethorpe	31 Y 26
Freevater Forest	67 F 10
Fremington	6 H 30
Frensham	10 R 30
Freshwater	9 P 31
Freshwater Bay	9 P 31
Freshwater East	14 F 29
Freshwater West	14 E 29
Fressingfield	31 X 26
Frettenham	31 X 25
Freuchie (Loch)	61 I 14
Friday Bridge	29 U 26
Fridaythorpe	40 S 21
Frimley	18 R 30
Frinton-on-Sea	23 X 28
Friockheim	63 M 14
Frisa (Loch)	59 B 14
Friskney	37 U 24
Frittenden	12 V 30
Frizington	43 J 20
Frodsham	34 L 24
Froggatt	35 P 24
Frome	17 N 30
Fuday	64 X 12
Fuiay	58 X 13
Fulbourn	29 U 27
Fulwood	38 M 22
Funzie	75 R 2
Furness Abbey	38 K 21
Furness Fells	44 K 20
Fyfield (Essex)	22 U 28
Fyfield (Hants.)	9 P 30
Fyvie	69 M 11

Egglescliffe	46 P 20
Eggleston	45 N 20
Egham	20 S 29
Egilsay	74 L 6
Eglingham	51 O 17
Egremont	43 J 20
Egton	47 R 20
Eigg	59 B 13
Eigheach (Loch)	60 G 13
Eil (Loch)	60 E 13
Eilde Mór (Loch)	60 F 13
Eilean a' Chalmain	59 A 15
Eilean Beag	66 C 11
Eilean Chathastail	59 B 13
Eilean Donan Castle	66 D 12
Eilean Flodigarry	65 B 10
Eilean Mullagrach	72 D 9
Eilean nan Each	59 B 13
Eilean Trodday	65 B 10
Eilt (Loch)	60 D 13
Einon	15 H 29
Eishort (Loch)	65 C 12
Elgin	68 K 11
Elgol	65 B 12
Elham	13 X 30
Elie	56 L 15
Elkesley	36 R 24
Elkstone	17 N 28
Elland	39 O 22

Ellastone	35 O 25
Ellesmere	34 L 25
Ellesmere Port	34 L 24
Ellon	69 N 11
Elmswell	30 W 27
Elphin	72 E 9
Elsenham	22 U 28
Elstead	18 R 30
Elstree	20 T 29
Elswick	38 L 22
Eltisley	29 T 27
Elton	29 S 26
Elvington	41 R 22
Ely	29 U 26
Emberton	28 R 27
Embleton	51 P 17
Embo	73 I 10
Embsay	39 O 22
Emneth	29 U 26
Empingham	28 S 26
Emsworth	10 R 31
Enard Bay	72 D 9
Enderby	28 Q 26
Endon	35 N 24
Enfield (London Borough)	20 T 29
Enford	17 O 30
Englefield Green	20 S 29
Enham Alamein	18 P 30
Enmore	7 K 30
Ensay	59 B 14
Enstone	18 P 28

Enville	27 N 26
Eoropie	71 B 8
Eorsa	59 B 14
Eport (Loch)	64 Y 11
Epping	21 U 28
Epping Forest	21 U 29
Epsom	20 T 30
Epworth	41 R 23
Eredine Forest	54 D 15
Eriboll (Loch)	72 F 8
Ericht (Loch)	61 H 13
Eriskay	64 Y 12
Erisort (Loch)	70 A 9
Ermington	4 I 32
Erpingham	31 X 25
Erraid	59 A 15
Errochty (Loch)	61 H 13
Errol	62 K 14
Ersary	64 X 13
Erskine Bridge	55 G 16
Esha Ness	75 P 2
Esher	20 S 29
Esk (Glen)	62 L 13
Esk (River)	50 K 19
Eskdale	50 K 18
Eskdalemuir	50 K 18
Essendon	19 T 28
Essex (County)	22 V 28
Essich	67 H 11
Eston	46 Q 20
Etchingham	12 V 30
Etherow (River)	39 N 23

Etherow Park	39 N 23
Etive (Glen)	60 F 14
Etive (Loch)	60 E 14
Eton	20 S 29
Ettington	27 P 27
Ettrick	50 K 17
Ettrick Forest	50 K 17
Ettrick Pen	50 K 17
Euxton	38 L 22
Evanton	67 G 11
Evercreech	8 M 30
Everleigh	17 O 30
Evershot	8 M 31
Everton	36 R 23
Evesham	27 O 27
Evesham (Vale of)	27 O 27
Ewe (Isle of)	66 D 10
Ewell	20 T 29
Ewelme	18 Q 29
Ewhurst	11 S 30
Exbourne	6 I 31
Exe (River)	7 J 31
Exebridge	7 J 31
Exeter	4 J 31
Exford	7 J 30
Exminster	4 J 31
Exmoor National Park	7 I 30
Exmouth	4 J 32
Exton	7 J 30
Eyam	35 O 24

G

Gainford	45	O 20
Gainsborough	36	R 23
Gairloch	66	C 10
Gairlochy	60	F 13
Gairsay	74	L 6
Galashiels	50	L 17
Galgate	38	L 22
Gallan Head	70	Y 9
Galloway Forest Park	48	G 18
Galmisdale	59	B 13
Galson	70	A 8
Galston	48	G 17
Galtrigill	64	Z 11
Gamlingay	29	T 27
Gamston	36	R 24
Ganton	47	S 21
Garboldisham	30	W 26
Gardenstown	69	N 10
Garelochhead	54	F 15
Garenin	70	Z 9
Garforth	40	P 22
Gargrave	39	N 22
Gargunnock	55	H 15
Garioch	69	M 12
Garlieston	42	G 19
Garmouth	68	K 11
Garrabost	71	B 9
Garrisdale Point	64	A 12
Garry (Glen) (Highland)	60	E 12
Garry (Glen) (Tayside)	61	H 13
Garry (Loch)	60	F 12
Garsdale Head	39	N 21
Garsington	18	Q 28
Garth	25	J 27
Gartmore	55	G 15
Garton-on-The-Wolds	41	S 21
Garve	66	F 11
Garvellachs	52	C 15
Garvock	54	F 16
Garynahine	70	Z 9
Gatehouse of Fleet	43	H 19
Gateshead	51	P 19
Gateside	56	K 15
Gatley	34	N 23
Gatwick Airport	11	T 30
Gaulden Manor	7	K 30
Gayton	30	V 25
Geddington	28	R 26
Gedney Drove End	37	U 25
Gedney Hill	29	T 25
Georgeham	6	H 30
Georth	74	K 6
Gerrards Cross	20	S 29
Gifford	56	L 16
Gigha (Sound of)	53	C 17
Gigha Island	52	C 16
Gighay	64	Y 12
Gildersome	39	P 22
Gillingham (Dorset)	8	N 30
Gillingham (Kent)	12	V 29
Gilmerton	61	I 14
Girvan	48	F 18
Gisburn	39	N 22
Glaisdale	47	R 20
Glamis	62	K 14
Glamis Castle	62	K 14
Glanaman	15	I 28
Glas Maol	62	J 13
Glasbury	25	K 27
Glascarnoch (Loch)	66	F 10
Glasgow	55	H 16
Glass (Loch)	67	G 10
Glasson	38	L 22
Glastonbury	8	L 30
Gleann Beag	66	F 10
Gleann Mór	67	G 10
Glemfield	28	Q 26
Glen Brittle Forest	65	B 12
Glen Finglas Reservoir	55	G 15
Glen More Forest Park	67	I 12
Glen Shee	62	J 13
Glenbarr	53	C 17
Glenborrodale	59	C 13
Glenbuck	49	I 17
Glencarse	56	K 14
Glencoe	60	E 13
Glencoul (Loch)	72	F 9
Glendurgan Garden	2	E 33
Gleneg	66	D 12
Glenelg Bay	66	D 12
Glenfarg	56	J 15
Glenfield	28	Q 26
Glenfinnan	60	D 13
Glenforsa Airport	59	C 14
Glengorm	59	B 14
Glengrasco	65	B 11
Glenkens (The)	49	H 18
Glenluce	42	F 19
Glenrothes	56	K 15
Glensford	22	V 27
Glentham	36	S 23
Glentress	56	K 17
Glentworth	36	S 23
Glinton	29	T 26
Glossop	39	O 23
Gloucester	17	N 28
Gloucestershire (County)	17	N 28
Glusburn	39	O 22
Glyn Ceiriog	33	K 25
Glyn-Ebwy/Ebbw Vale	16	K 28
Glyn-neath	15	J 28
Glyncorrwg	15	J 28
Glynde	12	U 31
Gnosall	35	N 25
Goat Fell	53	E 17
Goathland	47	R 20
Gobowen	33	K 25
Godalming	11	S 30
Godmanchester	29	T 27
Godmanstone	8	M 31
Godshill	10	Q 32
Godstone	20	T 30
Goil (Loch)	54	F 15
Golborne	38	M 23
Goldthorpe	40	Q 23
Golspie	73	I 10
Gomersal	39	O 22
Gometra	59	B 14
Gomshall	20	S 30
Goodrich	16	M 28
Goodrington	4	J 32
Goodwick	14	F 27
Goodwood House	10	R 31
Goole	41	R 22
Gordon	57	M 16
Gorebridge	56	K 16
Goring	18	Q 29
Gorm Loch Mór	72	F 9
Gorran Haven	3	F 33
Gorseinon	15	H 29
Gorsleston-on-Sea	31	Z 26
Gosberton	37	T 25
Gosforth (Cumbria)	43	J 20
Gosforth (Tyne and Wear)	51	P-18
Gosport	10	Q 31
Gotham	36	Q 25
Gott Bay	58	Z 14
Goudhurst	12	V 30
Gourdon	63	N 13
Gourock	54	F 16
Gowerton	15	H 29
Goxhill	41	T 22
Graemsay	74	K 7
Grain	12	W 29
Grampian (Region)	61	H 13
Grampian Mountains	61	G 14
Grandtully	61	I 14
Grange-over-Sands	44	L 21
Grangemouth	55	I 15
Grantham	36	S 25
Grantown-on-Spey	68	J 12
Grantshouse	57	N 16
Grasmere	44	K 20
Grassington	39	O 21
Gravesend	21	V 29
Grayrigg	45	M 20
Grays Thurrock	21	U 29
Grayshott	10	R 30
Grayswood	10	R 30
Great Ayton	46	Q 20
Great Baddow	22	V 28
Great Badminton	17	N 29
Great Bardfield	22	V 28
Great Barford	29	S 27
Great Barr	27	O 26
Great Bedwyn	17	P 29
Great Bentley	23	X 28
Great Bernera	70	Z 9
Great Bircham	30	V 25
Great Bookham	20	S 30
Great Bridon	46	P 20
Great Chalfield Manor	8	N 30
Great Chesterford	29	U 27
Great Chishill	29	U 27
Great Clifton	43	J 20
Great Coates	41	T 23
Great Cumbrae Island	54	F 16
Great Driffield	41	S 21
Great Dunmow	22	V 28
Great Easton (Essex)	22	U 28
Great Easton (Leics.)	28	R 26
Great Eccleston	38	L 22
Great Ellingham	30	W 26
Great Gonerby	36	S 25
Great Grimsby	41	T 23
Great Harwood	39	M 22
Great Hockham	30	W 26
Great Horwood	28	R 28
Great Houghton	40	P 23
Great Livermere	30	W 27
Great Malvern	26	N 27
Great Massingham	30	W 25
Great Milton	18	Q 28
Great Missenden	18	R 28
Great Musgrave	45	M 20
Great Oakley	23	X 28

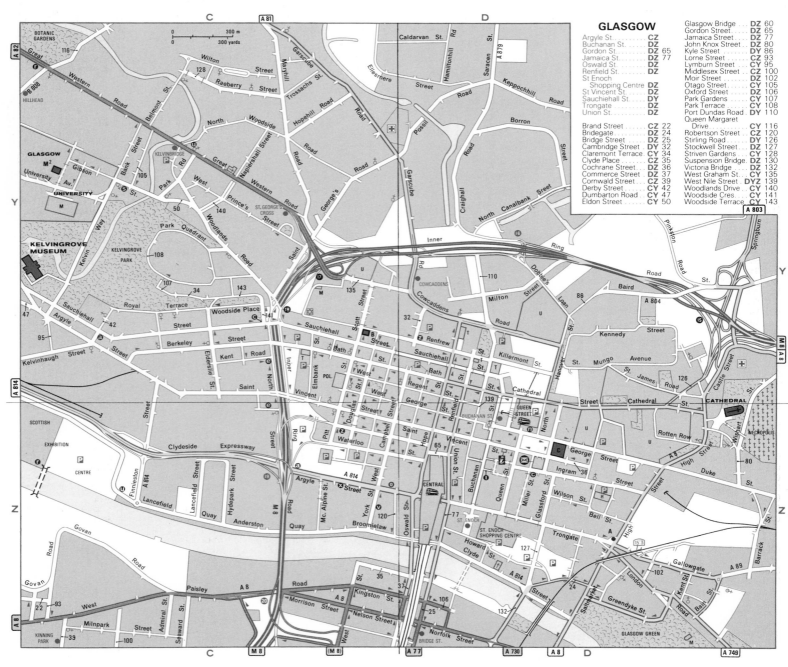

GLASGOW

Argyle St.	CZ
Buchanan St.	DZ
Gordon St.	DZ 65
Jamaica St.	DZ 77
Oswald St.	DZ
Renfield St.	DZ
St Enoch Shopping Centre	DZ
St Vincent St.	DZ
Sauchiehall St.	DY
Trongate	DZ
Union St.	DZ
Brand Street	CZ 22
Bridgate	DZ 24
Bridge Street	DZ 25
Cambridge Street	DY 32
Claremont Terrace	CY 34
Clyde Place	CZ 35
Cochrane Street	DZ 36
Commerce Street	DZ 37
Cornwald Street	CZ 39
Derby Street	CY 42
Dumbarton Road	CY 47
Eldon Street	CY 50
Glasgow Bridge	DZ 60
Gordon Street	DZ 65
Jamaica Street	DZ 77
John Knox Street	DZ 80
Kyle Street	DY 86
Lorne Street	CZ 93
Lymburn Street	CY 95
Middlesex Street	CZ 100
Moir Street	DZ 102
Otago Street	CY 105
Oxford Street	DZ 106
Park Gardens	CY 107
Park Terrace	CY 108
Port Dundas Road	DY 110
Queen Margaret Drive	CY 116
Robertson Street	CZ 120
Stirling Road	DY 126
Stockwell Street	DZ 127
Striven Gardens	CY 128
Suspension Bridge	DZ 130
Victoria Bridge	DZ 132
West Graham St.	CY 135
West Nile Street	DYZ 139
Woodlands Drive	CY 140
Woodside Cres.	CY 141
Woodside Terrace	CY 143

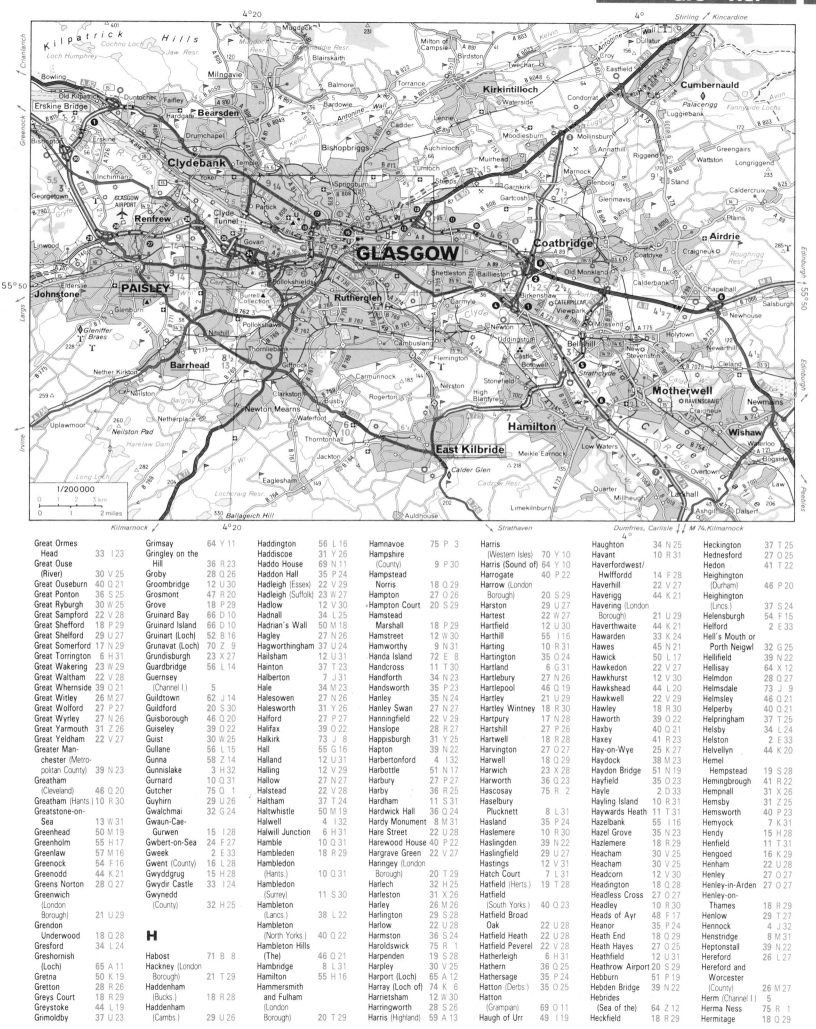

Great Ormes		Grimsay	64 Y 11	Haddington	56 L 16	Hamnavoe	75 P 3	Harris
Head	33 I 23	Gringley on the		Haddiscoe	31 Y 26	Hampshire		(Western Isles) 70 Y 10
Great Ouse		Hill	36 R 23	Haddo House	69 N 11	(County)	9 P 30	Harris (Sound of) 64 Y 10
(River)	30 V 25	Groby	28 Q 26	Haddon Hall	35 P 24	Hampstead		Harrogate	40 P 22
Great Ouseburn	40 Q 21	Groombridge	12 U 30	Hadleigh (Essex)	22 V 29	Norris	18 Q 29	Harrow (London
Great Ponton	36 S 25	Grosmont	47 R 20	Hadleigh (Suffolk)	23 W 27	Hampton	27 O 26	Borough)	20 S 29
Great Ryburgh	30 W 25	Grove	18 P 29	Hadlow	12 V 30	Hampton Court	20 S 29	Harston	29 U 27
Great Sampford	22 V 28	Gruinard Bay	66 D 10	Hadnall	34 L 25	Hamstead		Hartest	22 W 27
Great Shefford	18 P 29	Gruinard Island	66 D 10	Hadrian's Wall	50 M 18	Marshall	18 P 29	Hartfield	12 U 30
Great Shelford	29 U 27	Gruinart (Loch)	52 B 16	Hagley	27 N 26	Hamstreet	12 W 30	Harthill	55 I 16
Great Somerford	17 N 29	Grunavat (Loch)	70 Z 9	Hagworthingham 37 U 24		Hamworthy	9 N 31	Hartington	35 O 24
Great Torrington	6 H 31	Grundisburgh	23 X 27	Hailsham	12 U 31	Handa Island	72 E 8	Hartland	6 G 31
Great Wakering	23 W 29	Guardbridge	56 L 14	Hainton	37 T 23	Handcross	11 T 30	Hartlebury	27 N 26
Great Waltham	22 V 28	Guernsey		Hale	34 M 23	Handforth	34 N 23	Hartlepool	46 Q 19
Great Whernside 39 O 21		(Channel I.)	5	Halberton	7 J 31	Handsworth	35 P 23	Hartley	21 U 29
Great Witley	26 M 27	Guildtown	62 J 14	Halesowen	27 N 26	Hanley	35 N 24	Hartley Wintney	18 R 30
Great Wolford	27 P 27	Guildford	20 S 30	Halesworth	31 Y 26	Hanley Swan	27 N 27	Hartpury	17 N 28
Great Wyrley	27 N 26	Guisborough	46 Q 20	Halford	27 P 27	Hanningfield	22 V 28	Hartshill	27 P 26
Great Yarmouth	31 Z 26	Guiseley	39 O 22	Halifax	39 O 22	Hanslope	28 R 27	Hartwell	18 R 28
Great Yeldham	22 V 27	Guist	30 W 25	Halkirk	73 J 8	Happisburgh	31 Y 25	Harvington	27 O 27
Greater Man-		Gullane	56 L 15	Hall	55 G 16	Hapton	39 N 22	Harwell	18 Q 29
chester (Metro-		Gunna	58 Z 14	Halland	12 U 31	Harbertonford	4 I 32	Harwich	23 X 28
politan County) 39 N 23		Gunnislake	3 H 32	Halling	12 V 29	Harbottle	51 N 17	Harworth	36 Q 23
Greatham		Gurnard	10 Q 31	Hallow	27 N 27	Harbury	27 P 27	Hascosay	75 R 2
(Cleveland)	46 Q 20	Gutcher	75 Q 1	Halstead	22 V 28	Harby	36 R 25	Haselbury
Greatham (Hants.) 10 R 30		Guyhirn	29 U 26	Haltham	37 T 24	Hardham	11 S 31	Plucknett	8 L 31
Greatstone-on-		Gwalchmai	32 G 24	Haltwhistle	50 M 19	Hardwick Hall	36 Q 24	Hasland	35 P 24
Sea	13 W 31	Gwaun-Cae-		Halwell	4 I 32	Hardy Monument	8 M 31	Haslemere	10 R 30
Greenhead	50 M 19	Gurwen	15 I 28	Halwill Junction	6 H 31	Hare Street	22 U 28	Haslingden	39 N 22
Greenholm	55 H 17	Gwbert-on-Sea	24 F 27	Hamble	10 Q 31	Harewood House 40 P 22		Haslingfield	29 U 27
Greenlaw	57 M 16	Gweek	2 E 33	Hambleden	18 R 29	Hargrave Green	22 V 27	Hastings	12 V 31
Greenock	54 F 16	Gwent (County)	16 L 28	Hambledon		Haringey (London		Hatch Court	7 L 31
Greenodd	44 K 21	Gwyddgrug	15 H 28	(Hants.)	10 Q 31	Borough)	20 T 29	Hatfield (Herts.)	19 T 28
Greens Norton	28 Q 27	Gwydir Castle	33 I 24	Hambledon		Harlech	32 H 25	Hatfield
Greenwich		Gwynedd		(Surrey)	11 S 30	Harleston	31 X 26	(South Yorks.) 40 Q 23
(London		(County)	32 H 25	Hambleton		Harley	26 M 26	Hatfield Broad
Borough)	21 U 29			(Lancs.)	38 L 22	Harlington	29 S 28	Oak	22 U 28
Grendon		**H**		Hambleton		Harlow	22 U 28	Hatfield Heath	22 U 28
Underwood	18 Q 28			(North Yorks.) 40 Q 22		Harmston	36 S 24	Hatfield Peverel	22 V 28
Gresford	34 L 24	Habost	71 B 8	Hambleton Hills		Haroldswick	75 R 1	Hatherleigh	6 H 31
Greshornish		Hackney (London		(The)	46 Q 21	Harpenden	19 S 28	Hathern	36 Q 25
(Loch)	65 A 11	Borough)	21 T 29	Hambridge	8 L 31	Harpley	30 V 25	Hathersage	35 P 24
Gretna	50 K 19	Haddenham		Hamilton	55 H 16	Harport (Loch)	65 A 12	Hatton (Derbs.)	35 O 25
Gretton	28 R 26	(Bucks.)	18 R 28	Hammersmith		Harray (Loch of)	74 K 6	Hatton
Greys Court	18 R 29	Haddenham		and Fulham		Harrietsham	12 W 30	(Grampian)	69 O 11
Greystoke	44 L 19	(Cambs.)	29 U 26	(London		Harringworth	28 S 26	Hebrides
Grimoldby	37 U 23			Borough)	20 T 29	Harris (Highland) 59 A 13		(Sea of the)	64 Z 12
						Haugh of Urr	49 I 19	Heckfield	18 R 29
								Haughton	34 N 25	Heckington	37 T 25
								Havant	10 R 31	Hednesford	27 O 25
								Haverfordwest/		Hedon	41 T 22
								Hwlfford	14 F 28	Heighington
								Haverhill	22 V 27	(Durham)	46 P 20
								Haverigg	44 K 21	Heighington
								Havering (London		(Lincs.)	37 S 24
								Borough)	21 U 29	Helensburgh	54 F 15
								Haverthwaite	44 K 21	Helford	2 E 33
								Hawarden	33 K 24	Hell's Mouth or
								Hawes	45 N 21	Porth Neigwl	32 G 25
								Hawick	50 L 17	Hellifield	39 N 22
								Hawkedon	22 V 27	Hellisay	64 X 12
								Hawkshead	44 L 20	Helmdon	28 Q 27
								Hawkwell	22 V 29	Helmsdale	73 J 9
								Hawley	18 R 30	Helmsley	46 Q 21
								Haworth	39 O 22	Helperby	40 Q 21
								Haxby	40 Q 21	Helpringham	37 T 25
								Haxey	41 R 23	Helsby	34 L 24
								Hay-on-Wye	25 K 27	Helston	2 E 33
								Haydock	38 M 23	Helvellyn	44 K 20
								Haydon Bridge	51 N 19	Hemel
								Hayfield	35 O 23	Hempstead	19 S 28
								Hayle	2 D 33	Hemingbrough	41 R 22
								Hayling Island	10 R 31	Hempnall	31 X 26
								Haywards Heath	11 T 31	Hemsby	31 Z 25
								Hazelbank	55 I 16	Hemsworth	40 P 23
								Hazel Grove	35 N 23	Hemyock	7 K 31
								Hazlemere	18 R 29	Hendy	15 H 28
								Heacham	30 V 25	Henfield	11 T 31
								Heacham	30 V 25	Hengoed	16 K 29
								Headcorn	12 V 30	Henham	22 U 28
								Headington	18 Q 28	Henley	27 O 27
								Headless Cross	27 O 27	Henley-in-Arden	27 O 27
								Headley	10 R 30	Henley-on-
								Heads of Ayr	48 F 17	Thames	18 R 29
								Heanor	35 P 24	Henlow	29 T 27
								Heath End	18 Q 29	Hennock	4 J 32
								Heath Hayes	27 O 25	Henstridge	8 M 31
								Heathfield	12 U 31	Heptonstall	39 N 22
								Heathrow Airport 20 S 29		Hereford	26 L 27
								Hebburn	51 P 19	Hereford and
								Hebden Bridge	39 N 22	Worcester
										(County)	26 M 27
										Herm (Channel I.)	5
										Herma Ness	75 R 1
										Hermitage	18 Q 29

Hermitage Castle 50 L 18
Herne Bay 13 X 29
Herstmonceux 12 U 31
Hertford 19 T 28
Hertfordshire
(County) 19 T 28
Hessle 41 S 22
Hest Bank 38 L 21
Heswall 33 K 24
Hetton-le-Hole 46 P 19
Heveningham 31 Y 27
Hever 12 U 30
Heversham 44 L 21
Hevingham 30 X 25
Hexham 51 N 19
Heybridge 22 W 28
Heysham 38 L 21
Heyshott 10 R 31
Heytesbury 8 N 30
Heywood 39 N 23
Hibadstow 41 S 23
Hibaldstow 41 S 23
High Bentham 38 M 21
High Bickington 6 I 31
High Easter 22 V 28
High Ercall 34 M 25
High Force (The) 45 N 20
High Halstow 12 V 29
High Ham 8 L 30
High Holden 12 W 30
High Ongar 22 U 28
High Peak 35 O 23
High Willhays 4 I 31
High Wycombe 18 R 29
Higham (Kent) 12 V 29
Higham (Lancs.) 39 N 22
Higham (Suffolk) 30 V 27
Higham Ferrers 28 S 27
Highbridge 7 L 30
Highclere 18 P 29
Highcliffe 9 O 31
Higher
Penwortham 38 L 22
Highland (Region) 66 F 12
Highley 26 M 26
Highnam 17 N 28
Hightae 49 J 18
Hightown 38 K 23
Highworth 17 O 29
Hildenborough 12 U 30
Hilderstone 35 N 25
Hilgay 30 V 26
Hill 16 M 29
Hill of Fearn 67 I 10
Hill of Tarvit 56 L 15
Hillingdon
(London
Borough) 20 S 29
Hillside 63 M 13
Hillswick 75 P 2
Hilperton 17 N 30
Hilpsford Point 38 K 21
Hilton 35 P 25
Hinchingbrooke
House 29 T 27
Hinckley 27 P 26
Hinderwell 47 R 20
Hindhead 10 R 30
Hindley 38 M 23
Hindon 8 N 30
Hingham 30 W 26
Hinstock 34 M 25
Hintlesham 23 X 27
Hirwaun 15 J 28
Histon 29 U 27
Hitcham 23 W 27
Hitchin 29 T 28
Hockering 30 X 25
Hockley 22 V 29
Hockley Heath 27 O 26
Hockliffe 19 S 28
Hoddesdon 19 T 28
Hodnet 34 M 25
Hogsthorpe 37 U 24
Holbeach 37 T 25
Holbrook 23 X 28
Holbury 9 P 31
Holcombe 17 M 30
Holkam Hall 30 W 25
Hollesley Bay 23 Y 27
Hollingworth 39 O 23
Hollybush 48 G 17
Holme 44 L 21
Holme upon
Spalding-Moor 41 R 22
Holmes Chapel 34 M 24
Holmesfield 35 P 24
Holmfirth 39 O 23

Holmhead 49 H 17
Holsworthy 6 G 31
Holt (Clwyd) 34 L 24
Holt (Dorset) 9 O 31
Holt (Norfolk) 30 X 25
Holt (Wilts.) 17 N 29
Holton (Lincs.) 37 T 24
Holton (Norfolk) 31 Y 26
Holy Island
(Gwynedd) 32 F 24
Holy Island
(Northumb.) 57 O 16
Holy Island
(Strathclyde) 53 E 17
Holybourne 10 R 30
Holyhead/
Caergybi 32 G 24
Holystone 51 N 18
Holywell/
Treffynnon 33 K 24
Holywell Bay 2 E 32
Honiton 5 K 31
Hoo St.
Werburgh 12 V 29
Hook 18 R 30
Hooke 8 M 31
Hook Norton 27 P 28
Hope (Clwyd) 33 K 24
Hope (Derbs.) 35 O 23
Hope (Loch) 72 G 8
Hope
under Dinmore 26 L 27
Hopeman 68 J 10
Hopetoun House 56 J 16
Hopton 31 Z 26
Horam 12 U 31
Horbury 40 P 23
Horden 46 Q 19
Horeb 24 G 27
Horley 11 T 30
Hornby 38 M 21
Horncastle 37 T 24
Horning 31 Y 25
Horninglow 35 P 25
Hornsea 41 T 22
Horrabridge 3 H 32
Horseheath 22 V 27
Horsell 20 S 30
Horsforth 39 P 22
Horsham 11 T 30
Horsham
St. Faith 31 X 25
Horsmonden 12 V 30
Horsted Keynes 11 T 30
Horton 9 O 31
Horton Court 17 M 29
Horton-
in-Ribblesdale 39 N 21
Horwich 38 M 23
Houghton House 29 S 27
Houghton-le-
Spring 46 P 19
Hounslow
(London
Borough) 20 S 29
Hourn (Loch) 66 D 12
House of The
Binns (The) 56 J 16
Housesteads
Fort 50 N 18
Hove 11 T 31
Hoveton 31 Y 25
Hovingham 46 R 21
How Caple 26 M 28
Howden 41 R 22
Howe of the
Mearns 63 M 13
Howmore 64 X 12
Hoxa (Sound of) 74 K 7
Hoy 74 J 7
Hoylake 33 K 23
Hoyland Nether 40 P 23
Hucknall 36 Q 24
Huddersfield 39 O 23
Hugh Town
(I. of Scilly) 2
Hughenden 18 R 29
Huish Episcopi 8 L 30
Hull (River) 41 S 22
Hullbridge 22 V 29
Humber (River) 41 T 23
Humber Bridge 41 S 22
Humberside
(County) 41 S 22
Humberston 41 T 23
Hungerford 18 P 29
Hunmanby 47 T 21
Hunstanton 30 V 25

Huntingdon 29 T 26
Huntingtower
Castle 62 J 14
Huntly 68 L 11
Huntspill 7 L 30
Hurlford 48 G 17
Hursley 9 P 30
Hurst Green 12 V 30
Hurstbourne
Priors 18 P 30
Hurstbourne
Tarrant 18 P 30
Hurstpierpoint 11 T 31
Hurworth-on-
Tees 46 P 20
Husbands
Bosworth 28 Q 26
Huthwaite 36 Q 24
Huttoft 37 U 24
Hutton
Cranswick 41 S 22
Hutton Rudby 46 Q 20
Huyton 34 L 23
Hwlffordd/
Haverfordwest 14 F 28
Hyde 39 N 23
Hynish Bay 58 Z 14
Hythe (Hants.) 9 P 31
Hythe (Kent) 13 X 30

I

Ibstock 27 P 25
Ickleford 29 T 28
Icklingham 30 V 27
Ickworth House 22 V 27
Iden 12 W 31
Iden Green 12 V 30
Idrigill Point 65 A 12
Ightham 21 U 30
Ilchester 8 L 30
Ilderton 51 O 17
Ilfracombe 6 H 30
Ilkeston 36 Q 25
Ilkley 39 O 22
Illogan 2 E 33
Ilmington 27 O 27
Ilminster 7 L 31
Ilsington 4 I 32
Ilsley 18 Q 29
Immingham 41 T 23
Immingham Dock 41 T 23
Ince-in-
Makerfield 38 M 23
Inch Kenneth 59 B 14
Inchard (Loch) 72 E 8
Inchkeith 56 K 15
Inchlaggan 60 E 12
Inchmarnock 54 E 16
Inchnadamph 72 F 9
Inchture 62 K 14
Indaal (Loch) 52 A 16
Ingatestone 21 V 28
Ingham 30 W 27
Ingleton
(Durham) 45 O 20
Ingleton
(North Yorks.) 39 M 21
Inglewood Forest 44 L 19
Ingliston 56 J 16
Ingoldmells 37 V 24
Ingoldsby 36 S 25
Ings 44 L 20
Innellan 54 F 16
Inner Hebrides 58 Y 14
Inner Sound 65 C 11
Innerleithen 50 K 17
Insh 69 M 11
Instow 6 H 30
Inver (Loch) 72 E 9
Inver Bay 67 I 10
Inver Valley 72 E 9
Inverallochy 69 O 10
Inveraray 54 E 15
Inverbervie 63 N 13
Inverewe
Gardens 66 C 10
Inverey 62 J 13
Invergarry 60 F 12
Invergordon 67 H 10
Invergowrie 62 K 14
Inverkeithing 56 J 15
Inverkeithny 69 M 11
Inverkip 54 F 16
Inverkirkaig 72 E 9
Inverliever Forest 54 D 15
Invermoriston 67 G 12

Inverness 67 H 11
Inversanda 60 D 13
Inverurie 69 M 12
Iona 59 A 15
Ipplepen 4 J 32
Ipstones 35 O 24
Ipswich 23 X 27
Ireby 44 K 19
Irfon (River) 25 I 27
Irlam 39 M 23
Iron Acton 17 M 29
Iron-Bridge 26 M 26
Irthlingborough 28 S 27
Irvine 54 F 17
Irwell (River) 38 M 22
Isla (Glen) 62 K 13
Isla (River) 62 L 14
Islay (Sound of) 52 B 16
Isleham 30 V 26
Isle of Whithorn 42 G 19
Islington
(London
Borough) 20 T 29
Islip 18 Q 28
Ithon (River) 25 K 27
Iver 20 S 29
Iver Heath 20 S 29
Ivinghoe 19 S 28
Ivybridge 4 I 32
Ivychurch 12 W 30
Iwerne Minster 8 N 31
Ixworth 30 W 27

J

Jacobstowe 6 H 31
Janetstown 73 J 9
Jarrow 51 P 19
Jaywick 23 X 28
Jedburgh 50 M 17
Jedburgh Abbey 50 M 17
Jersey
(Channel I.) 5
Jevington 12 U 31
John o' Groats 74 K 8
Johnshaven 63 N 13
Johnston 14 F 28
Johnstone 55 G 16
Jura (Sound of) 53 C 16
Jura Forest 52 B 16
Jura Islay 52 B 16
Jurby West 42 G 20

K

Kames 54 E 16
Katrine (Loch) 55 G 15
Keal 37 U 24
Keal (Loch na) 59 B 14
Kearsley 39 M 23
Kebock Head 70 A 9
Kedleston Hall 35 P 25
Kegworth 36 Q 25
Keighley 39 O 22
Keinton
Mandeville 8 M 30
Keir Mill 49 I 18
Keiss 74 K 8
Keith 68 L 11
Kellas 62 L 14
Kellie Castle 56 L 15
Kelly Bray 3 H 32
Kelsall 34 L 24
Kelso 50 M 17
Keltneyburn 61 H 14
Kelty 56 J 15
Kelvedon 22 W 28
Kelvedon Hatch 21 U 29
Kemble 17 N 28
Kemnay 69 M 12
Kempsey 27 N 27
Kempston 29 S 27
Kemsing 21 U 30
Kendal 44 L 21
Kenilworth 27 P 26
Kenmore
(Highland) 66 C 11
Kenmore
(Tayside) 61 I 14
Kennet (River) 17 O 29
Kennethmont 69 L 11
Kenninghall 30 X 26
Kennington
(Kent) 12 W 30
Kennington
(Oxon.) 18 Q 28

Kennoway 56 K 15
Kenovay 58 Z 14
Kensaleyre 65 B 11
Kensington and
Chelsea
(London
Borough) 20 T 29
Kent (County) 12 V 30
Kentford 30 V 27
Kentisbeare 7 K 31
Kenton 4 J 32
Keoldale 72 F 8
Kerrera 59 D 14
Kerry 25 K 26
Kershader 70 A 9
Kesgrave 23 X 27
Kessingland 31 Z 26
Keswick 44 K 20
Kettering 28 R 26
Kettleshulme 35 N 24
Kettletoft 75 M 6
Kettlewell 39 N 21
Ketton 29 S 26
Kew 20 T 29
Kexby 36 R 23
Keyingham 41 T 22
Keymer 11 T 31
Keynsham 17 M 29
Keyworth 36 Q 25
Kibworth
Harcourt 28 R 26
Kidderminster 27 N 26
Kidlington 18 Q 28
Kidsgrove 34 N 24
Kidwelly/Cydweli 15 H 28
Kielder 50 M 18
Kielder Forest 50 M 18
Kielder Reservoir 50 M 18
Kilbarchan 55 G 16
Kilbirnie 54 F 16
Kilbrannan Sound 53 D 17
Kilbride 60 D 14
Kilcadzow 55 I 16
Kilchattan 54 E 16
Kilchenzie 53 C 17
Kilchoan 59 B 13
Kilchrenan 60 E 14
Kilconquhar 56 L 15
Kilcreggan 54 F 16
Kildonan 53 E 17
Kildrummy Castle 68 L 12
Kilham 41 S 21
Kilkhampton 6 G 31
Killearn 55 G 15
Killerton 7 J 31
Killichronan 59 C 14
Killin 61 H 14
Killinghall 40 P 21
Kilmacolm 55 G 16
Kilmaluag 65 B 10
Kilmany 62 L 14
Kilmarnock 54 G 17
Kilmartin 54 D 15
Kilmaurs 54 G 17
Kilmelford 54 D 15
Kilmorack 67 G 11
Kilmun 54 F 16
Kilninver 60 D 14
Kilnkadzow 55 I 16
Kilnsey 39 N 21
Kiloran 52 B 15
Kilrenny 56 L 15
Kilsyth 55 H 16
Kilt Rock 65 B 11
Kilwinning 54 F 17
Kimberley 30 X 26
Kimble 18 R 28
Kimbolton 29 S 27
Kimmeridge 8 N 32
Kimpton 19 T 28
Kinbrace 73 I 9
Kincardine 55 I 15
Kincardine
O' Neil 63 L 12
Kincraig 61 I 12
Kineton 27 P 27
Kinfauns 62 J 14
King's Bromley 35 O 25
King's Cliffe 29 S 26
King's Lynn 30 V 25
King's Somborne 9 P 30
King's Sutton 28 Q 27
Kingairloch 60 D 14
Kingarth 54 E 16
Kinghorn 56 K 15
Kingie (Loch) 66 E 12
Kinglassie 56 K 15
Kings Langley 20 S 28

Kings Worthy 10 Q 30
Kingsbarns 56 M 15
Kingsbridge 4 I 33
Kingsclere 18 Q 30
Kingsdown 13 Y 30
Kingskerswell 4 J 32
Kingskettle 56 K 15
Kingsland 26 L 27
Kingsley 35 O 24
Kingsmuir 62 L 14
Kingsnorth 12 W 30
Kingsteignton 4 J 32
Kingston (Devon) 4 I 33
Kingston
(Grampian) 68 K 10
Kingston
Bagpuize 18 P 28
Kingston Lacy 8 N 31
Kingston-upon-
Hull 41 S 22
Kingston-upon-
Thames
(London
Borough) 20 T 29
Kingstone 26 L 27
Kingswear 4 J 32
Kingswinford 27 N 26
Kingswood
(Avon) 16 M 29
Kingswood
(Glos.) 17 M 29
Kington 25 K 27
Kington Langley 17 N 29
Kingussie 61 H 12
Kinloch 65 B 12
Kinloch Rannoch 61 H 13
Kinlochard 55 G 15
Kinlochbervie 72 E 8
Kinlocheil 60 E 13
Kinlochewe 66 E 11
Kinlochleven 60 F 13
Kinlochmoidart 59 C 13
Kinloss 68 J 11
Kinneff 63 N 13
Kinnersley 26 L 27
Kinross 56 J 15
Kintbury 18 P 29
Kintore 69 M 12
Kintyre 53 D 17
Kinver 27 N 26
Kippax 40 P 22
Kippen 55 H 15
Kippford 43 I 19
Kirby 38 L 23
Kirby Cross 23 X 28
Kirby Hall 28 S 26
Kirby Muxloe 28 Q 26
Kirdford 11 S 30
Kirk Ella 41 S 22
Kirk Ireton 35 P 24
Kirk Michael 42 G 21
Kirkbean 43 J 19
Kirkbride 44 K 19
Kirkburton 39 O 23
Kirkby-in-
Ashfield 36 Q 24
Kirkby Lonsdale 45 M 21
Kirkby Malham 39 N 21
Kirkby Malzeard 39 P 21
Kirkby Stephen 45 M 20
Kirkby Thore 45 M 20
Kirkbymoorside 46 R 21
Kirkcaldy 56 K 15
Kirkcolm 48 E 19
Kirkconnel 49 I 17
Kirkcowan 48 G 19
Kirkcudbright 43 H 19
Kirkcudbright
Bay 43 H 19
Kirkfieldbank 55 I 16
Kirkham 38 L 22
Kirkhill 67 G 11
Kirkinner 42 G 19
Kirkintilloch 55 H 16
Kirklevington 46 P 20
Kirklington 36 R 24
Kirkmichael
(Strathclyde) 48 G 17
Kirkmichael
(Tayside) 62 J 13
Kirkmuirhill 55 I 17
Kirknewton 56 J 16
Kirkoswald 48 F 18
Kirkpatrick
Durham 49 I 18
Kirkpatrick-
Fleming 50 K 18
Kirkstone Pass 44 L 20

Kirkton
of Culsalmond 69 M 11
Kirkton of Durris 63 M 12
Kirkton of
Glenisla 62 K 13
Kirkton
of Kingoldrum 62 K 13
Kirkton of Largo 56 L 15
Kirkton of Skene 69 N 12
Kirkton of
Strathmartine 62 K 14
Kirktown
of Auchterless 69 M 11
Kirkwall 74 L 7
Kirriemuir 62 K 13
Kirtlebridge 50 K 18
Kirtlington 18 Q 28
Kirtomy 73 H 8
Kirton 37 T 25
Kirton-in-Lindsey 41 S 23
Kishorn (Loch) 66 D 11
Kitchener
Memorial 74 J 6
Knapdale 53 D 16
Knaresborough 40 P 21
Knarsdale 45 M 19
Knebworth 19 T 28
Kneesworth 29 T 27
Knighton/
Trefyclawdd 25 K 26
Knightshayes
Court 7 J 31
Kniveton 35 O 24
Knock (Grampian) 69 L 11
Knock
(Western Isles) 70 B 9
Knockie Lodge 67 G 12
Knockin 34 L 25
Knole 21 U 30
Knossington 28 R 25
Knottingley 40 Q 22
Knowle 27 O 26
Knowsley 34 L 23
Knoydart 65 D 12
Knutsford 34 M 24
Kyle Forest 48 G 17
Kyle of Durness 72 F 8
Kyle of Lochalsh 65 C 12
Kyle of
Sutherland 67 G 10
Kyle of Tongue 72 G 8
Kyleakin 65 C 12
Kylerhea 65 C 12
Kyles Scalpay 70 Z 10
Kylestrome 72 E 9
Kynance Cove 2 E 34

L

Laceby 41 T 23
Lacey Green 18 R 28
Lacock 17 N 29
Ladder Hills 68 K 12
Ladock 2 F 33
Ladybank 56 K 15
Ladybower
Reservoir 35 O 23
Lagg 53 C 16
Laggan
(near Invergarry) 60 F 12
Laggan (near
Newtonmore) 61 H 12
Laggan (Loch) 61 G 13
Laggan Point 52 B 16
Laide 66 D 10
Laindon 22 V 29
Lair 66 E 11
Lairg 73 G 9
Lake District
National Park 44 K 20
Lakenheath 30 V 26
Lamberhurst 12 V 30
Lambeth (London
Borough) 20 T 29
Lambourn 18 P 29
Lamerton 3 H 32
Lamlash 53 E 17
Lamlash Bay 53 E 17
Lammermuir Hills 56 L 16
Lampeter/
Llanbedr
Pont Steffan 24 H 27
Lanark 55 I 16
Lancashire
(County) 38 M 22
Lancaster 38 L 21
Lanchester 45 O 19

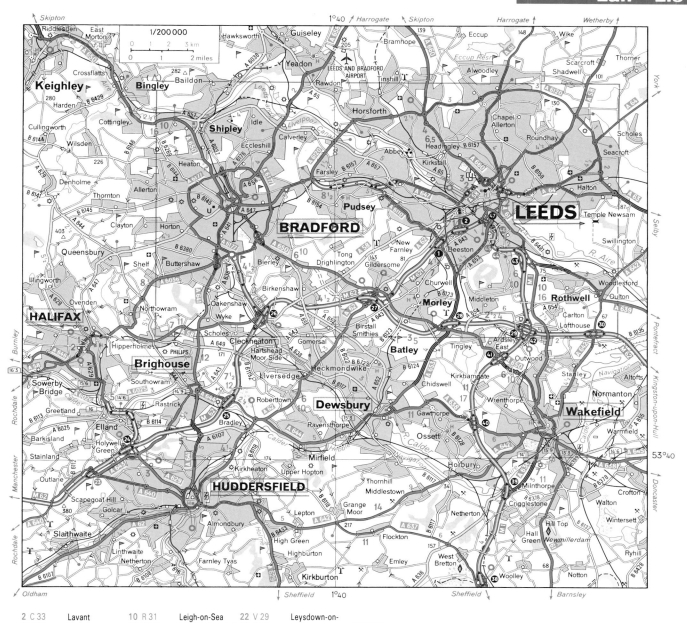

Land's End 2 C 33
Landrake 3 H 32
Lanercost 50 L 19
Langavat (Loch) (Lewis) 70 Z 9
Langavat (Loch) (South Harris) 70 Z 10
Langbank 55 G 16
Langdale Valley 44 K 20
Langenhoe 23 W 28
Langford 29 T 27
Langholm 50 L 18
Langley 20 S 29
Langold 36 Q 23
Langport 8 L 30
Langsett 39 O 23
Langstrothdale Chase 45 N 21
Langtoft 41 S 21
Langton Matravers 9 O 32
Langwathby 45 L 19
Lanhydrock 3 F 32
Lanivet 3 F 32
Lanreath 3 G 32
Lansallos 3 G 32
Lapford 6 I 31
Larbert 55 I 15
Largs 54 F 16
Larkhall 55 I 16
Larkhill 17 O 30
Lasswade 56 K 16
Latchingdon 22 W 28
Lauder 56 L 16
Lauderdale 56 L 16
Laugharne 14 G 28
Laughton 12 U 31
Launceston 3 G 32
Laurencekirk 63 M 13
Lauriston Castle 56 K 16

Lavant 10 R 31
Lavenham 23 W 27
Laverstoke 9 P 30
Lawford 23 X 28
Laxey 42 G 21
Laxey Bay 42 G 21
Laxfield 31 Y 27
Laxford (Loch) 72 E 8
Laxford Bridge 72 E 8
Laxo 75 Q 2
Layer-de-la-Haye 23 W 28
Layer Marney 22 W 28
Lazonby 44 L 19
Leaden Roding 22 U 28
Leadenham 36 S 24
Leadgate 45 M 19
Leadhills 49 I 17
Lealholm 47 R 20
Leasingham 37 S 24
Leathaid Bhuain (Loch an) 72 F 9
Leatherhead 20 S 30
Leathley 39 P 22
Lechlade 17 O 28
Lecht Road 68 K 12
Ledbury 26 M 27
Ledmore 72 F 9
Lee-on-the-Solent 10 Q 31
Leebotwood 26 L 26
Leeds (Kent) 12 V 30
Leeds (West Yorks.) 40 P 22
Leedstown 2 D 33
Leek 35 N 24
Leeming Bar 46 P 21
Leicester 28 Q 26
Leicestershire (County) 27 P 26
Leigh 38 M 23

Leigh-on-Sea 22 V 29
Leighton Buzzard 19 S 28
Leintwardine 26 L 26
Leiston 23 Y 27
Leith 56 K 16
Lemreway 70 A 9
Lenham 12 W 30
Lennoxlove 56 L 16
Lennoxtown 55 H 16
Leominster 26 L 27
Lerwick 75 Q 3
Lesbury 27 P 27
Leslie 56 K 15
Lesmahagow 55 I 17
Leswalt 48 E 19
Letchworth 29 T 28
Letham (Fife) 56 K 15
Letham (Tayside) 62 L 14
Letheringsett 30 X 25
Letterewe Forest 66 D 10
Letterston 14 F 28
Leuchars 62 L 14
Leven (Fife) 56 K 15
Leven (Highland) 60 E 13
Leven (Humberside) 41 T 22
Leven (Loch) 60 E 13
Levens 44 L 21
Levens Hall 44 L 21
Leverington 29 U 25
Leverton with Habblesthorpe 36 R 24
Lewes 11 U 31
Lewis (Isle of) 70 Z 9
Lewisham (London Borough) 21 T 29
Leyburn 45 O 21
Leyland 38 L 22

Leysdown-on-Sea 12 W 29
Lezant 3 G 32
Lhanbryde 68 K 11
Liathach 66 D 11
Lichfield 27 O 25
Liddesdale 50 L 18
Lidgate 22 V 27
Lifton 3 H 32
Ligger or Perran Bay 2 E 32
Lilleshall 34 M 25
Limpsfield 21 U 30
Lincoln 36 S 24
Lincolnshire (County) 36 S 24
Lincolnshire Wolds 37 T 23
Lindfield 11 T 30
Lindores 56 K 14
Lingay (near Eriskay) 64 X 12
Lingay (near Pabbay) 58 X 13
Lingfield 11 T 30
Linlithgow 56 J 16
Linn of Tummel 61 I 13
Linney Head 14 E 29
Linnhe (Loch) 60 D 14
Linslade 18 R 28
Lintmill 68 L 10
Linton 29 U 27
Linton-on-Ouse 40 Q 21
Lintrathen (Loch of) 62 K 13
Linwood 55 G 16
Liphook 10 R 30
Liskeard 3 G 32
Lismore 60 D 14
Liss 10 R 30

LEEDS

Albion Street.......... DZ 3
Bond Street........... DZ 8
Briggate.............. DZ 12
Commercial Street.... DZ 19
Headrow (The)........ DZ
Kirkgate.............. DZ 48
Lands Lane........... DZ 49
Merrion Centre........ DZ

Aire Street............ CZ 2
Blenheim Walk........ CY 6

Bridge Street......... DZ 10
City Square........... DZ 15
Cookridge Street...... DZ 20
Cross Stamford St..... DY 21
Duncan Street......... DZ 25
East Parade.......... CDZ 27
Eastgate............. DZ 31
Hanover Way.......... CZ 39
Infirmary Street...... DZ 44
King Street........... CZ 46
Marsh Lane........... DZ 51
Merrion Street........ DZ 53
Merrion Way.......... DZ 55
New Briggate......... DZ 57

New York Road....... DZ 60
Park Lane............ CZ 64
Portland Crescent..... DZ 65
Queen Street......... CZ 68
Roundhay Road....... DY 71
St. Paul's Street...... CZ 72
St. Peter's Street..... DZ 73
Sheepscar St. South........... DY 75
Skinner Lane......... DY 76
South Parade........ CDZ 78
Wade Lane........... DZ 82
West Street.......... CZ 84
Westgate............ CZ 85

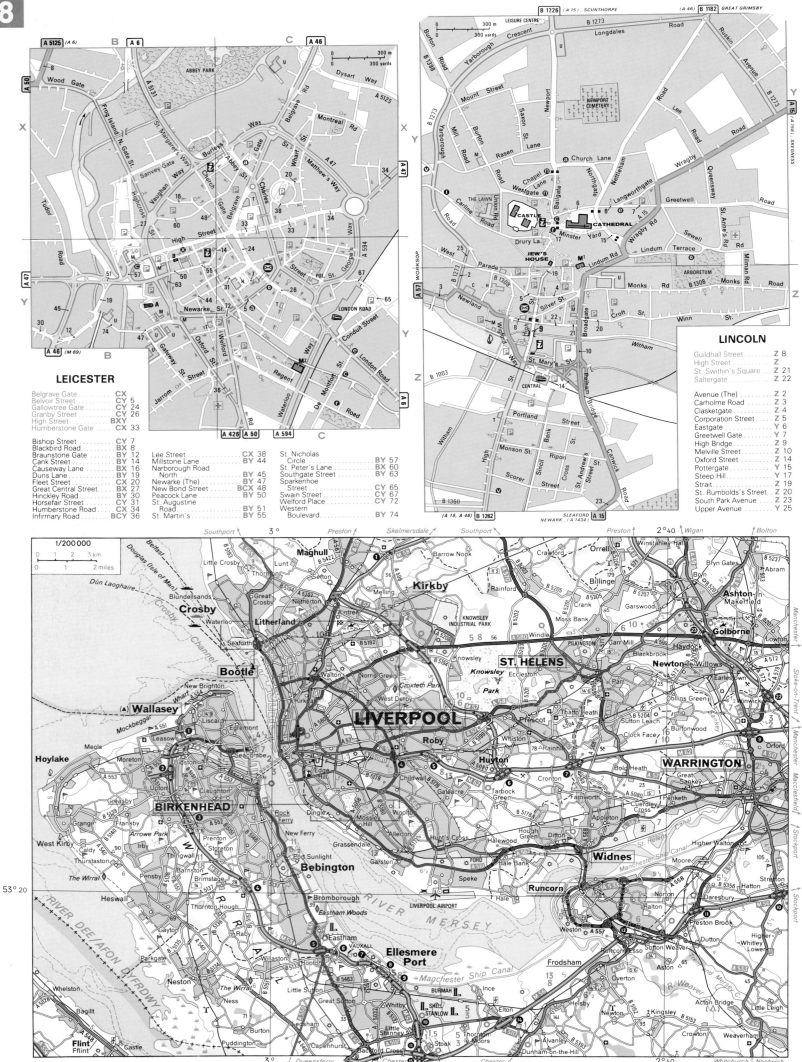

LEICESTER

Belgrave Gate	CX	
Belvoir Street	CY	5
Gallowtree Gate	CY	24
Granby Street	CY	26
High Street	BXY	
Humberstone Gate	CX	33

Bishop Street	CY	7
Blackbird Road	BX	8
Braunstone Gate	BY	12
Cank Street	CY	14
Causeway Lane	BX	16
Duns Lane	BY	19
Fleet Street	CX	20
Great Central Street	BX	27
Hinckley Road	BY	30
Horsefair Street	CY	31
Humberstone Road	CX	34
Infirmary Road	BCY	36

Lee Street	CX	38
Millstone Lane	BY	44
Narborough Road North	BY	45
Newarke (The)	BY	47
New Bond Street	BCX	48
Peacock Lane	BY	50
St. Augustine Road	BY	51
St. Martin's	BY	55
St. Nicholas Circle	BY	57
St. Peter's Lane	BX	60
Southgate Street	BY	63
Sparkenhoe Street	CY	65
Swain Street	CY	67
Welford Place	CY	72
Western Boulevard	BY	74

LINCOLN

Guildhall Street	Z	8
High Street	Z	
St. Swithin's Square	Z	21
Saltergate	Z	22

Avenue (The)	Z	2
Carholme Road	Z	3
Clasketgate	Z	4
Corporation Street	Z	5
Eastgate	Y	6
Greetwell Gate	Y	7
High Bridge	Z	9
Melville Street	Z	10
Oxford Street	Z	14
Pottergate	Y	15
Steep Hill	Z	17
Strait	Z	19
St. Rumbolds's Street	Z	20
South Park Avenue	Z	23
Upper Avenue	Y	25

LIVERPOOL

Bold Street . . . . DZ
Church Street . . . . DY
Lime Street . . . . DY
London Road . . . . DEY
Lord Street . . . . CDY
Parker Street . . . . DY 103
Ranelagh Street . . . . . . DY 108
Renshaw Street . . . . . . DEZ
St. Johns Centre . . . . . . DY

Argyle Street . . . . DZ 6
Blackburne Place . . . . . EZ 11
Brunswick Road . . . . . . EY 19
Canning Place . . . . CZ 23
Churchill Way . . . . DY 25
Clarence Street . . . . . . EYZ 26
College Lane . . . . DZ 28
Commutation Row . . . . DY 30
Cook Street . . . . CY 32
Crosshall Street . . . . . . DY 36
Daulby Street . . . . EY 40
Erskine Street . . . . EY 45
Fontenoy Street . . . . . . DY 48
Forrest Street . . . . DZ 49
George's Dock Gate . . . CY 51
Grafton Street . . . . DZ 53
Great Charlotte Street . . DY 54
Great Howard Street . . . CY 56
Hatton Garden . . . . DY 57
Haymarket . . . . DY 58
Hood Street . . . . DY 62
Houghton Street . . . . . . DY 65
Huskisson Street . . . . . . EZ 66
James Street . . . . CY 68
King Edward Street . . . . CY 69
Knight Street . . . . EZ 72
Leece Street . . . . EZ 73
Liver Street . . . . CDZ 76
Mansfield Street . . . . . . DEY 80
Mathew Street . . . . CDY 81
Moss Street . . . . EY 86
Mount Street . . . . EZ 88
Myrtle Street . . . . EZ 89
Newington . . . . DZ 92
New Quay . . . . CY 93
North John Street . . . . , CY 96
Norton Street . . . . DY 97
Pitt Street . . . . DZ 104
Prescot Street . . . . EY 105
Prince's Road . . . . EZ 107
Richmond Street . . . . . . DY 109
Roe Street . . . . DY 114
St. James Place . . . . . . EZ 117
St. John's Lane . . . . DY 118
School Lane . . . . DYZ 122
Scotland Place . . . . DY 123
Sefton Street . . . . DZ 129
Seymour Street . . . . . . EY 130
Skelhorne Street . . . . . . DY 133
Stanley Street . . . . CDY 135
Suffolk Street . . . . EZ 137
Tarleton Street . . . . DY 139
Victoria Street . . . . DY 143
Water Street . . . . CY 150
William Brown Street . . . DY 156
York Street . . . . DZ 157

Town plans : the names of main shopping streets are indicated in red at the beginning of the list of streets.

Litcham	30 W 25	Littlestone-on-Sea	13 W 31
Litherland	38 L 23	Liverpool	34 L 23
Little Berkhamsted	19 T 28	Liverton	46 R 20
Little Budworth	34 M 24	Livet (Glen)	68 K 12
Little Bytham	36 S 25	Livingston	56 J 16
Little Chalfont	20 S 29	Lizard Peninsula	2 E 33
Little Clacton	23 X 28	Llanarth	24 H 27
Little Colonsay	59 B 14	Llanbedr	32 H 25
Little Cumbrae Island	54 F 16	Llanbedr Pont Steffan/Lampeter	24 H 27
Little Hadham	22 U 28	Llanbedrog	32 G 25
Little Hallingbury	22 U 28	Llanberis	32 H 24
Little Loch Broom	66 D 10	Llanbister	25 K 26
Little Loch Roag	70 Z 9	Llanbrynmair	25 J 26
Little Minch (The)	64 Z 11	Llanddewi Brefi	24 I 27
Little Moreton Hall	34 N 24	Llandegai	32 H 24
		Llandeilo Ferwall	15 H 29
Little Ouse (River)	30 V 26	Llandenny	16 L 28
Little Ouseburn	40 Q 21	Llandissilio	14 F 28
Little Snoring	30 W 25	Llandovery/Llanymddyfri	15 I 28
Little Walsingham	30 W 25	Llandrindod	25 J 27
Little Waltham	22 V 28	Llandrinio	33 K 25
Littleborough	39 N 23	Llandudno	33 I 24
Littlebourne	13 X 30	Llandudno Junction	33 I 24
Littlebury	29 U 27	Llandybie	15 H 28
Littlecote House	18 P 29	Llandysul	24 H 27
Littlehampton	11 S 31	Llanegryn	24 H 26
Littleport	29 U 26	Llanelli	15 H 29
		Llanelltyd	32 I 25

Llanengan	32 G 25	Llanrhaeadr-ym-Mochnant	33 K 25
Llanerchymedd	32 G 24	Llanrhidian	15 H 29
Llanfair	32 H 25	Llanrhystud	24 H 27
Llanfair-Caereinion	25 K 26	Llanrwst	33 I 24
Llanfair-Pwllgwyngyll	32 H 24	Llansantffraid	33 I 24
Llanfair-ym-Muallt/Builth	25 J 27	Llansantffraid-ym-Mechain	33 K 25
Llanfairfechan	33 I 24	Llansawel	24 H 27
Llanfyllin	33 K 25	Llansilin	33 K 25
Llangadog	15 I 28	Llansoy	16 L 28
Llangammarch Wells	25 J 27	Llanthony	16 K 28
Llanuwchllyn	33 I 25	Llantwit Major	15 J 29
Llanwddyn	33 J 25	Llanuwchllyn	33 I 25
Llangefni	32 H 24	Llanwenog	24 H 27
Llangeinor	15 J 29	Llanwnda	24 H 27
Llangeitho	24 I 27	Llanwrda	15 I 28
Llangollen	33 K 25	Llanwrtyd Wells	25 J 27
Llangors	16 K 28	Llanybydder	24 H 27
Llangranog	24 G 27	Llanymddyfri/Llandovery	15 I 28
Llangunllo	25 K 26	Llanymynech	33 K 25
Llangurig	25 J 26	Lledrod	24 H 27
Llangwm	16 L 28	Lleyn Peninsula	32 G 25
Llangwnnadl	32 F 25	Llwyngwril	24 H 25
Llangwyryfon	24 H 27	Llwynmawr	33 K 25
Llangybi	24 H 27	Llyfnant Valley	25 I 26
Llangynidr	16 K 28	Llyn Brianne	25 I 27
Llangynog	33 J 25	Llyn Celyn	33 I 25
Llanhilleth	16 K 28	Llyn Tegid	33 J 25
Llanidloes	25 J 26	Llyswen	25 K 27
Llanilar	24 H 26	Llanmadoc	15 H 29
Llanmadoc	15 H 29	Llannefydd	33 J 24
Llannefydd	33 J 24	Loanhead	56 K 16
		Lochaber	66 D 12

Lochailort	59 D 13	Logiealmond	61 I 14
Lochaline	59 C 14	Lomond (Loch)	55 G 15
Lochans	42 E 19	LONDON	20 T 29
Locharbriggs	49 J 18	London Colney	19 T 28
Lochawe	60 E 14	Long (Loch) (Strathclyde)	54 F 15
Lochay (Glen)	61 G 14	Long (Loch) (Tayside)	62 K 14
Lochboisdale	64 Y 12	Long Bennington	36 R 25
Lochbuie	59 C 14	Long Buckby	28 Q 27
Lochcarron	66 D 11	Long Crendon	18 R 28
Lochearnhead	61 H 14	Long Eaton	36 Q 25
Locheport	64 Y 11	Long Hanborough	18 P 28
Lochgarthside	67 G 12	Long Man (The)	12 U 31
Lochgelly	56 K 15	Long Marston	40 Q 22
Lochgilphead	54 D 15	Long Melford	22 W 27
Lochgoilhead	54 F 15	Long Mountain	25 K 26
Lochinver	72 E 9	Long Mynd (The)	26 L 26
Lochluichart	66 F 11	Long Preston	39 N 21
Lochmaben	49 J 18	Long Stratton	31 X 26
Lochmaddy	64 Y 11	Long Sutton (Lincs.)	37 U 25
Lochore	56 K 15	Long Sutton (Somerset)	8 L 30
Lochranza	53 E 16	Longay	65 C 12
Lochsie (Glen)	62 J 13	Longbenton	51 P 18
Lochton	63 M 12	Longbridge Deverill	8 N 30
Lochwinnoch	55 G 16	Longburton	8 M 31
Lochy (Loch)	60 F 13	Longfield	21 U 29
Lockerbie	49 J 18	Longford	9 O 30
Locking	16 L 30	Longforgan	62 K 14
Loddon	31 Y 26	
Lode	29 U 27	
Lodsworth	10 R 31	
Loftus	47 R 20	
Logan Gardens	42 F 19	
Logie Coldstone	68 L 12	

Longhope	74 K 7	
Longhorsley	51 O 18	
Longhoughton	51 P 17	
Longleat House	8 N 30	
Longniddry	56 L 16	
Longnor	35 O 24	
Longridge	38 M 22	
Longside	69 O 11	
Longton	35 N 25	
Longtown	50 L 18	
Lonmore	65 A 11	
Lorn	60 E 14	
Lorn (Firth of)	59 D 14	
Lossiemouth	68 K 10	
Lostwithiel	3 G 32	
Lothian (Region)	56 J 16	
Loudwater	18 R 29	
Loughborough	36 Q 25	
Loughor (River)	15 H 29	
Loughton	21 U 29	
Louth	37 U 23	
Low Street	31 Y 25	
Lowca	43 J 20	
Lowdham	36 Q 24	
Lower Bentham	38 M 21	
Lower Cam	17 M 28	
Lower Diabaig	66 C 11	
Lowestoft	31 Z 26	
Lowick	57 O 17	
Lowther	49 I 17	
Lowther Hills	49 J 18	
Loxwood	11 S 30	
Loyal (Loch)	73 G 8	

LONDON

Brompton Road . . . . HY
Camden Passage . . . . NS 70
Kensington High Street . . . . EY
King's Road . . . . IZ
Knightsbridge . . . . HY
Middlesex Street . . . . PU
Oxford Street . . . . KU
Piccadilly . . . . JX
Portobello Road . . . . EV
Regent Street . . . . KV
Sloane Street . . . . HY

Tower Hill . . . . PV 425
Trebovir Rd. . . . . FZ 426
Upper Ground . . . . NX 428
Upper Thames St. . . . . . . OV 431
Upper Woburn Pl. . . . . . . LT 432
Vincent St. . . . . LZ 436
Warwick Av. . . . . FU 441
Westbourne Park Villas . . FU 449

Westbourne Ter. Rd. . . . FU 452
West Smithfield . . . . NU 454
Wharfdale Rd. . . . . LS 455
Whitechapel High St. . . . PU 456
Whitehall Court . . . . LX 460
Whitehall Pl. . . . . LX 462
Whitmore Rd. . . . . PS 464
Wormwood St. . . . . PU 472

Abington Rd. . . . . EY 2
Addison Cres . . . . EY 3
Allsop Pl. . . . . HU 4
Atterbury St. . . . . LZ 9
Battersea Park Rd. . . . . JZ 19
Belvedere Rd. . . . . MX 23
Bernard St. . . . . LT 25
Bessborough St. . . . . . . KZ 30
Bethnal Green Rd. . . . . . PT 32
Bevis Marks . . . . PU 34
Bishopsgate . . . . PU 36
Blackfriars Bridge . . . . . NV 38
Bloomsbury St. . . . . LU 39
Bowling Green La. . . . . . NT 43
Bridgefoot . . . . LZ 49
Broad Sanctuary . . . . . . LY 52
Byward St. . . . . PV 62
Calthorpe St. . . . . MT 65
Camomile St. . . . . PU 71
Carriage Drive North . . . IZ 75
Chapel Market . . . . NS 78
Charlbert St. . . . . HT 79
Chapel Market . . . . NU 81
Charterhouse Sq. . . . . . NU 83
Charterhouse St. . . . . . . KZ 91
Churton St. . . . . EV 107
Cornwall Cres . . . . MX 108
Cornwall Rd. . . . . NT 110
Corporation Row . . . . . . NU 113
Cowcross St. . . . . HU 116
Crawford Pl. . . . . EZ 119
Cromwell Cres. . . . . PX 125
Crucifix Lane . . . . PT 126
Curtain Rd. . . . . NZ 129
Dante Rd. . . . . LX 138
Downing St. . . . . OT 141
Dufferin St. . . . . PV 145
Duke's Pl. . . . . MZ 150
Durham St. . . . . EZ 151
Eardley Cres . . . . PV 154
Eastcheap . . . . IZ 156
Ebury Bridge . . . . EY 158
Edwardes Sq. . . . . OZ 163
Elephant Rd. . . . . OU 166
Fann St. . . . . NU 168
Farringdon St. . . . . NY 173
Fetter Lane . . . . OU 178
Garden Row . . . . EZ 182
Giltspur St. . . . . KU 184
Gliddon Rd. . . . . PV 187
Goodge St. . . . . PT 192
Gracechurch St. . . . . . . LY 193
Great Eastern St. . . . . . . LY 196
Great George St. . . . . . . PV 197
Great Smith St. . . . . KY 200
Great Tower St. . . . . FZ 202
Greycoat Pl. . . . . EZ 203
Gunter Grove . . . . EZ 207
Gunterstone Rd. . . . . . . MZ 211
Hammersmith Road . . . . LT 218
Harleyford St. . . . . MY 219
Herbrand St. . . . . EX 224
Hercules Rd. . . . . EY 225
Holland Park Gdns . . . . . LX 228
Holland Walk . . . . FY 229
Horseguards Av. . . . . . . KU 232
Hornton St. . . . . LT 233
Howland St. . . . . PS 235
Hunter St. . . . . FZ 245
Hyde Rd. . . . . OU 247
Kenway Rd. . . . . PV 250
King Edward St. . . . . . . PV 260
King William St. . . . . . . OU 264
Leadenhall St. . . . . MT 265
Little Britain . . . . PV 268
Lloyd Baker St. . . . . OU 270
Lombard St. . . . . PU 273
Long Lane . . . . MY 277
Lothbury . . . . PV 278
Lower Marsh . . . . PV 282
Lower Thames St. . . . . . LZ 290
Mansell St. . . . . OT 293
Miles St. . . . . NT 296
Moreland St. . . . . EZ 298
Myddelton St. . . . . EZ 299
Nevern Place . . . . NV 301
Nevern Sq. . . . . OZ 304
New Bridge St. . . . . OZ 306
New Change . . . . OY 307
Newington Butts . . . . . . LX 317
Newington Causeway . . . NV 318
Northumberland Av. . . . . PU 319
Old Bailey . . . . HU 324
Old Broad St. . . . . EY 326
Old Marylebone Rd. . . . . IU 333
Olympia Way . . . . IU 337
Paddington St. . . . . LY 340
Park Cres. . . . . LZ 341
Parliament St. . . . . EY 342
Parry St. . . . . PS 343
Pembroke Gdns . . . . MT 344
Penn St. . . . . MT 345
Penton Rise . . . . FZ 347
Penton St. . . . . EZ 348
Penywern Rd. . . . . PY 349
Philbeach Gdns . . . . PS 350
Pilgrimage St. . . . . FU 351
Poole St. . . . . OV 352
Porchester Rd. . . . . MZ 353
Poultry . . . . PV 357
Prima Rd. . . . . IZ 361
Princes St. . . . . OY 365
Queen's Circus . . . . HT 369
Queen St. . . . . EX 371
Rossmore Rd. . . . . NU 372
Royal Cres. . . . . KU 376
St. Andrew St. . . . . GT 378
St. Bride St. . . . . GS 379
St. John's Wood High St. . OU 380
St. John's Wood Park . . . PT 384
St. Martin's-le-Grand . . . LT 385
Shoreditch High St. . . . . NT 398
Sidmouth St. . . . . PX 386
Snows Fields . . . . LU 387
Southampton Row . . . . . PU 391
South Pl. . . . . OV 395
Southwark Bridge . . . . . NT 398
Spencer St. . . . . LY 399
Spital Sq. . . . . PU 402
Storeys Gate . . . . OY 408
Tabard St. . . . . LT 409
Tavistock St. . . . . EZ 410
Templeton Pl. . . . . PV 417
Threadneedle St. . . . . . . PU 418
Throgmorton St. . . . .

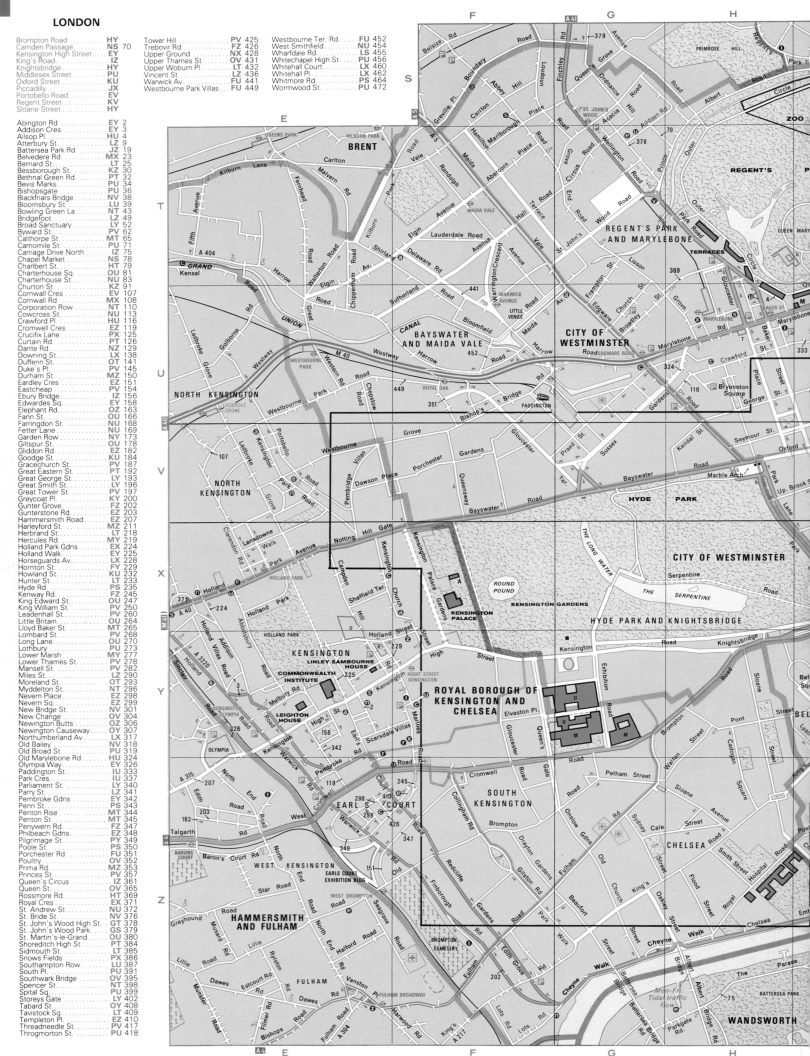

Loyne (Loch)	60 E 12	Luxborough	7 J 30	**M**		Maidstone	12 V 30	Mansfield	36 Q 24	Marlborough	17 O 29	Matlock	35 P 24
Lùb Score	65 A 10	Lybster	74 K 9			Mainland		Mansfield		Marldon	4 J 32	Matlock Bath	35 P 24
Lubenham	28 R 26	Lydbury North	26 L 26	Maaruig	70 Z 10	(Orkney Islands)	74 J 6	Woodhouse	36 Q 24	Marlow	18 R 29	Mattishall	30 X 26
Lubnaig (Loch)	55 H 15	Lydd	12 W 31	Mablethorpe	37 U 23	Mainland		Manton	28 R 26	Marnhull	8 N 31	Mauchline	48 G 17
Luccombe	7 J 30	Lydd-on-Sea	13 W 31	Macaskin (Island)	54 D 15	(Shetland		Manuden	22 U 28	Marple	35 N 23	Maud	69 N 11
Luce Bay	42 F 19	Lydford	3 H 32	Macclesfield	35 N 24	Islands)	75 R 3	Mar (Forest of)	62 J 12	Marsden	39 O 23	Maughold Head	42 H 21
Ludgershall		Lydham	26 L 26	Macduff	69 M 10	Maisemore	17 N 28	Marazion	2 D 33	Marshall	8 N 31	Mawbray	44 J 19
(Bucks.)	18 Q 28	Lydiard Park	17 O 29	Machars (The)	42 G 19	Malborough	4 I 33	March	29 U 26	Marsham	31 X 25	Maybole	48 F 17
Ludgershall		Lydney	16 M 28	Machir Bay	52 A 16	Malden Bradley	8 N 30	Marcham	18 P 29	Marshchapel	41 U 23	Mayfield	
(Wilts.)	17 P 30	Lyme Bay	5 L 32	Machrihanish	53 C 17	Maldon	22 W 28	Marchwood	9 P 31	Marshfield	17 N 29	(East Sussex)	12 U 30
Ludgvan	2 D 33	Lyme Park	35 N 23	Machrihanish Bay	53 C 17	Malham	39 N 21	Marden	12 V 30	Marske-by-the-		Mayfield (Staffs.)	35 O 24
Ludham	31 Y 25	Lyme Regis	7 L 31	Machynlleth	25 I 26	Mallaig	65 C 12	Maree (Loch)	66 D 10	Sea	46 Q 20	Mc Arthur's	
Ludlow	26 L 26	Lyminge	13 X 30	Madderty	61 I 14	Mallory Park	27 P 26	Mareham-le-Fen	37 T 24	Marston Magna	8 M 31	Head	52 B 16
Lugton	55 G 16	Lymington	9 P 31	Maddy (Loch)	64 Y 11	Mallwyd	25 I 25	Maresfield	12 U 31	Marston		Meadie (Loch)	72 G 8
Luichart (Loch)	67 F 11	Lymm	34 M 23	Madeley (Salop)	26 M 26	Malmesbury	17 N 29	Margam	15 I 29	Moretaine	29 S 27	Mealsgate	44 K 19
Luing	54 D 15	Lympne	13 X 30	Madeley (Staffs.)	34 M 24	Malpas	34 L 24	Margaretting	22 V 28	Martham	31 Y 25	Meare	8 L 30
Lulworth Cove	8 N 32	Lympstone	4 J 32	Madingley	29 U 27	Maltby	36 Q 23	Margate	13 Y 29	Martin (Isle)	66 E 10	Measach	
Lumphanan	69 L 12	Lyndhurst	9 P 31	Madron	2 D 33	Maltby-le-Marsh	37 U 24	Margnaheglish	53 E 17	Martley	26 M 27	(Falls of)	66 E 10
Lunanhead	62 L 14	Lyness	74 K 7	Maenclochog	14 F 28	Malton	40 R 21	Market Bosworth	27 P 26	Martock	8 L 31	Measham	27 P 25
Lundie (Loch)	66 C 11	Lynmouth	6 I 30	Maentwrog	32 I 25	Malvern Wells	26 N 27	Market Deeping	29 T 25	Marwell Zoo-		Medbourne	28 R 26
Lundin Links	56 L 15	Lynton	6 I 30	Maes Howe	74 K 7	Mamble	26 M 26	Market Drayton	34 M 25	logical Park	10 Q 31	Medmenham	18 R 29
Lundy	6 G 30	Lyon (Glen)	61 H 14	Maesteg	15 J 29	Mamore Forest	60 F 13	Market		Mary Tavy	3 H 32	Medway (River)	12 W 29
Lune (River)	44 L 20	Lyon (Loch)	60 G 14	Maghull	38 L 23	Man (Isle of)	42 G 21	Harborough	28 R 26	Maryburgh	67 G 11	Meidrim	14 G 28
Lurgainn		Lyonshall	26 L 27	Magor	16 L 29	Manaton	4 I 32	Market Lavington	17 O 30	Maryculter	69 N 12	Meigle	62 K 14
(Loch)	72 E 9	Lytchett Minster	8 N 31	Maiden Bradley	8 N 30	Manchester	39 N 23	Market Rasen	37 T 23	Marykirk	63 M 13	Melbost	70 B 9
Luss	55 G 15	Lytes Cary	8 L 30	Maiden Castle	8 M 31	Manderston	57 O 16	Market Weighton	40 S 22	Marypark	68 J 11	Melbourn	29 U 27
Luthrie	56 K 14	Lytham	38 L 22	Maiden Newton	8 M 31	Manea	29 U 26	Markfield	28 Q 25	Maryport	44 J 19	Melbourne	35 P 25
Luton	19 S 28	Lytham St.		Maidenhead	18 R 29	Mangotsfield	17 M 29	Markinch	56 K 15	Marywell	63 M 14	Melfort	54 D 15
Luton Hoo	19 S 28	Anne's	38 K 22	Maidens	48 F 17	Manningtree	23 X 28	Marks Tey	22 W 28	Masham	46 P 21	Melksham	17 N 29
Lutterworth	28 Q 26			Maidford	28 Q 27	Manorbier	14 F 29	Markyate	19 S 28			Mellerstain	50 M 17

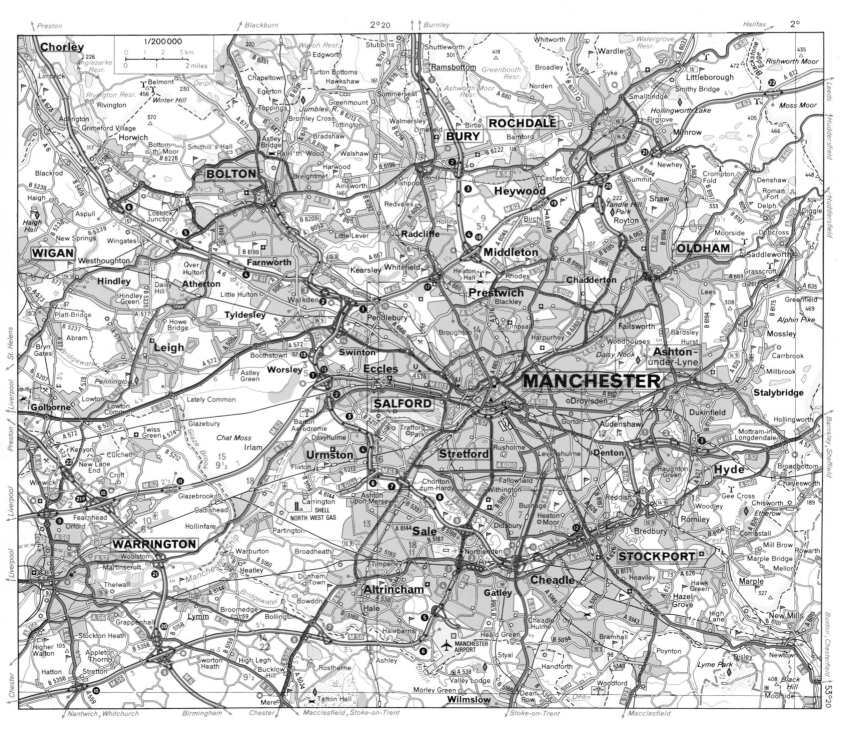

MANCHESTER

Street	Ref		Street	Ref
Deansgate	CYZ		Great Bridgewater Street	CZ 41
Lower Mosley			Great Ducie Street	CY 48
Street	DZ 56		High Street	DY 51
Market Place	CDY		John Dalton Street	DY 52
Market Street	DY		King Street	DY 53
Mosley Street	DYZ		Parker Street	DY 75
Princess Street	DZ		Peter Street	CZ 76
			St. Ann's Street	CY 84
Addington Street	DY 2		St. Peter's Square	DZ 87
Albert Square	CDYZ 5		Spring Gardens	DY 89
Aytoun Street	DZ 8		Viaduct Street	CY 92
Blackfriars Street	CY 13		Whitworth Street West	CZ 95
Cannon Street	DY 15		Withy Grove	DY 97
Cateaton Street	DY 16			
Cheetham Hill Road	DY 18			
Chepstow Street	DZ 19			
Chorlton Street	DZ 20			
Church Street	DY 21			
Dale Street	DY 27			
Dawson Street	CZ 28			
Ducie Street	DYZ 33			
Egerton Street	CZ 36			
Fairfield Street	DZ 39			

(Manchester and Salford city centre map with grid references C, D across and Y, Z down; roads A 56, A 576, A 664, A 62, A 635, A 6, A 57, A 57 (M), A 34, A 5103 marked. Scale 400 m / 400 yards.)

Place	Ref		Place	Ref		Place	Ref		Place	Ref
Melling	38 M 21		Meopham	21 V 29		Messingham	40 S 23		Mid Glamorgan	
Mellon Udrigle	71 D 10		Mere (Cheshire)	34 M 24		Metheringham	37 S 24		(County)	15 J 29
Melmerby	45 M 19		Mere (Wilts.)	8 N 30		Methil	56 K 15		Mid Sannox	53 E 17
Melrose	50 L 17		Mereworth	12 V 30		Methlick	69 N 11		Mid Yell	75 Q 2
Meltham	39 O 23		Meriden	27 P 26		Methven	62 J 14		Midbea	74 L 6
Melton Mowbray	36 R 25		Merrick	48 G 18		Methwold	30 V 26		Middle Wallop	9 P 30
Melvaig	66 C 10		Merriott	8 L 31		Mevagissey	3 F 33		Middleham	45 O 21
Melvich	73 I 8		Mersey (River)	38 M 23		Mexborough	40 Q 23		Middle Rasen	37 S 23
Menai Bridge/			Merseyside			Mhór (Loch)	67 G 12		Middlesbrough	46 Q 20
Porthaethwy	32 H 24		(Metropolitan			Miavaig	70 Z 9		Middlestown	39 P 23
Menai Strait	32 H 24		County-Liverpool)	34 L 23		Michelham			Middleton	
Mendip Hills	16 L 30		Merthyr Tydfil	16 J 28		Priory	12 U 31		(Gtr. Mches.)	39 N 23
Menston	39 O 22		Merton (Devon)	6 H 31		Mickleover	35 P 25		Middleton	
Menteith Hills	55 H 15		Merton (London			Mickleton	27 O 27		(Strathclyde)	58 Z 14
Mentmore	18 R 28		Borough)	20 T 29		Mid Ardlaw	69 N 10		Middleton	
Meonstoke	10 Q 31		Meshaw	6 I 31		Mid Calder	56 J 16		Cheney	28 Q 27

Place	Ref		Place	Ref		Place	Ref
Middleton-			Misterton			Morton	
in-Teesdale	45 N 20		(Somerset)	8 L 31		(near Bourne)	37 S 25
Middleton-			Mistley	23 X 28		Morton (near	
on-Sea	11 S 31		Mitcheldean	17 M 28		Gainsborough)	36 R 23
Middleton			Mitchell	2 E 32		Morven	73 J 9
St George	46 P 20		Modbury	4 I 32		Morvern	59 C 14
Middletown	33 K 25		Moelfre	32 H 23		Morville	26 M 26
Middlewich	34 M 24		Moffat	49 J 17		Morwelham	3 H 32
Midhurst	10 R 31		Moidart	59 C 13		Morwenstow	6 G 31
Midlem	74 L 7		Moira	35 P 25		Moss Bank	38 L 23
Midsomer Norton	17 M 30		Mold/Yr			Mossend	55 H 16
Migdale (Loch)	67 H 10		Wyddgrug	33 K 24		Mossley	39 N 23
Milborne Port	8 M 31		Monadhliath			Mosstodloch	68 K 11
Milborne St.			Mountains	67 H 12		Motherwell	55 I 16
Andrew	8 N 31		Monar (Loch)	66 E 11		Moulton (Lincs.)	37 T 25
Mildenhall	30 V 26		Monaughty			Moulton	
Mile End	23 W 28		Forest	68 J 11		(Northants.)	28 R 27
Milford	10 S 30		Moneydie	62 J 14		Moulton	
Milford Haven/			Moniaive	49 I 18		Chapel	37 T 25
Aberdaug-			Monifieth	62 L 14		Mountain Ash/	
leddau	14 E 28		Monikie	62 L 14		Aberpennar	16 J 28
Milford-on-Sea	9 P 31		Monk Fryston	40 Q 22		Mount's Bay	2 D 33
Millom	44 K 21		Monkoke-			Mountsorrel	36 Q 25
Millport	54 F 16		hampton	6 H 31		Mousa	75 Q 4
Milltown			Monks Eleigh	23 W 27		Mousehole	2 D 33
(Grampian)	69 L 11		Monksilver	7 K 30		Mouswald	49 J 18
Milltown			Monmouth/			Mow Cop	34 N 24
(Highland)	66 F 11		Trefynwy	16 L 28		Moy	67 H 11
Milnathort	56 J 15		Monreith	42 G 19		Much Hoole	38 L 22
Milngavie	55 H 16		Montacute	8 L 31		Much Wenlock	26 M 26
Milnrow	39 N 23		Montgarrie	69 L 12		Muchalls	63 N 12
Milnthorpe	44 L 21		Montgomery/			Muck	59 B 13
Milovaig	64 Z 11		Trefaldwyn	25 K 26		Muckle Roe	75 P 2
Milton (Cambs.)	29 U 27		Montrose	63 M 13		Mudford	8 M 31
Milton			Monymusk	69 M 12		Muick (Loch)	62 K 13
(Dumfries and			Moonen Bay	64 Z 11		Muir of Fowlis	69 L 12
Galloway)	42 F 19		Moorfoot Hills	56 K 16		Muir of Ord	67 G 11
Milton Abbas	8 N 31		Moors (The)	48 F 19		Muirdrum	63 L 14
Milton Abbot	3 H 32		Morar	59 C 13		Muirhead	55 H 16
Milton Bryan	28 S 28		Moray Firth	67 H 11		Muirkirk	49 H 17
Milton Ernest	29 S 27		Mordiford	26 M 27		Muirshearlich	60 E 13
Milton Keynes	28 R 27		More (Glen)	59 C 14		Muker	45 N 20
Milton Libourne	17 O 29		More (Loch)			Muldoanich	58 X 13
Milton of			(near Kinloch)	72 F 9		Mull (Isle of)	59 B 14
Campsie	55 H 16		More (Loch)			Mull (Sound of)	59 C 14
Milverton	7 K 30		(near			Mull of Oa	52 A 17
Milwich	35 N 25		Westerdale)	73 J 8		Mull	
Minard	54 E 15		Morebath	7 J 30		of Galloway	42 F 20
Minch (The)	71 C 9		Morecambe	38 L 21		Mullardoch	
Minehead	7 J 30		Morecambe			(Loch)	66 E 12
Minety	17 O 29		Bay	38 L 21		Mullion	2 E 33
Mingary	64 X 12		Moreton	22 U 28		Mumbles (The)	15 I 29
Minginish	65 B 12		Moreton-in-			Mundesley	31 Y 25
Mingulay	58 X 13		Marsh	27 O 28		Mundford	30 V 26
Minnigaff	48 G 19		Moreton-			Munlochy	67 H 11
Minster			hampstead	4 I 32		Munlochy Bay	67 H 11
(near Ramsgate)	13 X 29		Morfa Nefyn	32 G 25		Munslow	26 L 26
Minster			Moricambe Bay	44 K 19		Murrayfield	56 K 16
(near Sheerness)	12 W 29		Morie (Loch)	67 G 10		Murton	46 P 19
Minsterley	26 L 26		Moriston (Glen)	66 F 12		Musselburgh	56 K 16
Minsterworth	17 N 28		Morley	39 P 22		Muthill	55 I 15
Minterne Magna	8 M 31		Morlich (Loch)	67 I 12		Mwnt	24 G 27
Mintlaw	69 O 11		Morpeth	51 O 18		Mybster	73 J 8
Minto	50 L 17		Morte Bay	6 H 30		Mynach Falls	25 I 26
Mirfield	39 O 22		Mortehoe	6 H 30		Mynydd Eppynt	25 J 27
Misterton (Notts.)	41 R 23		Mortimer	18 Q 29		Mynydd Preseli	14 F 28

N

Na Cùiltean	53	C 16
Nafferton	41	S 21
Nailsworth	17	N 28
Nairn	67	I 11
Nant (Loch)	60	E 14
Nant-y-Moch Reservoir	25	I 26
Nantgwynant Valley	32	H 24
Nantwich	34	M 24
Nantyglo	16	K 28
Napton	28	Q 27
Narberth/Arberth	14	F 28
Narborough	30	V 25
Nash Point	15	J 29
Nateby	45	M 20
National Exhibition Centre (N.E.C.)	27	O 26
National Motor Museum	9	P 31
Navenby	36	S 24
Naver (Loch)	72	G 9
Nayland	23	W 28
Naze (The)	23	X 28
Neath (River)	15	I 28
Neath/Castell-nedd	15	I 29
Needham Market	23	X 27
Needles (The)	9	P 32
Nefyn	32	G 25
Neidpath Castle	56	K 17
Neilston	55	G 16
Neist Point	64	Z 11
Nelson	39	N 22
Nene (River)	29	T 26
Ness	71	B 8
Ness (Loch)	67	G 12
Neston	33	K 24
Nether Broughton	36	R 25
Nether Langwith	36	Q 24
Nether Stowey	7	K 30
Netheravon	17	O 30
Netherhampton	9	O 30
Nethertown	74	K 7

Nethy Bridge	68	J 12
Netley	9	P 31
Nettlebed	18	R 29
Nettleham	36	S 24
Nevis (Glen)	60	E 13
Nevis (Loch)	65	C 12
New Abbey	49	J 19
New Aberdour	69	N 11
New Alresford	10	Q 30
New Buckenham	30	X 26
New Byth	69	N 11
New Cumnock	49	H 17
New Deer	69	N 11
New Forest	9	P 31
New Forest Forest Park	9	P 31
New Galloway	49	H 18
New Holland	41	S 22
New Hythe	12	V 30
New Leeds	69	N 11
New Mills	35	O 23
New Milton	9	P 31
New Pitsligo	69	N 11
New Quay/Ceinewydd	24	G 27
New Romney	12	W 31
New Rossington	40	Q 23
New Sauchie	55	I 15
New Scone	62	J 14
New Tredegar	16	K 28
Newark-on-Trent	36	R 24
Newbiggin-by-the-Sea	51	P 18
Newbigging	62	L 14
Newbold Verdon	27	P 26
Newborough	32	G 24
Newbridge-on-Wye	25	J 27
Newburgh (Grampian)	69	N 12
Newburgh (Tayside)	56	K 14
Newburn	51	O 19
Newbury	18	Q 29
Newby Bridge	44	L 21
Newby Hall	40	P 21
Newcastle Airport	51	O 18

Newcastle Emlyn/Castell Newydd Emlyn	24	G 27
Newcastle-under-Lyme	34	N 24
Newcastle-upon-Tyne	51	O 18
Newcastleton	50	L 18
Newchurch	12	W 30
Newdigate	11	T 30
Newent	17	M 28
Newhall	34	M 24
Newham (London Borough)	21	U 29
Newhaven	11	U 31
Newick	11	U 31
Newington	12	V 29
Newland	16	M 28
Newlyn	2	D 33
Newmachar	69	N 12
Newmains	55	I 16
Newmarket (Lewis)	70	A 9
Newmarket (Suffolk)	22	V 27
Newmill	68	L 11
Newmilns	48	G 17
Newnham (Glos.)	17	M 28
Newnham (Kent)	12	W 30
Newnham Bridge	26	M 27
Newport (Dyfed)	14	F 27
Newport (Essex)	22	U 28
Newport/Casnewydd (Gwent)	16	L 29
Newport (I.O.W.)	10	Q 31
Newport (Salop)	34	M 25
Newport-on-Tay	62	L 14
Newport Pagnell	28	R 27
Newquay	2	E 32
Newstead	36	Q 24
Newstead Abbey	36	Q 24
Newton	39	M 22
Newton Abbot	4	J 32
Newton-Aycliffe	46	P 20
Newton Ferrers	3	H 33
Newton-le-Willows	34	M 23

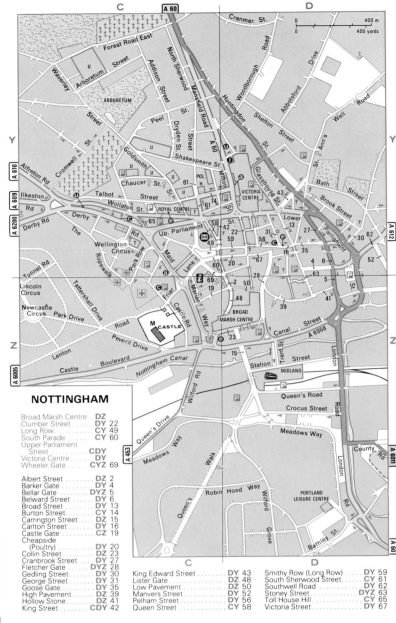

NOTTINGHAM

Broad Marsh Centre		DZ
Clumber Street	DY	22
Long Row	CY	49
South Parade	CY	60
Upper Parliament Street		CDY
Victoria Centre		DY
Wheeler Gate	CYZ	69

Albert Street	DZ	2
Barker Gate	DY	4
Bellar Gate	DYZ	5
Belward Street	DY	6
Broad Street	DY	13
Burton Street	CY	14
Carrington Street	DZ	15
Carlton Street	DY	16
Castle Gate	CZ	19
Cheapside (Poultry)	DY	20
Collin Street	DZ	23
Cranbrook Street	DY	27
Fletcher Gate	DYZ	28
Gedling Street	DY	30
George Street	DY	31
Goose Gate	DY	35
High Pavement	DZ	39
Hollow Stone	DZ	41
King Street	CDY	42

King Edward Street	DY	43
Lister Gate	DZ	48
Low Pavement	DZ	50
Manvers Street	DY	52
Pelham Street	DY	56
Queen Street	CY	58

Smithy Row (Long Row)	DY	59
South Sherwood Street	CY	61
Southwell Road	DY	62
Stoney Street	DYZ	63
Toll House Hill	CY	65
Victoria Street	DY	67

NORWICH

Elm Hill		Y
Gentleman's Walk		Y 17
London Street		YZ 26
St. Andrew's Street		Y 36
St. Stephen's Street		Z
Bank Plain		Y 2

Bethel Street		Z 4
Castle Meadow		Z 6
Cattle Market Street		Z 7
Chapel Field North		Z 9
Charing Cross		Y 10
Colegate		Y
Exchange Street		YZ 15
Grapes Hill		YZ 19
Market Avenue		Z 28
Rampant Horse Street		Z 32

Red Lion Street		Z 33
St. George's Street		Z 38
St. Giles Street		Y 40
Thorn Lane		Z 42
Timber Hill		Z 43
Tombland		Y 45
Upper King Street		Y 46
Wensum Street		Y 49
Westlegate		Z 50
Whitefriars		Y 51

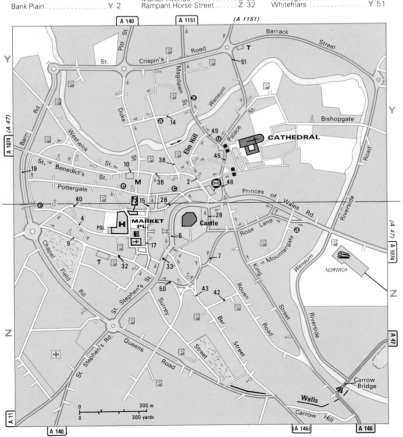

Newton Longville	28	R 28
Newton Mearns	55	H 16
Newton Poppleford	4	K 31
Newton St. Cyres	4	J 31
Newton Stewart	48	G 19
Newton Wamphray	49	J 18
Newtongrange	56	K 16
Newtonmore	61	H 12
Newtown (Cheshire)	35	N 23
Newtown (Heref. and Worc.)	26	M 27
Newtown/Drenewydd (Powys)	25	K 26
Newtown St. Boswells	50	L 17
Newtyle	62	K 14
Neyland	14	F 28
Nigg Bay	67	H 10
Ninfield	12	V 31
Nith (River)	49	J 19
Niths	49	I 18
Niton	10	Q 32
Norfolk (County)	30	W 25
Norham	57	N 16
Normandy	20	S 30
Normanton	40	P 22
North Ashton	38	L 23
North Baddesley	9	P 31
North Ballachulish	60	E 13
North Berwick	56	L 15
North Bradley	17	N 30
North Cadbury	8	M 30

North Cave	40	S 22
North Channel	53	D 18
North Creake	30	W 25
North Curry	7	L 30
North Downs	18	R 30
North Erradale	66	C 10
North Esk (River)	63	L 13
North Foreland	13	Y 29
North Grimston	40	R 21
North Harris	70	Z 10
North Hinksey	18	Q 28
North Holmwood	19	T 30
North Kelsey	41	S 23
North Kessock	67	H 11
North Leigh	18	P 28
North Morar	59	C 13
North Newbald	40	S 22
North Petherton	7	K 30
North Petherwin	3	G 31
North Ronaldsay	75	M 5
North Shields	51	P 18
North Somercotes	41	U 23
North Sound (The)	74	L 6
North Sunderland	51	P 17
North Thoresby	41	T 23
North Tidworth	17	P 30
North Uist	64	X 11
North Walsham	31	Y 25
North Warnborough	18	R 30
North Weald Bassett	22	U 28
North York Moors National Park	47	R 20

North Yorkshire (County)	39	O 21
Northallerton	46	P 20
Northam	6	H 30
Northampton	28	R 27
Northamptonshire (County)	28	R 26
Northchapel	10	S 30
Northchurch	19	S 28
Northfleet	21	V 29
Northiam	12	V 31
Northleach	17	O 28
Northop	33	K 24
Northton	70	Y 10
Northumberland (County)	50	M 18
Northumberland National Park	51	N 18
Northwich	34	M 24
Northwold	30	V 26
Norton	40	R 21
Norton Fitzwarren	7	K 30
Norton St. Philip	17	N 30
Norwich	31	Y 26
Noss Head	74	K 8
Noss (Isle of)	75	Q 3
Nottingham	36	Q 25
Nottinghamshire (County)	36	Q 24
Nuneaton	27	P 26
Nunney	17	M 30
Nunthorpe	46	Q 20
Nunton	64	X 11
Nutley	11	U 30

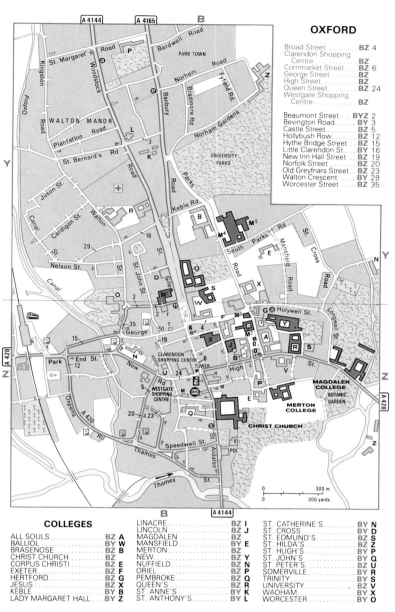

OXFORD

Broad Street	**BZ** 4
Clarendon Shopping Centre	**BZ**
Cornmarket Street	**BZ** 6
George Street	**BZ**
High Street	**BZ**
Queen Street	**BZ** 24
Westgate Shopping Centre	**BZ**
Beaumont Street	**BYZ** 2
Bevington Road	**BY** 3
Castle Street	**BZ** 5
Hollybush Row	**BZ** 12
Hythe Bridge Street	**BZ** 15
Little Clarendon St.	**BY** 16
New Inn Hall Street	**BZ** 19
Norfolk Street	**BZ** 20
Old Greyfriars Street	**BZ** 23
Walton Crescent	**BY** 29
Worcester Street	**BZ** 35

COLLEGES

ALL SOULS	**BZ** A	LINACRE	**BZ** I	ST. CATHERINE'S	**BY** N
BALLIOL	**BY** W	LINCOLN	**BZ** J	ST. CROSS	**BY** D
BRASENOSE	**BZ** B	MAGDALEN	**BZ**	ST. EDMUND'S	**BY** S
CHRIST CHURCH	**BZ**	MANSFIELD	**BY** E	ST. HILDA'S	**BZ** Z
CORPUS CHRISTI	**BZ** F	MERTON	**BZ**	ST. HUGH'S	**BY** P
EXETER	**BZ** G	NEW	**BZ** Y	ST. JOHN'S	**BZ**
HERTFORD	**BZ** X	NUFFIELD	**BZ** N	ST. PETER'S	**BZ**
JESUS	**BZ**	ORIEL	**BZ** P	SOMERVILLE	**BY**
KEBLE	**BY** B	PEMBROKE	**BZ** 23	TRINITY	**BY**
LADY MARGARET HALL	**BY** Z	QUEEN'S	**BZ** R	UNIVERSITY	**BZ**
		ST. ANNE'S	**BY** K	WADHAM	**BY** V
		ST. ANTHONY'S	**BY** L	WORCESTER	**BY** O

O

Oa (The)	52 B 17	Old Warden	29 S 27	Osdale	65 A 11		
Oadby	28 Q 26	Old Windsor	20 S 29	Osgaig (Loch)	72 E 9		
Oakengates	26 M 25	Oldany Island	72 E 9	Osmington	8 M 32		
Oakham	28 R 25	Oldbury	27 N 26	Ossett	39 P 22		
Oakhill	16 M 30	Oldcotes	36 Q 23	Oswaldtwistle	39 M 22		
Oare	12 W 30	Oldham	39 N 23	Oswestry	33 K 25		
Oathlaw	62 L 13	Oldmeldrum	69 N 11	Otford	21 U 30		
Oban	60 D 14	Ollaberry	75 P 2	Othery	8 L 30		
Ochil Hills	55 I 15	Ollay (Loch)	64 X 12	Otley (Suffolk)	23 X 27		
Ochiltree	48 G 17	Ollerton	36 Q 24	Otley (West Yorks.)	39 O 22		
Ockley	11 S 30	Olney	28 R 27	Otterbourne	9 P 30		
Odiham	18 R 30	Olveston	16 M 29	Otterburn	51 N 18		
Ogbourne St. George	17 O 29	Ombersley	27 N 27	Otterswick	75 Q 2		
Ogmore Vale	15 J 29	Onchan	42 G 21	Otterton	5 K 32		
Ogmore-by-Sea	15 J 29	Onich	60 E 13	Ottery St. Mary	5 K 31		
Oich (Loch)	60 F 12	Orchy (Glen)	60 F 14	Oulton Broad	31 Z 26		
Oidhche (Loch na h-)	66 D 11	Orford	23 Y 27	Oundle	29 S 26		
Oigh-Sgeir	58 Z 13	Orford Ness	23 Y 27	Ouse (River) (English Channel)	11 T 30		
Okeford Fitzpaine	8 N 31	Orkney Islands (Region)	74 K 7	Ouse (River) (North Sea)	40 Q 21		
Okehampton	4 H 31	Ormesby	46 Q 20	Out Skerries	75 R 2		
Old Alresford	10 Q 30	Ormesby St. Margaret	31 Z 25	Outer Hebrides	70 W 10		
Old Bolingbroke	37 U 24	Ormskirk	38 L 23	Outwell	29 U 26		
Old Deer	69 N 11	Oronsay	52 B 15	Overseal	35 P 25		
Old Fletton	29 T 26	Orosay (near Fuday)	64 X 12	Overstrand	31 Y 25		
Old Harry Rocks	8 O 32	Orosay (near Lochboisdale)	64 X 12	Overton (Clwyd)	34 L 25		
Old Head	74 L 7	Orphir	74 K 7	Overton (Hants.)	18 Q 30		
Old Kilpatrick	55 G 16	Orrin (Glen)	66 F 11	Overton (Lancs.)	38 L 21		
Old Knebworth	19 T 28	Orrin Reservoir	66 F 11	Overtown	55 I 16		
Old Leake	37 U 24	Orsay	52 A 16	Ower	9 P 31		
Old Man of Hoy	74 J 7	Orsett	21 V 29	Owermoigne	8 N 32		
Old Man of Storr	65 B 11	Orton	45 M 20	Owslebury	10 Q 30		
Old Radnor	25 K 27	Orwell	29 T 27	Oxburgh Hall	30 V 26		
Old Rayne	69 M 11	Orwell (River)	23 X 28	Oxford	18 Q 28		
Old' Sarum	9 O 30	Osborne House	10 Q 31	Oxfordshire (County)	18 P 28		

Oxted	21 T 30	Partney	37 U 24	Penalun	14 F 29		
Oxwich Bay	15 H 29	Parton	43 J 20	Penarth	16 K 29		
Oykel (Glen)	72 F 9	Partridge Green	11 T 31	Pencarrow	3 F 32		
Oykel Bridge	72 F 10	Pass of LLanberis	32 H 24	Pendine	14 G 28		
Oyne	69 M 12	Patchway	17 M 29	Pendine Sands	14 G 28		
		Pateley Bridge	39 O 21	Pendlebury	39 N 23		
		Path of Condie	56 J 15	Penfro/Pembroke	14 F 28		
P		Pathhead	56 L 16	Penicuik	56 K 16		
Pabay	65 C 12	Patna	48 G 17	Penifiler	65 B 11		
Pabbay (near Harris)	70 Y 10	Patrington	41 T 22	Penistone	39 P 23		
Pabbay (near Mingulay)	58 X 13	Patrixbourne	13 X 30	Penketh	34 L 23		
Pabbay (Sound of)	70 Y 10	Patterdale	44 L 20	Penkridge	35 N 25		
Padbury	28 R 28	Pattingham	27 N 26	Penmaenmawr	32 I 24		
Padiham	39 N 22	Paulerspury	28 R 27	Pennines (The)	45 N 19		
Padstow	2 F 32	Paull	41 T 22	Pennyghael	59 B 14		
Pagham	10 R 31	Paulton	17 M 30	Penpont	49 I 18		
Paignton	4 J 32	Peacehaven	11 T 31	Penrhyn Bay	33 I 24		
Painscastle	25 K 27	Peak District National Park	35 O 23	Penrhyn- deudraeth	32 H 25		
Painswick	17 N 28	Peasedown St. John	17 M 30	Penrith	44 L 19		
Paisley	55 G 16	Peasenhall	31 Y 27	Penryn	2 E 33		
Palnackie	43 I 19	Peasmarsh	12 W 31	Penshaw	46 P 19		
Pangbourne	18 Q 29	Peatknowe	69 M 11	Penshurst	12 U 30		
Papa Stour	75 O 3	Peebles	56 K 17	Pentire Point	2 F 32		
Papa Westray	74 L 5	Peel	42 F 21	Pentland Firth	74 K 7		
Paps of Jura	52 B 16	Peel Fell	50 M 18	Pentland Hills	56 J 16		
Parbh (The)	72 F 8	Pegwell Bay	13 Y 30	Pentland Skerries	74 L 7		
Parbold	38 L 23	Peldon	23 W 28	Penwith	2 D 33		
Parc Cefn Onn	16 K 29	Pelynt	3 G 32	Penybont	25 K 27		
Parham House	11 S 31	Pembridge	26 L 27	Penzance	2 D 33		
Park Gate	10 Q 31	Pembroke/Penfro	14 F 28	Perranporth	2 E 32		
Park of Pairc	70 A 9	Pembrokeshire Coast National Park	14 F 29	Pershore	27 N 27		
Parkeston	23 X 28	Pembury	12 V 30	Perth	62 J 14		
Parkhurst	10 Q 31	Pen-y-bont/ Bridgend	15 J 29	Peterborough	29 T 26		
Parnham House	8 L 31	Pen-y-groes	32 H 24	Peterculter	69 N 12		
Parrett (River)	7 K 30			Peterhead	69 O 11		
				Peterlee	46 P 19		
				Petersfield	10 R 30		
				Peterstow	16 M 28		
				Petham	13 X 30		

PORTSMOUTH AND SOUTHSEA

Arundel Street	**BY**	Hard (The)	**BY** 19
Cascade Centre	**BY**	Isambard Brunel Road	**BY** 20
Charlotte Street	**BY** 9	King's Terrace	**BZ** 21
Commercial Road	**BY**	Landport Terrace	**BZ** 23
Palmerston Road	**BZ**	Lennox Road South	**BZ** 24
Tricorn Centre	**BY**	Ordnance Row	**BY** 26
Alec Rose Lane	**BY** 2	St. Michael's Road	**BY** 33
Alfred Road	**BY** 5	Southsea Terrace	**BZ** 36
Bellevue Terrace	**BZ** 7	Stanhope Road	**BY** 37
Bradford Road	**BY** 8		
Edinburgh Road	**BY** 12		
Gordon Road	**BZ** 14		
Grove Road South	**BZ** 15		
Guildhall Walk	**BY** 16		
Gunwharf Road	**BZ** 17		
Hampshire Terrace	**BY** 18		

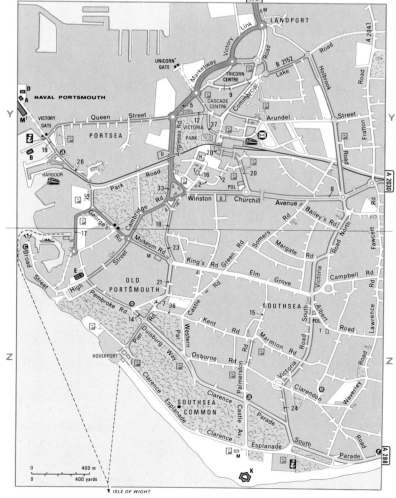

Pett 12 V 31
Pettaugh 23 X 27
Petworth 11 S 31
Pevensey Bay 12 V 31
Pewsey 17 O 29
Pickering 47 R 21
Piddletrenthide 8 M 31
Piercebridge 45 O 20
Pierowall 74 L 6
Pilgrims Hatch 21 U 29
Pillaton 3 H 32
Pilling 38 L 22
Pilning 16 M 29
Pilton 8 M 30
Pinchbeck 37 T 25
Pinhoe 4 J 31
Pirbright 20 S 30
Pirton 29 T 28
Pitcaple 69 M 12
Pitlochry 61 I 13
Pitmedden 69 N 11
Pitsea 22 V 29
Pittenween 56 L 15
Pladda 53 E 17
Plaistow 11 S 30
Plas Newydd 33 K 25
Pleasley 36 Q 24
Plockton 66 D 11
Pluckley 12 W 30
Plumbland 44 K 19
Plymouth 3 H 32
Plympton 3 H 32
Plymstock 3 H 32
Plynlimon (Pumlumon Fawr) 25 I 26
Pocklington 41 R 22
Point Lynas 32 H 23
Point of Ayr (Clwyd) 33 K 23
Point of Ayre (Isle of Man) 42 G 20
Polbain 72 D 9
Polegate 12 U 31
Polesden Lacey 20 S 30
Polesworth 27 P 26
Polkerris 3 F 32
Pollock House 55 H 16
Polmont 55 I 16
Polperro 3 G 33
Polruan 3 G 33
Pondersbridge 29 T 26
Pontardawe 15 I 28
Pontarddulais 15 H 28
Pontarfynach/ Devil's Bridge 25 I 26
Pontefract 40 Q 22
Ponteland 51 O 18
Ponterwyd 25 I 26
Pontesbury 26 L 26
Pontlottyn 16 K 28
Pontrhydygroes 25 I 26
Pontrilas 16 L 28
Pontsticill 16 J 28
Pontyclun 16 J 29
Pontycymer 15 J 29
Pontypool/ Pontypwl 16 K 28
Pontypridd 16 J 29
Pontypwl/ Pontypool 16 K 28
Poole 9 O 31
Poole Bay 9 O 31
Poolewe 66 D 10
Pooley Bridge 44 L 20
Pooltiel (Loch) 64 Z 11
Porlock 7 J 30
Port Appin 60 D 14
Port Askaig 52 B 16
Port Bannatyne 54 E 16
Port Charlotte 52 A 16
Port Dinorwic 32 H 24
Port Ellen 52 B 17
Port Erin 42 F 21
Port Glasgow 54 F 16
Port Henderson 66 C 10
Port Isaac 3 F 32
Port Lamont 54 E 16
Port Logan 42 F 19
Port Mór 59 B 13
Port of Menteith 55 H 15
Port of Ness 71 B 8
Port St. Mary 42 F 21
Port Talbot 15 I 29
Port William 42 G 19
Portchester 10 Q 31
Portesham 8 M 31
Portgordon 68 K 11
Porth 16 J 29
Porth Neigwl or Hell's Mouth 32 G 25
Porth Tywyn/ Burry Port 15 H 28
Porthaethwy/ Menai Bridge 32 H 24
Porthcawl 15 I 29
Porthcurno 2 D 33
Porthgwarra 2 C 33
Porthleven 2 E 33
Porthmadog 32 H 25
Porthyrhyd 15 H 28
Portinnisherrich 54 E 15
Portishead 16 L 29
Portknockie 68 L 10
Portland (Isle of) 8 M 32
Portlethen 63 N 12
Portmahomack 67 I 10
Portnacroish 60 D 14
Portnaguran 71 B 9
Portnahaven 52 A 16
Portobello 56 K 16
Portreath 2 E 33
Portree 65 B 11
Portscatho 2 F 33
Portskerra 73 I 8
Portskewett 16 L 29
Portslade 11 T 31
Portsmouth 10 Q 31
Portsoy 69 L 10
Portuairk 59 B 13
Postbridge 4 I 32
Potter Street 22 U 28
Potterne 17 N 30
Potters Bar 20 T 28
Potterspury 28 R 27
Potton 29 T 27
Poughill 6 G 31
Poulton-le-Fylde 38 L 22
Poundstock 6 G 31
Powburn 51 O 17
Powerstock 8 L 31
Powick 27 N 27
Powmill 56 J 15
Powys (County) 25 J 26
Poynings 11 T 31
Poynton 35 N 23
Praa Sands 2 D 33
Praze-an-Beeble 2 E 33
Prees 34 M 25
Preesall 38 L 22
Prescot 34 L 23
Prestatyn 33 J 23
Prestbury 35 N 24
Presteigne 25 K 27
Preston (Humberside) 41 T 22
Preston (Kent) 13 X 30
Preston (Lancs.) 38 L 22
Preston (West Sussex) 11 S 31
Preston Candover 10 Q 30
Prestonpans 56 L 16
Prestwich 39 N 23
Prestwick 48 G 17
Prestwood 18 R 28
Priest Island 72 D 10
Princes Risborough 18 R 28
Princethorne 27 P 26
Princetown 4 I 32
Priors Marston 28 Q 27
Probus 2 F 33
Prosen (Glen) 62 K 13
Prudhoe 51 O 19
Puckeridge 22 U 28
Puddletown 8 M 31
Pudsey 39 P 22
Pulborough 11 S 31
Pulham Market 31 X 26
Purbeck (Isle of) 8 N 32
Purbrook 10 Q 31
Purley 18 Q 29
Purse Caundle Manor 8 M 31
Purston Jaglin 40 P 22
Purton 17 O 29
Putsborough 6 H 30
Pwllheli 32 G 25
Pyecombe 11 T 31
Pyle 15 I 29

Q

Quainton 18 R 28
Quantock Hills 7 K 30
Quedgeley 17 N 28
Queen Camel 8 M 30
Queen Elizabeth Forest Park 55 G 15
Queenborough 12 W 29
Queensbury 39 O 22
Queensferry 33 K 24
Quinag 72 E 9
Quinish Point 59 B 14
Quiraing 65 B 11
Quoich (Loch) 60 E 12
Quorndon 36 Q 25

R

Raasay (Island of) 65 B 11
Raasay (Sound of) 65 B 11
Rackwick 74 J 7
Radcliffe 39 N 23
Radcliffe-on-Trent 36 Q 25
Radlett 20 T 29
Radnor Forest 25 K 27
Radstock 17 M 30
Radyr 16 K 29
Rafford 68 J 11
Raglan 16 L 28
Rainford 38 L 23
Rainham 12 V 29
Rainworth 36 Q 24
Ramsbottom 39 N 23
Ramsbury 18 P 29
Ramsey (Cambs.) 29 T 26
Ramsey (Isle of Man) 42 G 21
Ramsey Bay 42 G 21
Ramsey Island 14 D 28
Ramsey St. Mary's 29 T 26
Ramsgate 13 Y 30
Ramsgill 39 O 21
Ranfurly 55 G 16
Rannoch (Loch) 61 H 13
Rannoch Moor 60 F 14
Ranskill 36 Q 23
Rapness 74 L 6
Rappach 72 F 10
Ratby 28 Q 26
Rathen 69 O 11
Rattray 62 K 14
Rattray Head 69 O 11
Raunds 29 S 26
Ravenglass 43 J 20
Ravenstonedale 45 M 20
Rawcliffe 41 R 22
Rawmarsh 40 P 23
Rawtenstall 39 N 22
Rayleigh 22 V 29
Read 39 M 22
Reading 18 Q 29
Reay 73 I 8
Reay Forest 72 F 9
Reculver 13 X 29
Red Wharf Bay 32 H 24
Redbourn 19 S 28
Redbourne 41 S 23
Redbridge (London Borough) 21 U 29
Redcar 46 Q 20
Redcliff Bay 16 L 29
Redditch 27 O 27
Redford 63 L 14
Redhill 20 T 30
Redpoint 66 C 11
Redruth 2 E 33
Redwick 16 L 29
Reedham 31 Y 26
Reekie Linn 62 K 13
Reeth 45 O 20
Reigate 20 T 30
Reighton 41 T 21
Reiss 74 K 8
Rempstone 36 Q 25
Rendham 31 Y 27
Renfrew 55 G 16
Renish Point 70 Z 10
Renishaw 35 P 24
Renton 55 G 16
Resort (Loch) 70 Z 9
Restalrig 56 K 16
Restormel Castle 3 G 32
Rhaeadr/ Rhayader 25 J 27
Rhaeadr Ddu 32 I 25
Rhayader/ Rhaeadr 25 J 27
Rheidol (Vale of) 24 I 26
Rhiconich 72 F 8
Rhinns of Galloway (The) 42 E 19
Rhinns of Kells 48 G 18
Rhondda 16 J 29
Rhoose 16 J 29
Rhoscrowther 14 E 28
Rhosllanerchrugog 33 K 24
Rhosneigr 32 G 24
Rhossili 15 H 29
Rhu 54 F 15
Rhuddlan 33 J 24
Rhum 59 A 13
Rhuthun/Ruthin 33 K 24
Rhyd-Ddu 32 H 24
Rhydaman/ Ammanford 15 I 28
Rhydcymerau 24 H 27
Rhydd 27 N 27
Rhyddhywel 25 J 26
Rhydowen 24 H 27
Rhyl 33 J 24
Rhymney/ Rhymmi 16 K 28
Rhynie 68 L 12
Ribble (River) 38 N 22
Ribblesdale 39 N 21
Ribchester 38 M 22
Riccall 40 Q 22
Riccarton 48 G 17
Richmond 46 O 20
Richmond-upon-Thames (London Borough) 20 T 29
Rickmansworth 20 S 29
Ridgeway Path (The) 18 P 29
Rievaulx Abbey 46 Q 21
Rigside 49 I 17
Rillington 40 R 21
Rimsdale (Loch) 73 H 9
Ringford 43 H 19
Ringmer 12 U 31
Ringstead 29 S 26
Ringwood 9 O 31
Ringwould 13 Y 30
Rinnes (Glen) 68 K 11
Rinns of Islay 52 A 16
Rinns Point 52 A 16
Ripe 12 U 31
Ripley (Derbs.) 35 P 24
Ripley (North Yorks.) 39 P 21
Ripley (Surrey) 20 S 30
Ripon 40 P 21
Rippingale 37 S 25
Ripponden 39 O 22
Risca 16 K 29
Rishton 39 M 22
Ristol (Isle) 72 D 9
Roag (Loch) 70 Z 9
Roberton 50 L 17
Robertsbridge 12 V 31
Robin Hood's Bay 47 S 20
Roby 34 L 23
Rocester 35 O 25
Rochdale 39 N 23
Roche 3 F 32
Rochester 12 V 29
Rochford 22 W 29
Rock 2 F 32
Rockcliffe (Cumbria) 44 K 19
Rockcliffe (Dumfries and Galloway) 43 I 19
Rode 17 N 30
Rodel 70 Z 10
Rodmarton 17 N 28
Rogerstone 16 K 29
Rolleston (Notts.) 36 R 24
Rolleston (Staffs.) 35 P 25
Rolvenden 12 V 30
Romiley 35 N 23
Romney Marsh 12 W 30
Romsey 9 P 31
Romsley 27 N 26
Rona (Island of) 65 C 11
Ronaldsway 42 G 21
Ronas Voe 75 P 2
Ronay 64 Y 11
Roos 41 T 22
Rootpark 55 I 16
Ropsley 36 S 25
Rora Head 74 J 7
Rosehearty 69 N 10
Rosemarket 14 F 28
Rosemarkie 67 H 11
Roshven 59 C 13
Roslin 56 K 16
Ross of Mull 59 B 15
Ross-on-Wye 16 M 28
Rossall Point 38 K 22
Rossett 34 L 24
Rothbury 51 O 18
Rothbury Forest 51 O 18
Rotherfield 12 U 30
Rotherham 35 P 23
Rothes 68 K 11
Rothesay 54 E 16
Rothienorman 69 M 11
Rothiesholm 75 M 6
Rothwell (Northants.) 28 R 26
Rothwell (West Yorks.) 40 P 22
Rottingdean 11 T 31
Roughton 31 X 25
Rousay 74 K 6
Rowland's Castle 10 R 31
Rowland's Gill 51 O 19
Rownhams 9 P 31
Rowsley 35 P 24
Roxwell 22 V 28
Roy (Glen) 60 F 13
Royal Greenwich Observatory 12 V 31
Royal Leamington Spa 27 P 27
Royal Military Academy 18 R 29
Royal Tunbridge Wells 12 U 30
Roybridge 60 F 13
Roydon (Essex) 22 U 28
Roydon (Norfolk) 30 X 26
Royston (Herts.) 29 T 27
Royston (South Yorks.) 40 P 23
Royton 39 N 23
Ruabon 33 K 25
Ruan High Lanes 2 F 33
Ruan Minor 2 E 34
Ruardean 16 M 28
Rubbha na Faing 52 A 16
Rubh'an Dùnain 65 A 12
Rubha a' Mhail 52 B 16
Rubha Còigeach 72 D 9
Rubha Dubh 58 Z 14
Rubha Hunish 65 A 10
Rubha na h-Easgainne 65 B 12
Rubha Réidh 66 C 10
Rubha Suisnish 65 B 12
Ruddington 36 Q 25
Rudgeway 16 M 29
Rudgwick 11 S 30
Rudston 41 T 21
Rufford 38 L 23
Rufford Old Hall 38 L 23
Rugby 28 Q 26
Rugeley 35 O 25
Rumney 16 K 29
Runcorn 34 L 23
Runwell 22 V 29
Rushden 28 S 27
Ruskington 37 S 24
Rusper 11 T 30
Rustington 11 S 31
Ruswarp 47 S 20
Rutherglen 55 H 16
Ruthin/Rhuthun 33 K 24
Ruthven 62 K 14
Ruthven (Loch) 67 H 12
Ruthwell 49 J 19
Rutland Water 28 S 26
Ruyton of the Eleven Towns 34 L 25
Ryan (Loch) 48 E 19
Rycote 18 Q 28
Ryde 10 Q 31
Rye 12 W 31
Ryhall 29 S 25
Ryhill 40 P 23
Ryhope 46 P 19
Ryton 51 O 19

S

Sadberge 46 P 20
Saddell Bay 53 D 17
Saddleworth 39 O 23
Saffron Walden 29 U 27
St. Helier (Channel I.) 5
St. Peter Port (Channel I.) 5
St. Abb's Head 57 N 16
St. Agnes 2 E 33
St. Albans 19 T 28
St. Aldhelm's Head 8 N 32
St. Andrews 56 L 14
St. Ann's Head 14 E 28
St. Arvans 16 L 29
St. Asaph 33 J 24
St. Athan 16 J 29
St. Austell 3 F 32
St. Bees 43 J 20
St. Bees Head 43 J 20
St. Blazey 3 F 32
St. Breock 3 F 32
St. Briavels 16 M 28
St. Brides Bay 14 E 28
St. Brides Major 15 J 29
St. Buryan 2 D 33
St. Catherine's Point 10 Q 32
St. Clears/ Sanclêr 14 G 28
St. Cleer 3 G 32
St. Columb Major 2 F 32
St. Combs 69 O 11
St. Cyrus 63 M 13
St. David's Head 14 D 28
St. David's/ Tyddewi 14 E 28
St. Day 2 E 33
St. Dennis 3 F 32
St. Dogmaels 24 F 27
St. Donats 15 J 29
St. Ewe 3 F 33
St. Fagans 16 K 29
St. Fergus 69 O 11
St. Fillans 61 H 14
St. Gennys 6 G 31
St. Germans 3 H 32
St. Govan's Head 14 F 29
St. Helens (I.O.W.) 10 Q 31
St. Helens (Merseyside) 38 L 23
St. Ishmael's 14 E 28
St. Issey 2 F 32
St. Ive 3 G 32
St. Ives (Cambs.) 29 T 27
St. Ives (Cornwall) 2 D 33
St. John's 42 G 21
St. John's Loch 73 J 8
St. John's Chapel 45 N 19
St. John's Town of Dalry 49 H 18
St. Just 2 C 33
St. Just in Roseland 2 E 33
St. Keverne 2 E 33
St. Kew 3 F 32
St. Leonards (Dorset) 9 O 31
St. Leonards (East Sussex) 12 V 31
St. Mabyn 3 F 32
St. Magnus Bay 75 P 2
St. Margaret's at Cliffe 13 Y 30
St. Margaret's Bay 13 Y 30
St. Margaret's Hope 74 L 7
St. Martin's 33 K 25
St. Mary in the Marsh 12 W 30
St. Mary's 74 L 7
St. Mary's Loch 50 K 17
St. Mawes 2 E 33
St. Mawgan 3 F 32
St. Mellion 3 H 32
St. Merryn 2 F 32
St. Michael's Mount 2 D 33
St. Michaels-on-Wyre 38 L 22
St. Monance 56 L 15
St. Neot 3 G 32
St. Neots 29 T 27
St. Nicholas-at-Wade 13 X 29
St. Nicholas (Dyfed) 14 E 28
St. Nicholas (South Glam.) 16 K 29
St. Ninian's Isle 75 P 4
St. Osyth 23 X 28
St. Patrick's Isle 42 F 21
St. Paul's Walden 19 T 28
St. Peter's 13 Y 29
St. Stephen 2 F 32
St. Teath 3 F 32
St. Tudwal's Islands 32 G 25
St. Tudy 3 F 32
St. Vigeans 63 M 14
Salcombe 4 I 33
Sale 34 N 23
Salen (Highland) 59 C 14
Salen (Strathclyde) 59 C 13
Salfleet 41 U 23
Salford 39 N 23
Salfords 19 T 30
Saline 56 J 15
Salisbury 9 O 30
Salisbury Plain 17 O 30
Saltash 3 H 32
Saltburn 67 H 10
Saltcoats 54 F 17
Saltford 17 M 29
Saltram House 3 H 32
Samala 64 X 11
Samlesbury Old Hall 38 M 22
Sampford Courtenay 6 I 31
Sampford Peverell 7 J 31
Sanclêr/St. Clears 24 G 26
Sancreed 2 D 33
Sand Side 44 K 21
Sanda Island 53 D 18
Sanday (Highland) 65 A 12
Sanday (Orkney Islands) 75 M 6
Sandbach 34 M 24
Sandbank 54 F 16
Sandbanks 9 O 31
Sandend 69 L 10
Sandford 7 J 31
Sandford Orcas 8 M 31
Sandgate 13 X 30
Sandgreen 43 H 19
Sandhaven 69 N 10
Sandhurst (Berks.) 18 R 29
Sandhurst (Kent) 12 V 30
Sandleigh 18 Q 28
Sandlins 23 Y 27
Sandness 75 P 3
Sandon 35 N 25
Sandown 10 Q 32
Sandray 58 X 13
Sandridge 19 T 28
Sandringham House 30 V 25
Sandwell 27 O 26
Sandwich 13 Y 30
Sandwood Loch 72 E 8
Sandy 29 T 27
Sandygate 42 G 20
Sandyhills 43 I 19
Sanquhar 49 I 17
Santon Harcourt 18 P 28
Santon Head 42 G 21
Sarisbury 10 Q 31
Sark (Channel I.) 5
Sarre 13 X 29
Satterthwaite 44 K 21
Saundersfoot 14 F 28
Saunderton 18 R 28
Sawbridgeworth 22 U 28
Sawrey 44 L 20
Sawston 29 U 27
Sawtry 29 T 26
Saxilby 36 S 24
Saxlingham Nethergate 31 X 26
Saxmundham 23 Y 27
Saxtead Green 31 X 27

Scadavay (Loch)	64 Y 11
Scaddle (Glen)	60 D 13
Scafell Pikes	44 K 20
Scalasaig	52 B 15
Scalby	47 S 21
Scalloway	75 Q 3
Scalpay (Highland)	65 C 12
Scalpay	
(Western Isles)	70 A 10
Scampton	36 S 24
Scapa Flow	74 K 7
Scarba	52 C 15
Scarborough	47 S 21
Scarcliffe	36 Q 24
Scarisbrick	38 L 23
Scarp	70 Y 9
Scavaig (Loch)	65 B 12
Schiehallion	61 H 13
Scilly (Isles of)	2 B 34
Scone Palace	62 J 14
Scopwick	37 S 24
Scorton	46 P 20
Scotch-Corner	46 P 20
Scothern	37 S 24
Scotlandwell	56 K 15
Scotney	12 V 30
Scotter	40 S 23
Scourie	72 E 8
Scousburgh	75 Q 4
Scrabster	73 J 8
Scridain (Loch)	59 B 14
Scunthorpe	40 S 23
Sea Palling	31 Y 25
Seaford	11 U 31
Seaforth (Loch)	70 Z 10
Seaham	46 P 19
Seale	47 R 20
Sealga (Loch na)	66 E 10
Seasalter	13 X 29
Seascale	43 J 20
Seaton	5 K 31
Seaton Carew	46 Q 20
Seaton Delaval	51 P 18
Seaton Delaval	
Hall	51 P 18
Seaview	10 Q 31
Sebergham	44 L 19
Sedbergh	45 M 21
Sedgebrook	36 R 25
Sedgley	27 N 26
Sedlescombe	12 V 31
Seend	17 N 29
Seething	31 Y 26
Seil	54 D 15
Seilich	
(Loch an t-)	61 H 13
Selborne	10 R 30
Selby	40 Q 22
Selker Bay	43 J 21
Selkirk	50 L 17
Sellindge	13 W 30
Selmeston	12 U 31
Selsey	10 R 31
Selworthy	7 J 30
Semley	8 N 30
Senghenydd	16 K 29
Sennen	2 C 33
Sennybridge	15 J 28
Settle	39 N 21
Seven Sisters	
(West Glam.)	15 I 28
Seven Sisters	
(East Sussex)	12 U 31
Sevenoaks	21 U 30
Severn (River)	16 M 28
Severn Bridge	16 M 29
Sgibacleit (Loch)	70 A 9
Sgiwen	15 I 29
Sgurr Mór	66 E 10
Shaftesbury	8 N 30
Shalbourne	18 P 29
Shaldon	4 J 32
Shalford	19 S 30
Shandon	54 F 15
Shanklin	10 Q 32
Shap	45 L 20
Shapinsay	74 L 6
Sharnbrook	29 S 27
Sharpness	17 M 28
Shaw (Gtr	
Mches.)	39 N 23
Shaw (Wilts.)	17 N 29
Shawbost	70 Z 9
Shawbury	34 M 25
Shawford	9 P 30
Shebbear	6 H 31
Shebster	73 I 8
Sheepwash	6 H 31

Sheering	22 U 28
Sheerness	12 W 29
Sheffield	35 P 23
Sheffield Park	12 U 31
Shefford	29 S 27
Sheldon	17 N 29
Sheldon Manor	17 N 29
Sheldwich	12 W 30
Shell or Sealg	
(Loch)	70 A 9
Shenstone	27 O 26
Shenval	68 K 11
Shepley	39 O 23
Sheppey (Isle of)	12 W 29
Shepreth	29 U 27
Shepshed	36 Q 25
Shepton Mallet	8 M 30
Sherborne	8 M 31
Sherborne	
St. John	18 Q 30
Sherburn	47 S 21
Sherburn-in-	
Elmet	40 Q 22
Shere	20 S 30
Sheriff Hutton	40 Q 21
Sheriffhales	34 M 25
Sheringham	30 X 25
Sherston	17 N 29
Sherwood Forest	36 Q 24
Shetland Islands	
(Region)	75
Shiant (Sound of)	70 A 10
Shiel (Glen)	66 D 12
Shiel (Loch)	60 D 13
Shieldaig	66 D 11
Shieldaig (Loch)	66 C 11
Shifnal	26 M 25
Shilbottle	51 O 17
Shildon	46 P 20
Shillingford	7 J 30
Shillington	29 S 28
Shimpling	30 X 26
Shin (Loch)	72 G 9
Shinfield	18 R 29
Shipdham	30 W 26
Shipley (Salop)	27 N 26
Shipley	
(West Yorks.)	39 O 22
Shipston-on-	
Stour	27 P 27
Shipton	26 M 26
Shipton-under-	
Wychwood	18 P 28
Shira (Lochan)	60 F 14
Shirebrook	36 Q 24
Shirley	27 O 26
Shobdon	26 L 27
Shoeburyness	23 W 29
Shoreham	11 T 31
Shorne	12 V 29
Shorwell	9 P 32
Shotley Bridge	45 O 19
Shotley Gate	23 X 28
Shottermill	10 R 30
Shotton Colliery	
Thornley	46 P 19
Shotts	55 I 16
Shrewsbury	26 L 25
Shrewton	17 O 30
Shrivenham	17 P 29
Shropshire	
(County)	26 M 26
Shuna Sound	54 D 15
Shurdington	17 N 28
Sible Hedingham	22 V 28
Sibsey	37 U 24
Sidbury	5 K 31
Siddlington	34 N 24
Sidford	5 K 31
Sidlaw Hills	62 K 14
Sidlesham	10 R 31
Sidmouth	5 K 31
Sighthill	56 K 16
Sileby	36 Q 25
Silecroft	44 K 21
Silkstone	35 P 23
Silloth	49 J 19
Silsden	39 O 22
Silver End	22 V 28
Silverdale	38 L 21
Silverstone	28 Q 27
Silverton	7 J 31
Simonsbath	7 I 30
Sinclair's Bay	74 K 8
Sionascaig (Loch)	72 E 9
Sissinghurst	12 V 30
Sittingbourne	12 W 29
Skara Brae	74 J 6

Skares	49 H 17
Skegness	37 V 24
Skellingthorpe	36 S 24
Skelmanthorpe	35 P 23
Skelmersdale	38 L 23
Skelmorlie	54 F 16
Skelton	
(Cleveland)	46 R 20
Skelton (Cumbria)	44 L 19
Skelwith Bridge	44 K 20
Skenfrith	16 L 28
Skerray	73 H 8
Skervuile	
Lighthouse	53 C 16
Skiddaw	44 K 20
Skilgate	7 J 30
Skipness	53 D 16
Skipport (Loch)	64 Y 12
Skipsea	41 T 22
Skipton	39 N 22
Skirza	74 K 8
Skokholm Island	14 E 28
Skomer Island	14 E 28
Skye (Isle of)	65 B 12
Slaidburn	38 M 22
Slaithwaite	39 O 23
Slamannan	55 I 16
Slapin (Loch)	65 B 12
Slapton	4 J 33
Sleaford	37 S 25
Sleat (Sound)	65 C 12
Sledmere	41 S 21
Sleekburn	51 P 18
Sleights	47 S 20
Sligachan	65 B 12
Sligachan (Loch)	65 B 12
Slindon	11 S 31
Slockavullin	54 D 15
Slough	20 S 29
Sloy (Loch)	54 F 15
Small Hythe	12 W 30
Smallfield	11 T 30
Smarden	12 W 30
Smedmore	8 N 32
Snaefell	42 G 21
Snainton	47 S 21
Snaith	40 Q 22
Snape	23 Y 27
Snettisham	30 V 25
Snizort (Loch)	65 A 11
Snodland	12 V 30
Snowdon	32 H 24
Snowdonia	
Forest and	
National Park	32 I 24
Soa	58 Z 14
Soa Island	59 A 15
Soar (River)	36 Q 25
Soay	65 B 12
Soay Sound	65 B 12
Soham	30 V 26
Solent (The)	10 Q 31
Solihull	27 O 26
Sollas	64 X 11
Solva	14 E 28
Solway Firth	43 J 19
Somercotes	35 P 24
Somerset	
(County)	8 M 30
Somersham	29 U 26
Somerton	
(Norfolk)	31 Y 25
Somerton (Oxon.)	28 Q 28
Somerton	
(Somerset)	8 L 30
Sompting	11 S 31
Sonning	
Caversham	18 R 29
Sonning	
Common	18 R 29
Sopley	9 O 31
Sorbie	42 G 19
Sorn	49 H 17
Sound (The)	3 H 32
South Brent	4 I 32
South Cave	40 S 22
South Cerney	17 O 28
South Downs	10 R 31
South Elmsall	40 Q 23
South Esk (River)	63 L 13
South Foreland	13 Y 30
South Glamorgan	
(County)	16 J 29
South	
Hanningfield	22 V 29
South Harris	70 Z 10
South Harris	
Forest	70 Z 10

SHEFFIELD

Blonk Street	DY 6
Castle Gate	DY 13
Charter Row	CZ 14
Church Street	CZ 15
Cumberland Street	CZ 17
Fitzwilliam Gate	CZ 19
Flat Street	DY 20
Furnival Gate	CZ 21
Furnival Street	CZ 22

Angel Street	DY 3
Commercial Street	DZ 16
Fargate	CZ
High Street	DZ
Leopold Street	CZ 31
West Street	CZ

Haymarket	DY 25
Moorfields	CY 35
Pinstone Street	CZ 37
Queen Street	CY 38
St. Mary's Gate	CZ 40
Shalesmoor	CY 41
Snig Hill	DY 42
Waingate	DY 44
West Bar Green	CY 45

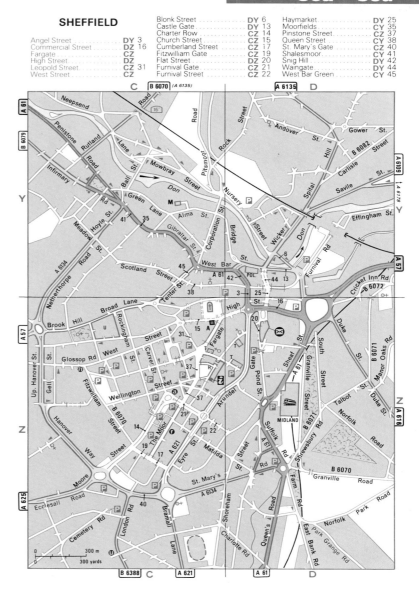

SOUTHAMPTON

Above Bar Street	
High Street	
Avenue (The)	3

Bargate Street	4
Brunswick Place	6
Central Bridge	7
Central Station	
Bridge	8
Civic Centre	
Road	13

Cumberland Place	14
Hanover Buildings	17
Houndwell Place	20
Inner Avenue	22
Marsh Lane	26
Mountbatten Way	27
Orchard Place	32
Oxford Avenue	33
Portland Street	34
Pound Tree Road	35
Queen's Terrace	38
Queen's Way	39
Radcliffe Road	41
St. Andrew's	
Road	43
South Front	48
Terminus Terrace	52
Threefield Lane	56
Town Quay	57

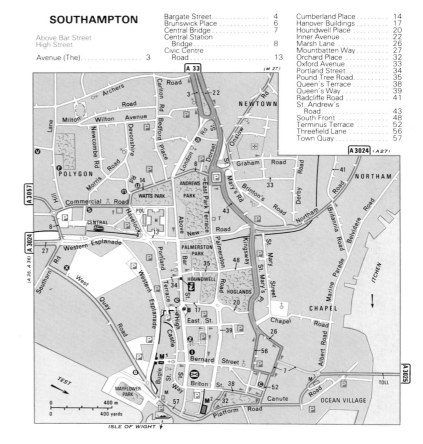

South Hayling 10 R 31
South Kelsey 41 S 23
South Kirkby 40 Q 23
South Lancing 11 T 31
South Leverton 36 R 24
South Lopham 30 X 26
South Mimms 20 T 28
South Molton 6 I 30
South Morar 59 C 13
South Normanton 35 P 24
South Ockendon 21 U 29
South Oxhey 20 S 29
South Petherton 8 L 31
South Petherwin 3 G 32
South Queensferry 56 J 16
South Ronaldsay 74 L 7
South Shields 51 P 19
South Stack 32 F 24
South Tawton 6 I 31
South Uist 64 X 12
South Walls 74 K 7
South Warnborough 18 R 30
South Woodham Ferrers 22 V 29
South Yorkshire (County) 39 O 23
South Zeal 6 I 31
Southam 27 P 27
Southampton 9 P 31
Southborough 12 U 30
Southbourne (Dorset) 9 O 31
Southbourne (West Sussex) 10 R 31
Southend 53 D 18
Southend-on-Sea 22 W 29
Southery 30 V 26
Southminster 23 W 29
Southport 38 K 23
Southsea 10 Q 31
Southwark (London Borough) 20 T 29
Southwater 11 S 30
Southwell 36 R 24
Southwick (West Sussex) 11 T 31
Southwick (Wilts.) 17 N 30
Southwick Widley 10 Q 31
Southwold 23 Z 27
Sowerby Bridge 39 O 22
Spalding 37 T 25
Spaldwick 29 S 26
Spanish Head 42 F 21
Sparkford 8 M 30
Spean (Glen) 60 F 13
Spean Bridge 60 F 13
Spelve (Loch) 59 C 14
Spennymoor 46 P 19
Spey (River) 61 G 12
Spey Bay 68 K 10
Speymouth Forest 68 K 11
Spilsby 37 U 24
Spinningdale 67 H 10

Spithead 10 Q 31
Spittal (Highland) 73 J 8
Spittal (Northumb.) 57 O 16
Spittal of Glenshee 62 J 13
Spofforth 40 P 22
Spondon 35 P 25
Spreyton 6 I 31
Springfield 56 K 15
Sprotbrough 40 Q 23
Spurn Head 41 U 23
Stack (Loch) 72 F 8
Stack Island 64 Y 12
Stacks Rocks 14 E 29
Staffa 59 A 14
Staffin Bay 65 B 11
Stafford 35 N 25
Staffordshire (County) 35 N 25
Staindrop 45 O 20
Staines 20 S 29
Stainforth (North Yorks.) 39 N 21
Stainforth (South Yorks.) 40 Q 23
Staithes 47 R 20
Stalbridge 8 M 31
Stalham 31 Y 25
Stalmine 38 L 22
Stalybridge 39 N 23
Stamford 29 S 26
Stanbridge 19 S 28
Standing Stones 70 Z 9
Standish 38 M 23
Standlake 18 P 28
Standford-in-the-Vale 18 P 29
Stanford-le-Hope 22 V 29
Stanford-on-Avon 28 Q 26
Stanhope 45 N 19
Stanley (Durham) 46 O 19
Stanley (Tayside) 62 J 14
Stanley (West Yorks.) 40 P 22
Stanmer Park 11 T 31
Stanstead Abbotts 22 U 28
Stansted Mountfitched 22 U 28
Stanton 30 W 27
Stanton Harcourt 18 P 28
Stanwell 20 S 29
Stapleford (Notts.) 36 Q 25
Stapleford (Wilts.) 9 O 30
Staplehurst 12 V 30
Start Point 4 J 33
Startforth 45 O 20
Stathern 36 R 25
Staughton Highway 29 S 27
Staunton 26 N 28
Staveley (Cumbria) 44 L 20
Staveley (Derbs.) 35 P 24
Staxigoe 74 K 8
Staxton 47 S 21

Staylittle 25 J 26
Stedham 10 R 31
Steeple 22 W 28
Steeple Ashton 17 N 30
Steeple Aston 18 Q 28
Steeple Bumpstead 22 V 27
Steeple Claydon 18 R 28
Steeple Morden 29 T 27
Stenhousemuir 55 I 15
Stenness (Orkney Islands) 74 K 7
Stenness (Shetland Islands) 75 P 2
Stevenage 19 T 28
Stevenston 54 F 17
Steventon 18 Q 29
Stewartby 29 S 27
Stewarton 55 G 16
Stewkley 18 R 28
Steyning 11 T 31
Sticklepath 4 I 31
Stilligarry 64 X 12
Stillington 40 Q 21
Stilton 29 T 26
Stirling 55 I 15
Stithians 2 E 33
Stob Choire Claurigh 60 F 13
Stock 22 V 29
Stockbridge 9 P 30
Stockland 7 K 31
Stockport 35 N 23
Stocksbridge 39 P 23
Stockton Heath 34 M 23
Stockton-on-Tees 46 P 20
Stockton-on-Teme 26 M 27
Stoer 72 D 9
Stogumber 7 K 30
Stogursey 7 K 30
Stoke Albany 28 R 26
Stoke-by-Nayland 23 W 28
Stoke Climsland 3 H 32
Stoke Fleming 4 J 33
Stoke Gabriel 4 J 32
Stoke Lacy 26 M 27
Stoke Mandeville 18 R 28
Stoke-on-Trent 35 N 24
Stoke Poges 20 S 29
Stoke sub Hamdon 8 L 31
Stokenchurch 18 R 29
Stokenham 4 I 33
Stokesay 26 L 26
Stokesley 46 Q 20
Stone (Bucks.) 18 R 28
Stone (Staffs.) 35 N 25
Stonehaven 63 N 13
Stonehenge 9 O 30
Stonehouse (Devon) 3 H 32
Stonehouse (Glos.) 17 N 28
Stonehouse (Strathclyde) 55 I 16
Stonesfield 18 P 28
Stoneybridge 64 X 12
Stoneykirk 42 E 19
Stoneywood 69 N 12
Stony Stratford 28 R 27
Stornoway 70 A 9
Storr (The) 65 B 11
Storrington 11 S 31
Stort (River) 22 U 28
Stotfold 29 T 27
Stottesdon 26 M 26
Stour (River) (English Channel) 8 N 31
Stour (River) (North Sea) 22 V 27
Stour (River) (R. Severn) 27 N 26
Stourbridge 27 N 26
Stourhead House 8 N 30
Stourport-on Severn 27 N 26
Stow 56 L 16
Stow-on-the-Wold 17 O 28
Stowe School 28 Q 27
Stowmarket 23 W 27
Strachan 63 M 12

Strachur 54 E 15
Stradbroke 31 X 27
Stradishall 22 V 27
Stradsett 30 V 26
Straiton 48 G 18
Straloch 62 J 13
Stranraer 42 E 19
Stratfield Saye 18 Q 29
Stratford St. Mary 23 W 28
Stratford-upon-Avon 27 P 27
Strath Brora 73 H 9
Strath Dearn 67 I 11
Strath Halladale 73 I 8
Strath Isla 68 K 11
Strath More 66 E 10
Strath Mulzie 72 F 10
Strath of Kildonan 73 I 9
Strath Oykel 72 F 10
Strath Skinsdale 73 H 9
Strath Tay 62 J 14
Strathallan 55 I 15
Strathardle 62 J 13
Strathaven 55 H 16
Strathbeg (Loch of) 69 O 11
Strathblane 55 H 16
Strathbogie 68 L 11
Strathbraan 61 I 14
Strathcarron 66 D 11
Strathclyde (Region) 55 G 16
Strathconon Forest 66 F 11
Strathdon 68 K 12
Strathearn 55 I 14
Stratherrick 67 G 12
Strathkinness 56 L 14
Strathmiglo 56 K 15
Strathmore 62 K 14
Strathnairn 67 H 11
Strathnaver 73 H 8
Strathpeffer 67 G 11
Strathspey 68 J 11

Strathvaich Lodge 67 F 10
Strathy 73 I 8
Strathy Point 73 H 8
Strathyre 55 H 15
Stratton (Cornwall) 6 G 31
Stratton (Glos.) 17 O 28

Stratton-on-the-Fosse 17 M 30
Stratton-St. Margaret 17 O 29
Streatley 18 Q 29
Street 8 L 30
Strensall 40 Q 21
Stretford 39 N 23

Stretham 29 U 26
Stretton (Cheshire) 34 M 23
Stretton (Staffs.) 27 N 25
Strichen 69 N 11
Striven (Loch) 54 E 16
Stroma (Island of) 74 K 7

STOKE-ON-TRENT
BUILT UP AREA

Alexandra Road U 3
Bedford Road U 4
Brownhills Road U 12
Church Lane U 19
Cobridge Road U 21
Davenport Street U 23
Elder Road U 24
Etruria Vale Road U 27
Grove Road V 30
Hanley Road U 31
Heron Street U 34
High Street U 35
Higherland V 37
Manor Street V 44
Mayne Street V 45
Moorland Road U 48
Park Hall Road V 54
Porthill Road U 59
Snow Hill U 63
Stoke Road U 68
Strand (The) Road U 75
Victoria Park Road U 75
Watlands View V 76
Williamson Street U 77

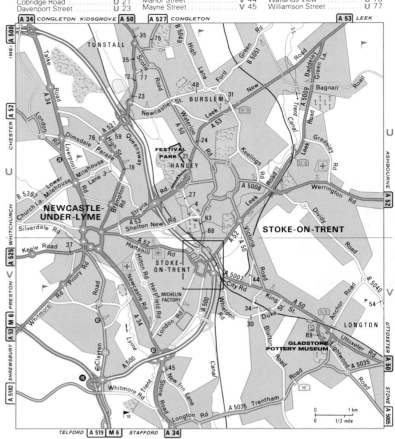

STOKE-ON-TRENT

Church Street

Campbell Place ... 14
Campbell Road ... 16
Elenora Street 26
Fleming Road 28
Hartshill Road..... 33
Lichfield Street.... 40
London Road 42
Shelton Old Road 62
Station Road 66
Vale Street 72

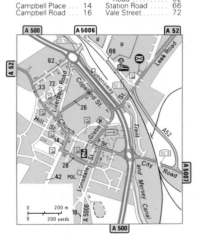

STRATFORD-UPON-AVON

Bridge Street B 8
High Street A 31
Sheep Street AB 35
Wood Street A 47

Banbury Road B 2
Benson Road B 3
Bridge Foot B 6
Chapel Lane A 13
Chapel Street A 14

Church Street A 16
Clopton Bridge B 18
College Lane A 19
Ely Street A 22
Evesham Place A 24
Great William Street A 25
Greenhill Street A 27
Guild Street A 28
Scholars Lane A 33
Tiddington Road B 38
Trinity Street A 40
Warwick Road B 42
Waterside B 43
Windsor Street A 45

SUNDERLAND

Fawcett Street
High Street West 15
Holmeside
John Street 16
Three Bridges
Albion Place 2
Bedford Street 4
Borough Road 5
Bridge Street 6
Chester Road 10
Crowtree Road 11
Derwent Street 12
Livingstone Road 18
New Durham Road 19
Park Lane 23
St. Mary's Way 27
Southwick Road 30
Vine Place 36

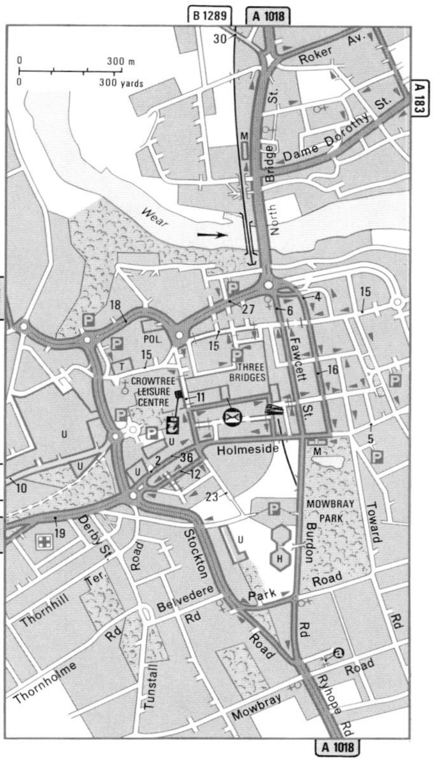

Stromeferry 66 D 11
Stromemore 66 D 11
Stromness 74 K 7
Stronachlachar 55 G 15
Stronchreggan 60 E 13
Stronsay 75 M 6

SWANSEA/ ABERTAWE

College Street 13
Kingsway (The)
Oasis Park Shopping Centre
Oxford Street
Princess Way
Quadrant Centre
St. David's Square
Alexandra Road 2
Belle Vue Way 4
Carmarthen Road 7
Christina Street 9
Clarence Terrace 10
De La Beche Street 14
Dillwyn Street 15
Fabian Way 17
East Bank Way 16
Grove Place 18
Nelson Street 20
New Cut Bridge 21
St. Mary's Square 28
Tawe Bridge 29
Union Street 32
Wellington Street 37
West Way 38
William Street 39

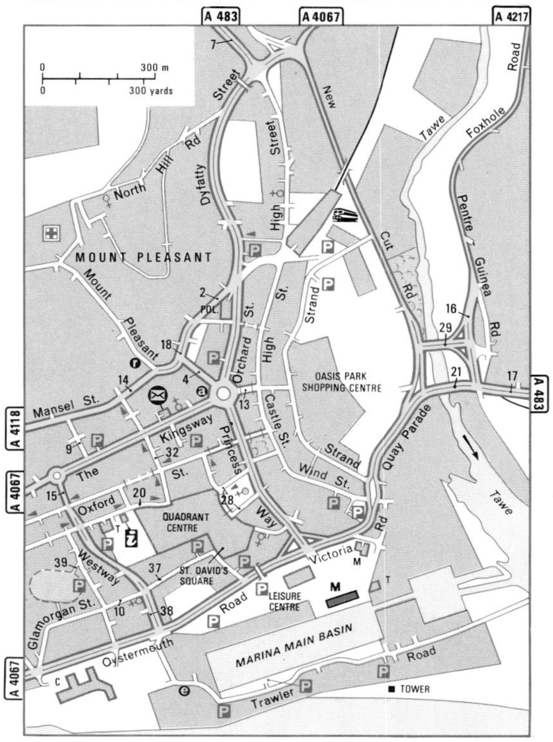

Stronsay Firth 74 L 6
Stroud 17 N 28
Strumble Head 14 E 27
Stuartfield 69 N 11
Stubbington 10 Q 31
Studland 9 Q 32
Studley (Warw.) 27 O 27
Studley (Wilts.) 17 N 29
Studley Royal Gardens 39 P 21
Stuley 64 Y 12
Sturminster Marshall 8 N 31
Sturminster Newton 8 N 31
Sturry 13 X 30
Sturton-le-Steeple 36 R 23
Suainaval (Loch) 70 Z 9
Sudbury (Derbs.) 35 O 25
Sudbury (Suffolk) 22 W 27
Sudbury Hall 35 O 25
Sudeley Castle 17 O 28
Suffolk (County) 30 X 27
Sùil Ghorm 59 A 13
Sulby 42 G 21
Sulgrave 28 Q 27
Sullom Voe 75 P 2
Sumburgh 75 Q 4
Sumburgh Roost 75 P 4
Summer Bridge 39 O 21
Summer Island 72 D 9
Summercourt 2 F 32
Sunart 59 D 13
Sunart (Loch) 59 C 13
Sunbury 20 S 29
Sunderland 46 P 19
Sunningdale 20 S 29
Sunninghill 20 S 29
Surfleet 37 T 25
Surrey (County) 11 S 30
Sutterton 37 T 25
Sutton (Cambs.) 29 U 26
Sutton (London Borough) 20 T 29
Sutton (Salop) 34 M 25
Sutton Bank 46 Q 21
Sutton Benger 17 N 29
Sutton Bridge 37 U 25
Sutton Coldfield 27 O 26
Sutton Courtenay 18 Q 29
Sutton-in-Ashfield 36 Q 24
Sutton-on-Forest 40 Q 21
Sutton-on-Hull 41 T 22
Sutton-on-Sea 37 U 24
Sutton-on-Trent 36 R 24
Sutton Scotney 9 P 30
Sutton Valence 12 V 30
Swadlincote 35 P 25
Swaffham 30 W 26
Swaffham Bulbeck 29 U 27
Swale (River) 40 P 21
Swale (The) 12 W 29
Swale Dale 45 O 20
Swallow 41 T 23
Swallow Falls 33 I 24
Swanage 9 O 32
Swanland 41 S 22
Swanley 21 U 29
Swanscombe 21 U 29
Swansea/Abertawe 15 I 29
Swarbacks Minn 75 P 2
Sway 9 P 31
Swaythling 9 P 31
Swimbridge 6 I 30
Swinbrook 18 P 28
Swindon 17 O 29
Swineshead 37 T 25
Swinton (Borders) 57 N 16
Swinton (South Yorks.) 40 Q 23
Swynnerton 34 N 25
Symbister 75 Q 2
Symonds Yat 16 M 28
Symonds Yat Rock 16 M 28
Symondsbury 8 L 31
Syresham 28 Q 27
Syston 28 Q 25

T

Tadcaster 40 Q 22
Tadley 18 Q 29
Tadmarton 27 P 27
Tadworth 20 T 30
Taff (River) 16 K 29
Taibach 15 I 29
Tain 67 H 10
Takeley 22 U 28
Tal-y-bont (Dyfed) 24 I 26
Tal-y-Llyn Lake 32 I 25
Talgarth 25 K 28
Talke 34 N 24
Talladale 66 D 10
Talley 15 I 28
Talsarnau 32 H 25
Talybont (Powys) 16 K 28
Tamanavay (Loch) 70 Y 9
Tamar (River) 6 G 31
Tamworth 27 O 26
Tan Hill 45 N 20
Tanera Beg 72 D 9
Tanera Mór 72 D 9
Tannadice 62 L 13
Tantallon Castle 56 M 15
Taransay 70 Y 10
Taransay (Sound of) 70 Z 10
Tarbat Ness 67 I 10
Tarbert (Strathclyde) 53 D 16
Tarbert (Western Isles) 70 Z 10
Tarbert (Loch) 53 C 16
Tarbet 54 F 15
Tarbolton 48 G 17
Tardy Gate 38 L 22
Tarland 68 L 12
Tarleton 38 L 22
Tarn (The) 44 L 20
Tarporley 34 L 24
Tarrant Hinton 8 N 31
Tarrant Keyneston 8 N 31
Tarrington 26 M 27
Tarskavaig Point 65 B 12
Tarves 69 N 11
Tarvin 34 L 24
Tatton Hall 34 M 24
Taunton 7 K 30
Taunton Deane 7 K 30
Taverham 30 X 25
Tavistock 3 H 32
Taw (River) 6 I 31
Tay (Firth of) 62 K 14
Tay (Loch) 61 H 14
Tay (River) 61 H 14
Tay Road Bridge 62 L 14
Taynuilt 60 E 14
Tayport 62 L 14
Tayside (Region) 62 J 13
Tayvallich 54 D 15
Teacuis (Loch) 59 C 14
Tebay 45 M 20
Tedburn St. Mary 7 I 31
Tees (River) 46 P 20
Teesdale 45 N 20
Teifi (River) 24 G 27
Teignmouth 4 J 32
Telford 26 M 25
Teme (River) 26 M 27
Temple Ewell 13 X 30
Temple Sowerby 45 M 20
Templeton 14 F 28
Tempsford 29 T 27
Tenbury Wells 26 M 27
Tenby/Dinbych y-pysgod 14 F 28
Tendring 23 X 28
Tenterden 12 W 30
Terling 22 V 28
Tern Hill 34 M 25
Terrington St. Clement 37 U 25
Test (River) 18 P 30
Tetbury 17 N 29
Tetford 37 T 24
Tetney 41 T 23
Tettenhall 27 N 26
Teviotdale 50 L 17
Tewin 19 T 28
Tewkesbury 27 N 28
Texa 52 B 17
Teynham 12 W 30
Thakeham 11 S 31
Thame 18 R 28
Thame (River) 18 R 28
Thames (River) 18 Q 29
Thanet (Isle of) 13 Y 29
Thatcham 18 Q 29
Thaxted 22 V 28
Theale (Berks.) 18 Q 29
Theale (Somerset) 16 L 30
Theddlethorpe St. Helen 37 U 23
Thetford 30 W 26
Theydon Bois 21 U 28
Thirsk 46 P 21
Thornaby-on-Tees 46 Q 20
Thornaganby 41 R 22
Thornbury (Avon) 16 M 29
Thornbury (Heref. and Worc.) 26 M 27
Thornby 28 Q 26
Thorne 41 R 23
Thorner 40 P 22
Thorney 29 T 26
Thornham 30 V 25
Thornhill (Central) 55 H 15
Thornhill (Dumfries and Galloway) 49 I 18
Thornley 46 P 19
Thornton (Fife) 56 K 15
Thornton (Lancs.) 38 K 22
Thornton Curtis 41 S 23
Thornton Dale 47 R 21
Thornton-in-Craven 39 N 22
Thornyhive Bay 63 N 13
Thorpe (Derbs.) 35 O 24
Thorpe (Essex) 22 W 29
Thorpe-le-Soken 23 X 28
Thorpe-on-the-Hill 36 S 24
Thorpeness 23 Y 27
Thorrington 23 X 28
Thorverton 7 J 31
Thrapston 29 S 26
Three Cocks 25 K 27
Threlkeld 44 K 20
Throckley 51 O 19
Throwleigh 4 I 31
Thundersley 22 V 29
Thurcroft 36 Q 23
Thurlby 37 S 25
Thurlestone 4 I 33
Thurlow 22 V 27
Thurmaston 28 Q 25
Thursby 44 K 19
Thurso 73 J 8
Thwaite 45 N 20
Tibberton (Glos.) 17 M 28
Tibberton (Salop) 34 M 25
Tibshelf 35 P 24
Ticehurst 12 V 30
Tickhill 36 Q 23
Ticknall 35 P 25
Tideswell 35 O 24
Tigerton 63 L 13
Tigharry 64 X 11
Tighnabruaich 54 E 16
Tilbury 21 V 29
Tillicoultry 55 I 15
Tillington 11 S 31
Tilshead 17 O 30
Tilt (Glen) 61 I 13
Tilton-on-the-Hill 28 R 26
Timberscombe 7 J 30
Timsbury 17 M 30
Tingwall (Loch) 75 P 3
Tintagel 3 F 32
Tintern Abbey 16 M 28
Tintinhull 8 L 31
Tipton 27 N 26
Tiptree 22 W 28
Tiree 58 Z 14
Tirga Mór 70 Z 10
Tisbury 8 N 30
Titchfield 10 Q 31
Tiumpan Head 71 B 9
Tiverton 7 J 31
Tobermory 59 B 14
Toberonochy 54 D 15
Tobson 70 Z 9
Toddington 19 S 28
Todmorden 39 N 22
Toe Head 70 Y 10
Toll of Birness 69 O 11
Tollerton 40 Q 21
Tollesbury 23 W 28
Tolleshunt d'Arcy 22 W 28
Tolpuddle 8 N 31
Tolsta 71 B 8
Tolsta Chaolais 70 Z 9
Tolsta Head 71 B 8
Tomatin 67 I 11
Tombreck 67 H 11
Tomintoul 68 J 12
Tonbridge 12 U 30
Tongland 43 H 19
Tongue 73 G 8
Tonna 15 I 28
Tonypandy 15 J 29
Tonyrefail 16 J 29
Topcliffe 46 P 21
Topsham 4 J 31
Tor Ness 74 K 7
Torbay 4 J 32
Torcross 4 J 33
Torksey 36 R 24
Torlundy 60 E 13
Torphichen 55 J 16
Torphins 69 M 12
Torpoint 3 H 32
Torquay 4 J 32
Torridon (Loch) 66 C 11
Torrisdale Bay 73 H 8
Torthorwald 49 J 18
Torver 44 K 20
Totland 9 P 31
Totnes 4 I 32
Totton 9 P 31
Tow Law 45 O 19
Towcester 28 R 27
Tower Hamlets (London Borough) 21 T 29
Town Yetholm 50 N 17
Towneley Hall 39 N 22
Traborton 48 G 17
Trallwng/Welshpool 25 K 26
Tranent 56 L 16
Traquair House 50 K 17
Trawden 39 N 22
Trawsfynydd 25 I 25
Trealaval (Loch) 70 A 9
Trearddur Bay 32 G 24
Trecastle 15 J 28
Trefaldwyn/Montgomery 25 K 26
Treffynnon/Holywell 33 K 24
Trefnant 33 J 24
Trefyclawdd/Knighton 25 K 26
Trefynwy/Monmouth 16 L 28
Tregaron 24 I 27
Tregony 2 F 33
Treharris 16 K 29
Treherbert 15 J 28
Treig (Loch) 60 F 13
Trelech 14 G 28
Trelissick Gardens 2 E 33
Trelleck 16 L 28
Tremadog 32 H 25
Tremadog Bay 32 H 25
Trengwainton Garden 2 D 33
Trent (River) 36 N 25
Trentham 35 N 25
Treorchy 15 J 29
Trerice 2 E 32
Treshnish Isles 59 A 14
Treshnish Point 59 A 14
Tretower 16 K 28
Trevone 2 F 32
Trevor 32 G 25
Trevose Head 2 E 32
Trewithen 2 F 33
Trimdon 46 P 19
Trimley Heath 23 X 28
Trimsaran 15 H 28
Tring 19 S 28
Trispen 2 E 33
Trochry 62 J 14
Troedyrhiw 16 J 28
Trollamarig (Loch) 70 Z 10
Tromie (Glen) 61 H 12
Troon 48 G 17
Trossachs (The) 55 G 15
Trotternish 65 B 11
Troutbeck 44 L 20
Trowbridge 17 N 30
Truim (Glen) 61 H 13
Trull 7 K 31
Trumpington 29 U 27
Truro 2 E 33
Trwyn Cilan 32 G 25
Tuath (Loch) 59 B 14
Tuddenham 30 V 27
Tudweiliog 32 G 25
Tugford 26 M 26
Tulla (Loch) 60 F 14
Tullibody 55 I 15
Tumble 15 H 28
Tummel (Loch) 61 I 13
Tunstall (Staffs.) 35 N 24
Tunstall (Suffolk) 31 Y 25
Turnberry 48 F 18
Turnditch 35 P 24
Turret (Loch and Reservoir) 61 I 14
Turriff 69 M 11
Turvey 28 S 27
Tusker Rock 15 I 29
Tutbury 35 O 25
Tuxford 36 R 24
Twatt 74 K 6
Tweed (River) 49 J 17
Tweeddale 49 J 17
Tweedmouth 57 N 16
Tweedsmuir Hills 49 J 17
Twickenham 20 S 29
Twyford (Berks.) 18 R 29
Twyford (Hants.) 10 Q 30
Twyford (Leics.) 28 R 25
Twynholm 43 H 19
Tyddewi/St. David's 14 E 28
Tyldesley 34 M 23
Tyne (River) 51 P 19
Tyne and Wear (Metropolitan County Newcastle) 51 P 19
Tynemouth 51 P 18
Tynewydd 15 J 28
Tytherington 17 M 29
Tywardreath 3 F 32
Tywi (River) 25 I 27
Tywyn 24 H 26

U

Uckfield	12	U 31
Uddingston	55	H 16
Uffculme	7	K 31
Ufford	23	Y 27
Ugadale Bay	53	D 17
Ugborough	4	I 32
Uig	65	A 11
Uisg (Loch)	59	C 14
Uiskevagh (Loch)	64	Y 11
Uley	17	N 28
Ullapool	72	E 10
Ulleskelf	40	Q 22
Ullesthorpe	28	Q 26
Ullswater	44	L 20
Ulpha	44	K 21
Ulsta	75	Q 2
Ulva	59	B 14
Ulverston	44	K 21
Unapool	72	E 9
Unst	75	R 1
Upavon	17	O 30
Uphall	56	J 16
Uphill	16	L 30
Uplyme	7	L 31
Upottery	7	K 31
Upper Badcall	72	E 9
Upper Beeding	11	T 31
Upper Chapel	25	J 27
Upper Dicker	12	U 31
Upper Knockando	68	J 11
Upper Loch Torridon	66	D 11
Upper Poppleton	40	Q 22
Upper Tean	35	O 25
Uppertown	74	K 7
Uppingham	28	R 26
Upton (Dorset)	8	N 31
Upton (Notts.)	36	R 24
Upton Grey	18	Q 30
Upton House	27	P 27
Upton Magna	26	M 25
Upton-upon-Severn	27	N 27
Upwell	29	U 26
Urchfont	17	O 30
Ure (River)	40	Q 21
Urigill (Loch)	72	F 9
Urmston	39	M 23
Urquhart Castle	67	G 12
Urquhart (Glen)	67	G 11
Urrahag (Loch)	70	A 8
Urswick	38	K 21
Usk (River)	15	J 28
Usk/Brynbuga	16	L 28
Uttoxeter	35	O 25
Uyea	75	R 2
Uyeasound	75	R 1

V

Vallay Strand	64	X 11
Valley	32	G 24
Valtos	70	Z 9
Vamden (London Borough)		
Vatersay	58	X 13
Ve Skerries	75	O 2
Venachar (Loch)	55	H 15
Ventnor	10	Q 32
Verwood	9	O 31
Veryan	2	F 33
Veyatie (Loch)	72	E 9
Vindolanda	50	M 19
Voe	75	Q 2
Voil (Loch)	61	G 14
Vowchurch	26	L 27
Vyrnwy (Lake)	33	J 25

W

Waddesdon	18	R 28
Waddington (Lancs.)	39	M 22
Waddington (Lincs.)	36	S 24
Wadebridge	3	F 32
Wadhurst	12	U 30
Wainfleet All Saints	37	U 24
Wakefield	40	P 22
Wakes Colne	22	W 28
Walberswick	31	Y 27

Walderslade	12	V 29
Walkden	39	M 23
Walkeringham	36	R 23
Walkern	19	T 28
Wall	27	O 26
Wallace Monument	55	I 15
Wallasey	34	K 23
Wallingford	18	Q 29
Walls	75	P 3
Wallsend	51	P 18
Walney (Isle of)	38	K 21
Walpole St. Andrew	37	U 25
Walsall	27	O 26
Waltham (Humberside)	41	T 23
Waltham (Kent)	13	X 30
Waltham Abbey	21	U 28
Waltham Forest (London Borough)	21	T 29
Waltham-on-the-Wolds	36	R 25
Walton-le-Dale	38	M 22
Walton-on-Thames	20	S 29
Walton-on-the-Naze	23	X 28
Wanborough	17	O 29
Wandsworth (London Borough)	20	T 29
Wanlockhead	49	I 17
Wansford	29	S 26
Wanstrow	8	M 30
Wantage	18	P 29
Wappenham	28	Q 27
Warboys	29	T 26
Wardington	28	Q 27
Wardour Castle	8	N 30
Ware	19	T 28
Wareham	8	N 31
Wargrave	18	R 29
Wark	57	N 17
Wark Forest	50	M 18
Warkworth	51	P 17
Warley	27	O 26
Warlingham	21	T 30
Warmington	27	P 27
Warminster	17	N 30
Warmsworth	40	Q 23
Warren (The)	13	X 30
Warrington	38	M 23
Warsash	10	Q 31
Warsop	36	Q 24
Warton (near Morecambe)	38	L 21
Warton (near Preston)	38	L 22
Warwick	27	P 27
Warwickshire (County)	27	P 27
Warwickshire (County)	27	P 27
Wasbister	74	K 6
Wash (The)	37	U 25
Washington (Tyne and Wear)	51	P 19
Washington (West Sussex)	11	S 31
Wast Water	44	K 20
Watchet	7	K 30
Watchfield	17	P 29
Watchgate	44	L 20
Water Orton	27	O 26
Waterbeach	29	U 27
Watergate Bay	2	E 32
Waterhouses	35	O 24
Wateringbury	12	V 30
Waterlooville	10	Q 31
Waternish Point	65	A 11
Waters Upton	34	M 25
Waterside	54	G 17
Watford	20	S 29
Wath-upon-Dearne	40	P 23
Watlington	18	Q 29
Watten	74	K 8
Watton	30	W 26
Watton at Stone	19	T 28
Waunfawr	32	H 24
Waveney (River)	31	Y 26
Weald (The)	12	U 30
Wear (River)	45	O 20
Weardale	45	N 19
Weaver (River)	34	M 24
Weaverthorpe	41	S 21

Wedmore	16	L 30
Wednesbury	27	N 26
Wednesfield	27	N 26
Weedon-Bec	28	Q 27
Week St. Mary	6	G 31
Weeley	23	X 28
Weem	61	I 14
Welcombe	6	G 31
Welham Green	19	T 28
Welland	26	N 27
Welland (River)	37	T 25
Wellesbourne	27	P 27
Wellingborough	28	R 27
Wellington (Salop)	26	M 25
Wellington (Somerset)	7	K 31
Wells	16	M 30
Wells-next-the-Sea	30	W 25
Welshpool/Trallwng	25	K 26
Welton	36	S 24
Welwyn	19	T 28
Welwyn Garden City	19	T 28
Wem	34	L 25
Wembdon	7	K 30
Wembley	20	T 29
Wembury	3	H 33
Wembworthy	6	I 31
Wemyss Bay	54	F 16
Wendens Ambo	29	U 27
Wendover	18	R 28
Wendron	2	E 33
Wenlock Edge	26	L 26
Wennington	38	M 21
Wensley	45	O 21
Wensleydale	45	O 21
Weobley	26	L 27
Wereham	30	V 26
West Alvington	4	I 33
West Auckland	45	O 20
West Bridgford	36	Q 25
West Bromwich	27	O 26
West Calder	56	J 16
West Camel	8	M 30
West Charleton	4	I 33
West Chiltington	11	S 31
West Coker	8	L 31
West Dean	9	P 30
West Down	6	H 30
West End	10	Q 31
West Farleigh	12	V 30
West Geirinish	64	X 11
West Glamorgan (County)	15	I 28
West Harptree	16	M 30
West Hoathly	11	T 30
West Kilbride	54	F 16
West Kingsdown	21	U 29
West Kirby	34	K 23
West Linton	56	J 16
West Loch Roag	70	Z 9
West Loch Tarbert (Strathclyde)	53	D 16
West Loch Tarbert (Western Isles)	70	Z 10
West Looe	3	G 32
West Lulworth	8	N 32
West Malling	12	V 30
West Malvern	26	M 27
West Meon	10	Q 30
West Mersea	23	W 28
West Midlands (Metropolitan County Birmingham)	27	O 26
West Moors	9	O 31
West Runton	30	X 25
West Sussex (County)	11	S 30
West Tanfield	46	P 21
West Thorney	10	R 31
West Wellow	9	P 31
West Wittering	10	R 31
West Wycombe	18	R 29
West Yorkshire (Metropolitan County Leeds)	39	O 23
West Bay	8	M 32
West Bergholt	23	W 28
Westbourne	10	R 31
Westbury (Cheshire)	26	L 25
Westbury (Wilts.)	17	N 30

Westbury-on-Severn	17	M 28
Westcliff	22	W 29
Westcott	20	S 30
Wester Ross	66	D 11
Westerham	21	U 30
Western Cleddau	14	E 28
Western Isles (Region)	70	X 10
Westfield	12	V 31
Westgate-on-Sea	13	Y 29
Westham	12	U 31
Westhoughton	38	M 23
Westleton	31	Y 27
Westmill	19	T 28
Westminster (London Borough)	20	T 29
Westnewton	44	J 19
Weston (Devon)	7	K 31
Weston (Staffs.)	35	N 25
Weston-on-the-Green	18	Q 28
Weston-on-Trent	35	P 25
Weston-super-Mare	16	K 29
Weston Turville	18	R 28
Weston-under-Lizard	27	N 25
Weston-under-Penyard	16	M 28
Westonzoyland	7	L 30
Westray	74	K 6
Westruther	56	M 16
Westward Ho	6	H 30
Westwood	17	N 30
Westwood Manor	8	N 31
Wetheral	44	L 19
Wetherby	40	P 22
Wethersfield	22	V 28
Wetwang	41	S 21
Wey (River)	18	R 30
Weybourne	30	X 25
Weybridge	20	S 29
Weyhill	18	P 30

Weymouth	8	M 32
Whaley Bridge	35	O 24
Whalley	39	M 22
Whalsay	75	R 2
Whaplode	37	T 25
Wharfe (River)	40	O 22
Wharfedale	39	O 22
Whauphill	42	G 19
Whauphill	42	G 19
Wheathampstead	19	T 28
Wheatley (Notts.)	36	R 23
Wheatley (Oxon.)	18	Q 28
Wheatley Hill	46	P 19
Wheaton Aston	34	N 25
Wheldrake	41	R 22
Whernside	38	M 21
Wherwell	9	P 30
Whickham	51	O 19
Whimple	4	J 31
Whipsnade	19	S 28
Whissendine	36	R 25
Whitburn (Lothian)	55	I 16
Whitburn (Tyne and Wear)	51	P 19
Whitby	47	S 20
Whitchurch (Avon)	17	M 29
Whitchurch (Bucks.)	18	R 28
Whitchurch (Devon)	3	H 32
Whitchurch (Heref. and Worc.)	16	M 28
Whitchurch (Oxon.)	18	Q 29
Whitchurch (Salop)	34	L 25
White Coomb	50	K 17
White Horse Hill	18	P 29
White Waltham	18	R 29
Whitefield	39	N 23
Whitehaven	43	J 20
Whitehill	10	R 30
Whitehills	69	M 10

Whitehouse	53	D 16
Whiten Head	72	G 8
Whiteness Sands	67	I 10
Whiteparish	9	P 30
Whiterashes	69	N 12
Whitesand Bay (Corwall)	2	C 33
Whitesand Bay (Dyfed)	14	E 28
Whitfield	13	X 30
Whithorn	42	G 19
Whiting Bay	53	E 17
Whitland	14	G 28
Whitley	18	R 29
Whitley Bay	51	P 18
Whitsand Bay	3	H 32
Whitstable	13	X 29
Whitstone	6	G 31
Whittingham	51	O 17
Whittington (Derbs.)	35	P 24
Whittington (Lancs.)	38	L 21

WINCHESTER

High Street

Andover Road	3
Bridge Street	6
Broadway (The)	8
City Road	10
Clifton Terrace	12
East Hill	15
Eastgate Street	16
Friarsgate	19
Magdalen Hill	23
Middle Brook Street	24
St. George's Street	32
St. Paul's Hill	33
St. Peter's Street	34
Southgate Street	35
Stockbridge Road	37
Sussex Street	38
Union Street	39
Upper High Street	40

WOLVERHAMPTON

Darlington Street	
Mander Centre	
Victoria Street	24
Wulfrun Centre	
Cleveland Street	7
Garrick Street	8
Lichfield Street	12
Market Street	14
Princess Street	15
Queen Square	17
Railway Drive	20
Salop Street	22

Whittington (Salop) 34 L 25
Whittle le Woods 38 M 22
Whittlebury 28 R 27
Whittlesey 29 T 26
Whitton (Powys) 25 K 27
Whitton (Suffolk) 23 X 27
Whittonstall 51 O 19
Whitwell (Derbs.) 36 Q 24
Whitwell (I.O.W.) 10 Q 32
Whitwell-on-the-Hill 40 R 21
Whitwick 35 P 25
Whitworth 39 N 23
Wiay (Highland) 65 A 11
Wiay (Western Isles) 64 Y 11
Wick (Avon) 17 M 29
Wick (Highland) 74 K 8
Wicken 28 R 27
Wickenby 37 S 24
Wickford 22 V 29
Wickham 10 Q 31
Wickham Market 23 Y 27
Wickwar 17 M 29
Widecombe-in-the-Moor 4 I 32
Wideford Hill Cairn 74 K 7
Widford 22 U 28
Widnes 34 L 23
Wigan 38 M 23
Wiggenhall St. Mary Magdalen 30 V 25
Wight (Isle of) (County) 9 P 32
Wigmore 12 V 29
Wigston 28 Q 26
Wigton 44 K 19
Wigtown 42 G 19
Wigtown Bay 43 H 19
Wilberfoss 41 R 22
Wilcot 17 O 29
Wild Animal Kingdom 28 S 28
Willand 7 J 31
Willenhall 27 N 26
Willerby 41 S 22
Willersey 27 O 27
Willingdon 12 U 31
Willingham 29 U 26
Willingham Forest 37 T 23
Willington (Beds.) 29 S 27
Willington (Derbs.) 35 P 25

Willington (Durham) 45 O 19
Williton 7 K 30
Wilmcote 27 O 27
Wilmington (East Essex) 12 U 31
Wilmington (Kent) 21 U 29
Wilmslow 34 N 24
Wilton 9 O 30
Wiltshire (County) 17 O 30
Wimbledon 20 T 29
Wimblington 29 U 26
Wimborne Minster 9 O 31
Wimborne St. Giles 9 O 31
Wincanton 8 M 30
Winchcombe 27 O 28
Winchelsea 12 W 31
Winchester 9 P 30
Windermere 44 L 20
Windlesham 20 S 29
Windrush 17 O 28
Windrush (River) 17 O 28
Windsor 20 S 29
Windsor Great Park 20 S 29
Windygates 56 K 15
Winfarthing 30 X 26
Winfrith Newburgh 8 N 32
Wing 18 R 28
Wingate 46 P 19
Wingfield 35 P 24
Wingham 13 X 30
Wingrave 18 R 28
Winkfield 18 R 29
Winkleigh 6 I 31
Winnersh 18 R 29
Winscombe 16 L 30
Winsford (Cheshire) 34 M 24
Winsford (Somerset) 7 J 30
Winshill 35 P 25
Winslow 28 R 28
Winster 35 P 24
Winterborne Kingston 8 N 31
Winterborne Stickland 8 N 31
Winterborne Whitechurch 8 N 31
Winterbourne 17 M 29
Winterbourne Abbas 8 M 31
Winterbourne Stoke 9 O 30
Winteringham 41 S 22
Winterton 41 S 23

Winterton-on-Sea 31 Z 25
Winton 45 N 20
Winwick 29 S 26
Wirksworth 35 P 24
Wirral 33 K 24
Wisbech 29 U 25
Wisborough Green 11 S 30
Wishaw 55 I 16
Wisley 20 S 30
Wissey (River) 30 V 26
Witchford 29 U 26
Witham 22 V 28
Witham (River) 37 T 24
Witheridge 7 I 31
Withernsea 41 U 22
Withington 17 O 28
Withycombe 4 J 32
Withypool 7 J 30
Witley 10 S 30
Witney 18 P 28
Wittering 29 S 26
Wittersham 12 W 30
Wiveliscombe 7 K 30
Wivenhoe 23 W 28
Woburn 28 S 28
Woburn Abbey 28 S 28
Woburn Sands 28 S 27
Woking 20 S 30
Wokingham 18 R 29
Woldingham 21 T 30
Wollaston 28 S 27
Wollaton Hall 36 Q 25
Wolsingham 45 O 19
Wolvercote 18 Q 28
Wolverhampton 27 N 26
Wolverton 28 R 27
Wolviston 46 Q 20
Wombourn 27 N 26
Wombwell 40 P 23
Womersley 40 Q 22
Wonersh 19 S 30
Wood Dalling 30 X 25
Woodbridge 23 X 27
Woodbury 4 J 31
Woodchurch 12 W 30
Woodcote 18 Q 29
Woodford Halse 28 Q 27
Woodhall Spa 37 T 24
Woodham Ferrers 22 V 29
Woodingdean 11 T 31
Woodnesborough 13 X 30
Woodseaves 34 N 25
Woodstock 18 P 28
Woodton 31 Y 26
Woody Bay 6 I 30
Wookey Hole 16 L 30
Wool 8 N 31

Woolacombe 6 H 30
Wooler 51 N 17
Woolfardisworthy 6 G 31
Woolpit 23 X 27
Woolsthorpe 36 R 25
Woore 34 M 25
Wootton Bassett 17 O 29
Wootton Courtenay 7 J 30
Wootton-Wawen 27 O 27
Worcester 27 N 27
Workington 43 J 20
Worksop 36 Q 24
Worle 16 L 29
Wormit 62 L 14
Worms Head 15 H 29
Worplesdon 20 S 30
Worsbrough 40 P 23
Worsley 39 M 23
Worthen 26 L 26
Worthing 11 S 31
Wortwell 31 Y 26
Wotton-under-Edge 17 M 29
Wragby 37 T 24
Wrangle 37 U 24
Wrawby 41 S 23
Wray 38 M 21
Wrea Green 38 L 22
Wrecsam/Wrexham 34 L 24
Wremtham 31 Z 26
Wrexham/Wrecsam 34 L 24
Wrington 16 L 29
Writtle 22 V 28
Wrotham 21 U 30
Wroughton 17 O 29
Wroxham 31 Y 25
Wroxton 27 P 27
Wyche 26 M 27
Wye 12 W 30
Wye (River) 16 M 28
Wylam 51 O 19
Wylye 9 O 30
Wymondham (Leics.) 36 R 25
Wymondham (Norfolk) 30 X 26
Wyre 74 L 6

Y

Y-Fenni/Abergavenny 16 L 28
Y Ffor 32 G 25
Y Llethr 32 I 25
Y Maerdy 15 J 28
Yafforth 46 P 20

Yalding 12 V 30
Yapton 11 S 31
Yardley Hastings 28 R 27
Yare (River) 30 W 26
Yarm 46 P 20
Yarmouth 9 P 31
Yate 17 M 29
Yateley 18 R 29
Yatton 16 L 29
Yaxham 30 W 26
Yaxley 29 T 26
Yeadon 39 O 22
Yealmpton 4 I 32

Yedingham 47 S 21
Yell 75 Q 1
Yelverton 3 H 32
Yeolmbridge 3 G 32
Yeovil 8 M 31
Yesnaby 74 J 6
Yetminster 8 M 31
Yetts o' Muckhart 56 J 15
Ynys/Lochtyn 24 G 27
York 40 Q 22
Yorkletts 13 X 30
Yorkley 16 M 28

Yorkshire Dales National Park 45 N 21
Yorkshire Wolds 41 S 21
Youlgreave 35 O 24
Yoxall 35 O 25
Yoxford 31 Y 27
Yr Wyddgrug/Mold 33 K 24
Ysbyty Ifan 33 I 24
Ystalyfera 15 I 28
Ystrad-Aeron 24 H 27
Ystradgynlais 15 I 28
Ystwyth (River) 24 H 26

YORK

Blake Street . . . . CY 5
Coney Street . . . . CY 13
Davygate . . . . CY 16
Lendal . . . . CY 32
Parliament Street DY 42
Shambles (The) DY 54
Stonegate . . . . . . CY 58

Bishopgate Street CZ 3
Bishophill Senior CZ 4

Church Street . . . . . DY 8
Clifford Street . . . . . DY 10
Colliergate . . . . DY 12
Cromwell Road . . . . CZ 15
Deangate . . . . DY 18
Duncombe Place . . CY 20
Fawcett Street . . . . DZ 21
Fetter Lane . . . . . . CY 22
Goodramgate . . . . . DY 25
High Ousegate . . . . DY 26
High Petergate . . . . CY 28
Leeman Road . . . . . CY 30
Lord Mayor's Walk . DX 33

Low Petergate . . . . DY 35
Museum Street . . . . CY 39
Pavement . . . . DY 43
Peasholme Green . . DY 45
Penley's Grove Street . . . . DX 46
Queen Street . . . . . CZ 49
St. Leonard's Place CY 52
St. Maurice's Road . . . . DXY 53
Station Road . . . . . CY 55
Stonebow (The) . . . DY 56
Tower Street . . . . . DZ 59

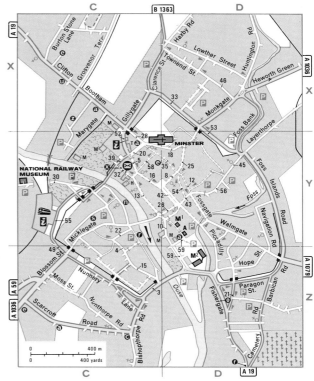

Ireland

A

Abbey Leix/ Mainistir Laoise	86 J 9
Abbeydorney	82 C 10
Abbeyfeale	83 E 10
Abbeylara	91 J 6
Achill Head	94 B 6
Achill Island	94 B 6
Achill Sound/ Gob an Choire	94 C 6
Achillbeg Island	94 C 6
Aclare	95 F 5
Acoose (Lough)	76 C 11
Adamstown	81 L 10
Adare	84 F 10
Adrigole	76 C 12
Aghaboe	86 J 9
Aghabullogue	78 F 12
Aghada	79 H 12
Aghalee	98 N 4
Aghavannagh	87 M 9
Aghaville	77 D 13
Aghla Mountain	100 H 3
Aghowle Church	87 M 9
Aglish	79 I 11
Ahakista	76 D 13
Ahalia (Loughs)	88 D 7
Ahascragh	89 G 7
Ahenny	80 J 10
Aherlow (Glen of)	85 H 10
Ahoghill	102 M 3
Aillwee Cave	89 E 8
Ailt an Chorráin/ Burtonport	100 G 3
Aird Mhór/ Ardmore	79 I 12
Allen (Bog of)	86 K 8
Allen (Lough)	96 H 5
Allenwood	86 L 8
Allihies	76 B 13
Allua (Lough)	77 E 12
Altan Lough	100 H 2
An Blascaod Mór/Blasket Islands	82 A 11
An Bun Beag/ Bunbeg	100 H 2
An Cabhán/ Cavan	97 J 6
An Caiseal/ Cashel	88 C 7
An Caisleán Nua/ Newcastle West	83 E 10
An Caisleán Riabhach/ Castlerea	96 G 6
An Charraig/ Carrick	100 G 4
An Chathair/ Caher	85 I 10
An Cheathrú Rua/ Carraroe	88 D 8
An Chloich Mhóir/ Cloghmore	94 C 6
An Clochán/ Clifden	88 B 7
An Clochán/ Cloghan (Donegal)	100 I 3
An Clochán Liath/ Dunglow	100 G 3
An Cloigeann/ Cleegan	88 B 7
An Cóbh/Cobh	78 H 12
An Coimín/ Commeen	100 I 3
An Coireán/ Waterville	76 B 12
An Corrán/ Currane	94 C 6
An Creagán/ Mount Bellew	89 G 7
An Daingean/ Dingle	82 B 11
An Dúchoraidh/ Doocharry	100 H 3

An Fál Carrach/ Falcarragh	100 H 2
An Fhairche/ Clonbur	88 D 7
An Geata Mór	94 B 5
An Gleann Garbh/ Glengarriff	77 D 12
An Gort/Gort	89 F 8
An Gort Mór/ Gortmore	88 D 7
An Leacht/ Lahinch	88 D 9
An Longfort/ Longford	90 I 6
An Mám/ Maam Cross	88 D 7
An Mhala Raithní/ Mulrany	94 C 6
An Móta/Moate	90 I 7
An Muileann gCearr/ Mullingar	91 J 7
An Nás/Naas	87 M 8
An Ráth/Rath Luirc (Charleville)	84 F 10
An Ráth/ Charleville	84 F 10
An Ros/Rush	92 N 7
An Scairbh/ Scarriff	84 G 9
An Sciobairín/ Skibbereen	77 E 13

An Seanchaisleán/ Oldcastle	91 K 6
An Spidéal/ Spiddle	88 E 8
An tAonach/ Nenagh	84 H 9
An Teampall Mór/ Templemore	85 I 9
An Tearmann/ Termon	101 I 2
An tInbhear Mór/ Arklow	87 N 9
An tSraith/Srah	95 E 6
An Tulach/ Tullow	86 L 9
An Uaimh/ Navan	92 L 7
Anascaul	82 B 11
Annacarriga	84 G 9
Annacotty	84 G 9
Annagary	100 H 2
Annagassan	92 M 6
Annageeragh	83 D 9
Annagh Head	94 B 5
Annaghmore Lough	90 H 6
Annalee	97 J 5
Annalong	98 O 5
Annamoe	87 N 8
Annestown	80 K 11
Antrim	103 N 3
Antrim (County)	102 M 3
Antrim Coast	103 O 2

Antrim (Glens of)	103 N 2
Antrim Mountains	103 N 2
Anure (Lough)	100 H 3
Araglin	79 H 11
Árainn Mhór/ Aran or Aranmore Island	100 G 2
Árainn (Oileáin)/ Aran Islands	88 C 8
Aran Islands/ Oileáin Árainn	88 C 8
Aran or Aranmore Island/Árainn Mhór	100 G 2
Archdale (Castle)	97 I 4
Ardagh	83 E 10
Ardara	100 G 3
Ardboe	98 M 4
Ardcath	92 M 7
Ardcrony	85 H 9
Ardea	76 C 12
Ardee/Baile Átha Fhirdhia	92 M 6
Ardfert	82 C 11
Ardfinnan	85 I 11
Ardglass	99 P 5
Ardgroom	76 C 12
Ardkeen	99 P 4
Ardmore/Aird Mhór	79 I 12
Ardrahan	89 F 8

Ardress House	98 M 4
Ards Forest Park	101 I 2
Ards Peninsula	99 P 4
Ardscull (Mote of)	86 L 8
Argideen	78 F 13
Argory (The)	98 M 4
Arigna	96 H 5
Arklow/ An tInbhear Mór	87 N 9
Armagh	98 M 4
Armagh (County)	98 L 5
Armoy	103 N 2
Arney	97 I 5
Arrow (Lough)	96 H 5
Arthurstown	80 L 11
Arvagh	97 J 6
Ashbourne	92 M 7
Ashford	87 N 8
Ashford Castle	89 E 7
Astee	83 D 10
Áth Cinn/ Headford	89 E 7
Athassel Abbey	85 I 10
Athboy	92 L 7
Athea	83 E 10
Athenry/ Baile Átha an Rí	89 F 8
Athleague	90 H 7
Athlone/ Baile Átha Luain	90 I 7
Baile Átha an Rí/ Athenry	89 F 8

Athy/ Baile Átha Í	86 L 9
Attymon	89 G 8
Audley's Castle	99 P 4
Augher	97 K 4
Aughils	82 C 11
Aughnacloy	97 L 4
Aughnanure Castle	89 E 7
Aughrim (Galway)	90 H 8
Aughrim (Wicklow)	87 N 9
Aughris Head	95 F 5
Avoca	87 N 9
Avoca (River)	87 N 9
Avoca (Valle of)	87 N 9
Avonbeg	87 M 9
Avondale Forest Park	87 N 9

B

Bagenalstown	86 L 9
Baile an Fheirtéaraigh/ Ballyferriter	82 A 11
Baile an Mhóta/ Ballymote	96 G 5
Baile an Róba/ Ballinrobe	89 E 7
Baile an Sceilg/ Ballinskelligs	76 B 12
Baile Átha an Rí/ Athenry	89 F 8

Baile Átha Cliath/Dublin	87 N 8
Baile Átha Fhirdhia/ Ardee	92 M 6
Baile Átha Í/Athy	86 L 9
Baile Átha Luain/ Athlone	90 I 7
Baile Átha Troim/Trim	92 L 7
Baile Bhuirne/ Ballyvourney	77 E 12
Baile Brigín/ Balbriggan	92 N 7
Baile Chláir/ Claregalway	89 F 7
Baile Locha Riach/ Loughrea	89 G 8
Baile Mhic Andáin/ Thomastown	80 K 10
Baile Mhic Íre/ Ballymakeery	77 E 12
Baile Mhistéala/ Mitchelstown	79 H 11
Baile na Finne/ Fintown	100 H 3
Baile na Lorgan/ Castleblayney	98 L 5
Baile Uí Bhuaigh/ Ballyvoge	77 E 12
Baile Uí Fhiacháin/ Newport	94 D 6

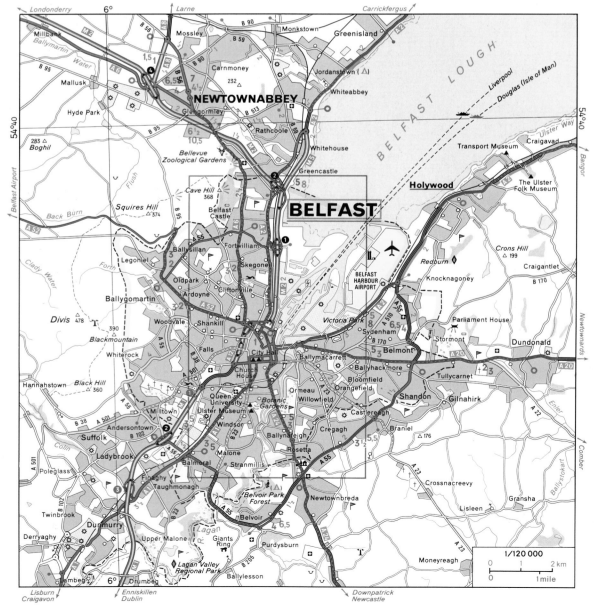

BELFAST

Castle Place	**BZ**	
Donegal Place	**BZ**	
Royal Avenue	**BYZ**	
Albert Bridge Road	**BZ** 2	
Albert Square	**BY** 3	
Ann Street	**BZ** 5	
Bradbury Place	**BZ** 7	
Bridge Street	**BZ** 8	
Clifton Street	**BY** 10	
Corporation Square	**BY** 12	
Donegall Quay	**BYZ** 13	
Donegall Square	**BZ** 14	
High Street	**BYZ** 16	
Howard Street	**BZ** 17	
Mountpottinger Road	**BZ** 22	
Newtownards Road	**BZ** 23	
Queen Elizabeth Bridge	**BZ** 25	
Queen's Quay Road	**BY** 26	
Queen's Bridge	**BZ** 27	
Queen's Square	**BY** 29	
Rosemary Street	**BZ** 30	
Station Street	**BZ** 35	
University Road	**BZ** 37	
Waring Street	**BY** 38	
Wellington Place	**BZ** 39	

Belfast city map

Baile Uí Mhatháin/ Ballymahon	90	I 7
Bailieborough/ Coill an Chollaigh	97	L 6
Balbriggan/ Baile Brigín	92	N 7
Baldoyle	92	N 7
Balla	95	E 6
Ballagan Point	98	N 5
Ballaghaderreen/ Bealach an Doirín	96	G 6
Ballaghbeama Gap	76	C 12
Ballaghisheen Pass	76	C 12
Ballina/ Béal an Átha	95	E 5
Ballina (Tipperary)	84	G 9
Ballinaboy	88	B 7
Ballinadee	78	G 12
Ballinafad	96	G 5
Ballinagar	86	J 8
Ballinakill	86	K 9
Ballinalack	91	J 7
Ballinalea	87	N 8
Ballinalee	91	J 6
Ballinamallard	97	J 4
Ballinamore/ Béal an Átha Mhóir	96	I 5
Ballinamore Bridge	89	G 7

Ballinascarty	78	F 12
Ballinasloe/Béal Átha na Sluaighe	90	H 8
Ballincollig	78	G 12
Ballincrea	80	K 11
Ballincurrig	79	H 12
Ballindarragh	97	J 5
Ballindine	95	F 6
Ballineen	78	F 12
Ballingarry (Galway)	85	H 8
Ballingarry (Limerick)	84	F 10
Ballingarry (Tipperary)	80	J 10
Ballingeary/Béal Átha an Ghaorthaidh	77	E 12
Ballinhassig	78	G 12
Ballinlough	96	G 6
Ballinrobe/ Baile an Róba	89	E 7
Ballinskelligs		
Baile an Sceilg	76	B 12
Ballinskelligs Bay	76	B 12
Ballinspittle	78	G 12
Ballintober	96	G 6
Ballintoy	103	M 2
Ballintra	96	H 4
Ballinure	85	I 10
Ballitore	86	L 8
Ballivor	92	L 7
Ballon	86	L 9
Ballyagran	84	F 10

Ballybay	97	L 5
Ballybofey/ Bealach Féich	101	I 3
Ballyboghil	92	N 7
Ballyboy	90	I 8
Ballybrittas	86	K 8
Ballybrophy	86	J 9
Ballybunnion	83	D 10
Ballycanew	81	N 10
Ballycarney	81	M 10
Ballycastle (Antrim)	103	N 2
Ballycastle (Mayo)	95	D 5
Ballycastle Bay	103	N 2
Ballyclare (Antrim)	103	N 3
Ballyclare (Roscommon)	90	I 6
Ballyclogh	78	F 11
Ballycolla	86	J 9
Ballyconneely	88	B 7
Ballyconneely Bay	88	B 7
Ballyconnell	97	J 5
Ballycotton	79	H 12
Ballycotton Bay	79	H 12
Ballycroy	94	C 5
Ballydavid	82	A 11
Ballydavid Head	82	A 11
Ballydavis	86	K 8
Ballydehob	77	D 13
Ballydesmond	83	E 11
Ballydonegan	76	B 13
Ballyduff (Dingle)	82	B 11

Ballyduff (Kerry)	83	D 10
Ballyduff (Waterford)	79	H 11
Ballyeighter Loughs	84	F 9
Ballyfarnan	96	H 5
Ballyferriter/ Baile an Fheirtéaraigh	82	A 11
Ballyforan	90	H 7
Ballygalley	103	O 3
Ballygalley Head	103	O 3
Ballygar	90	H 7
Ballygawley (Sligo)	96	G 5
Ballygawley (Tyrone)	97	K 4
Ballygorman	101	K 1
Ballygowan	99	O 4
Ballyhack	80	L 11
Ballyhahill	83	E 10
Ballyhaise	97	K 5
Ballyhalbert	99	P 4
Ballyhale	80	K 10
Ballyhaunis/Béal Átha hAmhnais	95	F 6
Ballyhean	95	E 6
Ballyheige	82	C 10
Ballyheige Bay	82	C 10
Ballyhoe Lough	92	L 6
Ballyhooly	78	G 11
Ballyhoura Mountains	84	G 11
Ballyjamesduff	91	K 6
Ballykeeran	90	I 7

Ballykelly	102	K 2
Ballylanders	84	G 10
Ballylickey	77	D 12
Ballyliffin	101	J 2
Ballylongford	83	D 10
Ballylongford Bay	83	D 10
Ballylynan	86	K 9
Ballymacarbry	79	I 11
Ballymacdermot Cairn	98	M 5
Ballymacoda	79	I 12
Ballymagorry	101	J 3
Ballymahon/ Baile Uí Mhatháin	90	I 7
Ballymakeery/ Baile Mhic Íre	77	E 12
Ballymartin	98	O 5
Ballymena	103	N 3
Ballymoe	96	G 6
Ballymoney	102	M 2
Ballymore	91	I 7
Ballymore Eustace	87	M 8
Ballymote/ Baile an Mhóta	96	G 5
Ballymurphy	81	L 10
Ballynabola	81	L 10
Ballynacarrigy	91	J 7
Ballynacorra	79	H 12
Ballynagore	91	J 7
Ballynagree	78	F 12
Ballynahinch	98	O 4
Ballynahinch Lake	88	C 7
Ballynahown	88	D 8
Ballynakill Harbour	88	B 7
Ballyneety	84	G 10
Ballynoe	79	H 11
Ballynure	103	O 3
Ballyorgan	84	G 11
Ballypatrick	80	J 10
Ballyporeen	79	H 11
Ballyquintin Point	99	P 5
Ballyragget	86	K 9
Ballyroan	86	K 9
Ballyronan	102	M 3
Ballyroney	98	N 5
Ballysadare	96	G 5
Ballyshannon/ Béal Átha Seanaidh	96	H 4
Ballysteen	84	F 10
Ballyteige Bay	81	L 11
Ballyvaughan	89	E 8
Ballyvaughan Bay	89	E 8
Ballyvourney/ Baile Bhuirne	77	E 12
Ballywalter	99	P 4
Ballywilliam	81	L 10
Balrath	92	M 7
Baltimore	77	D 13
Baltinglass/ Bealach Conglais	87	L 9
Baltray	92	N 6
Banagher	90	I 8
Banbridge	98	N 4
Bandon/ Droichead na Bandan	78	F 12
Bandon River	77	F 12
Bangor (Down)	103	O 4
Bangor (Mayo)	94	C 5
Bann (River) (Lough Neagh)	98	N 5
Bann (River) (R. Slaney)	81	M 10
Banna Strand	82	C 11
Bannow	81	L 11
Bansha	85	H 10
Banteer	78	F 11
Bantry/Beanntraí	77	D 12
Bantry Bay	76	C 13
Barefield	84	F 9
Barley Cove	76	C 13
Barna/Bearna	89	E 8
Barnaderg	89	F 7
Barnatra/ Barr na Trá	94	C 5
Barnesmore Gap	100	I 3
Baronscourt Forest	101	J 3
Barra (Lough)	100	H 3
Barr na Trá/ Barnatra	94	C 5

Barrow	86	J 8
Barrow Harbour	82	C 11
Barrow (River)	86	K 8
Beagh (Lough)	101	I 2
Béal an Átha/ Ballina	95	E 5
Béal an Átha Mhóir/ Ballinamore	96	I 5
Béal an Mhuirthead/ Belmullet	94	C 5
Béal Átha an Ghaorthaidh/ Ballingeary	77	E 12
Béal Átha hAmhnais/ Ballyhaunis	95	F 6
Béal Átha na Muice/ Swinford	95	F 6
Béal Átha na Sluaighe/ Ballinasloe	90	H 8
Béal Átha Seanaidh/ Ballyshannon	96	H 4
Béal Deirg/ Belderrig	94	D 5
Béal Tairbirt/ Belturbet	97	J 5
Bealach an Doirín/ Ballaghaderreen	96	G 6
Bealach Conglais/ Baltinglass	87	L 9
Bealach Féich/ Ballybofey	101	I 3
Bealaclugga	89	E 8
Bealadangan	88	D 8
Bealaha	83	D 9
Beanntraí/ Brantry	77	D 12
Beara	76	C 12
Bearna/Barna	89	E 8
Beaufort	77	D 11
Beenoskee	82	B 11
Beg (Lough)	102	M 3
Behy	76	C 11
Belcarra	95	E 6
Belclare	89	F 7
Belcoo	96	I 5
Belderrig/ Béal Deirg	94	D 5
Belfast	103	O 4
Belfast Lough	103	O 3
Belgooly	78	G 12
Belhavel Lough	96	H 5
Bellacorick	94	D 5
Bellaghy	102	M 3
Bellanagare	96	G 6
Bellanaleck	97	J 5
Bellananagh	97	J 6
Bellavary	95	E 6
Belleek (Armagh)	98	M 5
Belleek (Fermanagh)	96	H 4
Belmullet/Béal an Mhuirthead	94	C 5
Beltany Stone Circle	101	J 3
Beltra	94	D 6
Beltra Lough	94	D 6
Belturbet/ Béal Tairbirt	97	J 5
Benbane Head	102	M 2
Benbrack	96	I 5
Benbulben	96	G 4
Benburb	98	L 4
Bencroy or Gubnaveagh	96	I 5
Benmore or Fair Head	103	N 2
Benettsbridge	80	K 10
Benwee Head	94	C 4
Beragh	97	K 4
Bere Island	76	C 13
Bertraghboy Bay	88	C 7
Bessbrook	98	M 5
Bettystown	92	N 6
Binevenagh	102	L 2
Binn Éadair/ Howth	92	N 7
Biorra/Birr	90	I 8
Birdhill	84	G 9
Birr/Biorra	90	I 8

Black Head (Antrim)	103	O 3
Black Head (Clare)	88	E 8
Black Ball Head	76	B 13
Black Bull	92	M 7
Black Gap (The)	96	I 4
Blacklion	96	I 5
Blackrock	87	N 8
Blackrock (Louth)	98	M 6
Blacksod Bay	94	B 5
Blacksod Point	94	B 5
Blackstairs Mountains	81	L 10
Blackwater	81	M 10
Blackwater (River) (R. Boyne)	92	L 6
Blackwater Bridge	76	C 12
Blackwater (River)	78	F 11
Blackwater (River) (Lough Neagh)	98	L 4
Blarney	78	G 12
Blasket Islands/ An Blascaod Mór	82	A 11
Blennerville	82	C 11
Blessington	87	M 8
Bloody Foreland	100	H 2
Blue Ball	86	J 8
Blue Stack Mountains	100	H 3
Boderg (Lough)	96	I 6
Bodyke	84	G 9
Bofin (Lough) (Galway)	88	D 7
Bofin (Lough) (Roscommon)	96	I 6
Boggeragh Mountains	77	E 12
Boheraphuca	85	I 8
Boherboy	77	E 11
Bohermeen	92	L 7
Bola (Lough)	88	C 7
Boley	86	L 8
Boliska Lough	88	E 8
Bolus Head	76	A 12
Bonet	96	H 5
Boobyglass	80	K 10
Borris	80	L 10
Borris in Ossory	86	J 9
Borrisokane		
Buiríos Uí Chéin	85	H 9
Borrisoleigh	85	I 9
Bouladuff	85	I 9
Boyle/ Mainistir na Búille	96	H 6
Boyle (River)	96	H 6
Boyne (River)	91	K 7
Bracklin	91	K 7
Brandon/ Cé Bhréanainn	82	B 11
Brandon Bay	82	B 11
Brandon Head	82	B 11
Brandon Hill	81	L 10
Bray/Bré	87	N 8
Bray Head (Kerry)	76	A 12
Bray Head (Wicklow)	87	N 8
Bré/Bray	87	N 8
Breenagh	100	I 3
Bride (River)	78	F 12
Bride (River)	79	I 11
Bridebridge	79	H 11
Bridge End	101	J 2
Bridgeland	87	M 9
Bridget Lough	84	G 9
Bridgetown	81	M 11
Briensbridge	84	G 9
Brinlack/ Bun na Leaca	100	H 2
Brittas	87	M 8
Brittas Bay	87	N 9
Broad Haven	94	C 5
Broad Meadow	92	N 7
Broadford (Clare)	84	G 9
Broadford (Limerick)	84	F 10
Broadway	81	M 11
Brookeborough	97	J 5
Brosna	83	E 11
Brosna (River)	90	I 8

Broughshane 103 N 3
Brow Head 76 C 13
Brown Flesk 83 D 11
Brownstown
  Head 80 K 11
Bruff 84 G 10
Bruree 84 G 10
Buckode 96 H 4
Buiríos Uí Chéin/
  Borrisokane 85 H 9
Bull Point 103 N 2
Bull's Head 82 B 11
Bullaun 89 G 8
Bun an Phobail/
  Moville 101 K 2
Bun Cranncha/
  Buncrana 101 J 2
Bun Dobhráin/
  Bundoran 96 H 4
Bun na hAbhna/
  Bunnahowen 94 C 5
Bun na Leaca/
  Brinlack 100 H 2
Bunacurry 94 C 6
Bunbeg/
  An Bun Beag 100 H 2
Bunclody 81 M 10
Buncrana/
  Bun Cranncha 101 J 2
Bundoran/
  Bun Dobhráin 96 H 4
Bunmahon 80 J 11
Bunnahowen/
  Bun na hAbhna 94 C 5
Bunnanaddan 96 G 5
Bunny (Lough) 89 F 8
Bunnyconnellan 95 E 5
Bunowen 94 C 6
Bunratty 84 F 9
Burncourt 85 H 11
Burnfort 78 G 11
Burren (The) 89 E 8
Burrishoole
  Abbey 94 D 6
Burtonport/
  Ailt an
  Chorráin 100 G 3
Bush 102 M 2
Bushfield 84 G 9
Bushmills 102 M 2
Butler's Bridge 97 J 5
Butlerstown 78 F 13
Buttevant 84 F 11
Bweeng 78 F 11

C

Caha Mountains 76 C 12
Caher/An
  Chathair 85 I 10
Caher Island 94 B 6
Caherbarnagh 77 E 11
Caherconlish 84 G 10
Caherdaniel 76 B 12
Cahersiveen/
  Cathair
  Saidhbhín 76 B 12
Cahore Point 81 N 10
Caiseal/Cashel 85 I 10
Caisleán an
  Bharraigh/
  Castlebar 95 E 6
Caisleán an
  Chomair/
  Castlecomer 86 K 9
Calafort Ros
  Láir/
  Rosslare
  Harbour 81 M 11
Caledon 98 L 4
Callainn/Callan 80 J 10
Callan/Callainn 80 J 10
Caltra 89 G 7
Camlough 98 M 5
Camolin 81 M 10
Camp 82 C 11
Campile 80 L 11
Canglass Point 76 B 12
Canningstown 97 K 6
Cappagh White 84 H 10
Cappamore 84 G 10
Cappoquin/
  Ceapach
  Choinn 79 I 11
Car (Slieve) 94 D 5
Caragh (Lough) 76 C 11
Caragh (River) 76 C 12

Carbery's
  Hundred
  Isles 77 D 13
Carbury 92 L 7
Carhan House 76 B 12
Cark Mountain 101 I 3
Carlanstown 92 L 6
Carlingford 98 N 5
Carlingford
  Lough 98 N 5
Carlow/
  Ceatharlach 86 L 9
Carlow (County) 86 L 9
Carn Domhnach/
  Cardonagh 101 K 2
Carna 88 C 8
Carncastle 103 O 3
Carndonagh/
  Carn
  Domhnach 101 K 2
Carnew 87 M 9
Carney 96 G 4
Carnlough 103 O 3
Carnlough Bay 103 O 3
Carnsore Point 81 M 11
Carra (Lough) 95 E 6
Carraig Airt/
  Carrigart 101 I 2
Carraig
  Mhachaire
  Rois/
  Carrickmacross 98 L 6
Carraig na Siúire/
  Carrick-on-Suir 80 J 10
Carran 89 E 8
Carrantuohill 76 C 11
Carraroe/
  An Cheathrú
  Rua 88 D 8
Carrick/
  An Charraig
  (Donegal) 100 G 4
Carrick (Wexford) 81 L 11
Carrick-on-
  Shannon-Cora
  Droma Rúisc 96 H 6
Carrick-on-Suir/
  Carraig na
  Siúire 80 J 10
Carrickboy 91 I 7
Carrickfergus 103 O 3
Carrickmacross/
  Carraig
  Mhachaire Rois 98 L 6
Carrickmore 97 K 4
Carrigafoyle
  Castle 83 D 10
Carrigaholt 82 C 10
Carrigaline 78 G 12
Carrigallen 97 J 6
Carriganimmy 77 E 12
Carrigans 101 J 3
Carrigart/
  Carraig Airt 101 I 2
Carrigkerry 83 E 10
Carrigtohill 78 H 12
Carrowkeel 101 J 2
Carrowmore 96 G 5
Carrowmore
  Lake 94 C 5
Carrownisky 94 C 6
Carrowteige/
  Ceathrú
  Thaidhg 94 C 5
Carrybeg 80 J 10
Carryduff 98 O 4
Cashel/An
  Caiseal
  (Galway) 88 C 7
Cashel/Caiseal
  (Tipperary) 85 I 10
Cashel (Rock of) 85 I 10
Cashen River 83 D 10
Cashla Bay 88 D 8
Casla/Costelloe 88 D 8
Castle Gardens 78 F 13
Castle Haven 77 E 13
Castle Point 82 C 10
Castlebaldwin 96 G 5
Castlebar/
  Caisleán
  an Bharraigh 95 E 6
Castlebellingham 92 M 6
Castleblakeney 89 G 7
Castleblayney/
  Baile na Lorgan 98 L 5
Castlebridge 81 M 10
Castlecaulfield 98 L 4

Castlecomer/
  Caisleán an
  Chomair 86 K 9
Castleconnell 84 G 9
Castlecove 76 B 12
Castledawson 102 M 3
Castlederg 101 J 3
Castledermot 86 L 9
Castlefinn 101 J 3
Castlefreke 78 F 13
Castlegal 96 G 4
Castlegregory 82 B 11
Castlehill 94 C 6
Castleisland/
  Oileán Ciarraí 83 D 11
Castlelyons 79 H 11
Castlemaine 82 C 11
Castlemaine
  Harbour 82 C 11
Castlemartyr 79 H 12
Castleplunket 96 G 6
Casltepollard 91 K 6
Castlerea/An
  Caisleán
  Riabhach 96 G 6
Castlerock 102 L 2
Castletown
  (Laois) 86 J 9
Castletown
  (Westmeath) 91 J 7
Castletown
  (Wexford) 87 N 9
Castletownbere 76 C 13
Castletownroche 78 G 11
Castletownshend 77 E 13
Castleward
  House 99 P 4
Castlewellan 98 O 5
Castlewellan
  Forest Park 98 O 5
Cathair na Mart/
  Westport 94 D 6
Cathair
  Saidhbhín/
  Cahersiveen 76 B 12
Causeway 82 C 10
Cavan/An
  Cabhán 97 J 6
Cavan (County) 91 J 6
Cé Bhréanainn/
  Brandon 82 B 11
Ceanannas/
  Ceanannus Mór
  (Kells) 92 L 6
Ceanannus Mór
  (Kells) 92 L 6
Ceanannas 92 L 6
Ceann Toirc/
  Kanturk 78 F 11
Ceapach Choinn/
  Cappoquin 79 I 11
Ceatharlach/
  Carlow 86 L 9
Ceathrú Thaidhg/
  Carrowteige 94 C 5
Cecilstown 78 F 11
Celbridge 92 M 7
Chapeltown 99 P 5
Charles's Fort 78 G 12
Charlestown
  (Armagh) 98 M 4
Charlestown
  (Mayo) 95 F 6
Charleville (Ráth
  Luirc)/An Ráth 84 F 10
Church Hill 101 I 3
Church Quarter 103 N 2
Churchtown 80 L 11
Cill Airne/
  Killarney 77 D 11
Cill Chainnigh/
  Kilkenny 80 K 10
Cill Chaoi/Kilkee 83 D 9
Cill Chiaráin/
  Kilkieran 88 C 8
Cill Dalua/Killaloe 84 G 9
Cill Dara/Kildare 86 L 8
Cill Mhantáin/
  Wicklow 87 N 9
Cill Mocheallóg/
  Kilmallock 84 G 10
Cill Orglan/
  Killorglin 76 C 11
Cill Rois/Kilrush 83 D 10
Cill Rónáin/
  Kilronan 88 C 8
Cionn tSáile/
  Kinsale 78 G 12

Clady 101 J 3
Clane 87 L 8
Clár Chlainne
  Mhuiris/
  Claremorris 95 F 6
Clara/Clóirtheach
  (Offaly) 91 J 7
Clara (Wicklow) 87 N 9
Clare (County) 84 F 9
Clare Island 94 B 6
Clare (River) 89 F 7
Clarecastle 84 F 9
Claregalway 86 K 9
Claremorris/Clár
  Chlainne
  Mhuiris 95 F 6
Clarinbridge 89 F 8
Clashmore 79 I 11
Claudy 102 K 3
Clear (Cape) 77 D 13

Clear Island/
  Cléire (Oileán) 77 D 13
Cleegan Bay 88 B 7
Cleggan/
  An Cloigeann 88 B 7
Cléire (Oilean)/
  Clear Island 77 D 13
Clew Bay 94 C 6
Clifden/An
  Clochán 88 B 7
Cliffony 96 G 4
Clogh (Antrim) 103 N 3
Clogh (Kilkenny) 86 K 9
Clogh (Wexford) 81 M 10
Clogh Mills 103 N 3
Cloghan/An
  Clochán
  (Donegal) 100 I 3
Cloghan (Offaly) 90 I 8
Cloghan
  (Westmeath) 91 K 7

Cloghane 82 B 11
Cloghaneely 100 H 2
Cloghbrack 88 D 7
Clogheen 79 I 11
Clogher 97 K 4
Clogher Head
  (Kerry) 82 A 11
Clogher Head 92 N 6
Clogherhead 92 N 6
Cloghjordan 85 H 9
Cloghmore
  An Chloich
  Mhóir 94 C 6
Cloghy 99 P 4
Clohamon 81 M 10
Cloich na Coillte/
  Clonakilty 78 F 13
Clóirtheach/Clara 91 J 7
Clonakilty/
  Cloich na
  Coillte 78 F 13

Clonakilty Bay 78 F 13
Clonalis House 96 G 6
Clonaslee 86 J 8
Clonbern 89 G 7
Clonbulloge 86 K 8
Clonbur/
  An Fhairche 88 D 7
Clonco Bridge 89 G 8
Clondalkin 87 M 8
Clonea 80 J 11
Clonea Bay 80 J 11
Clonee 92 M 7
Cloneen 80 J 10
Clonegall 87 M 9
Clones/
  Cluain Eois 97 K 5
Clonfert 90 H 8
Clonmacnoise 90 I 8
Clonmany 101 J 2
Clonmel/
  Cluain Meala 85 I 10

DUBLIN/ BAILE ÁTHA CLIATH

Anne Street South........ BY 2
Dawson Street.......... BY
Duke Street........... BY 27
Grafton Street......... BY
Henry Street........... BY
Irish Life Mall Centre... BY
O'Connell Street....... BXY

Belvidere Place.......... BX 4
Blessington Street....... BX 6
Brunswick Street North... BY 8

Bull Alley........... BY 9
Chancery Street........ BY 13
Charlotte Street....... BZ 15
College Street........ BY 19
Denmark Street........ BX 23
D'Olier Street........ BY 24
Essex Quay........... BY 30
Fitzgibbon Street...... BX 31
Fitzwilliam Place...... BZ 32
Frederick Street North... BX 33
Gardiner Place........ BX 35
George's Quay........ BY 36
Golden Lane.......... BY 39
Harrington Street...... BZ 44
Kevin Street Upper..... BZ 47
Kildare Street........ BYZ 48
King Street South...... BZ 49

Marlborough Street...... BY 53
Merchants Quay....... BY 56
Montague Street....... BZ 59
Mountjoy Street....... BX 62
Nicholas Street....... BY 64
Parnell Square East.... BX 67
Parnell Square North... BX 68
Parnell Square West.... BY 69
St. Alphonsus Rd...... AY 76
Stephen Street....... BY 80
Tara Street......... BY 81
Wellington Quay....... BY 95
Westland Row........ BY 96
Westmoreland Street.... BY 97
Wexford Street....... BZ 99
Winetavern Street..... BY 100
Wood Quay.......... BY 103

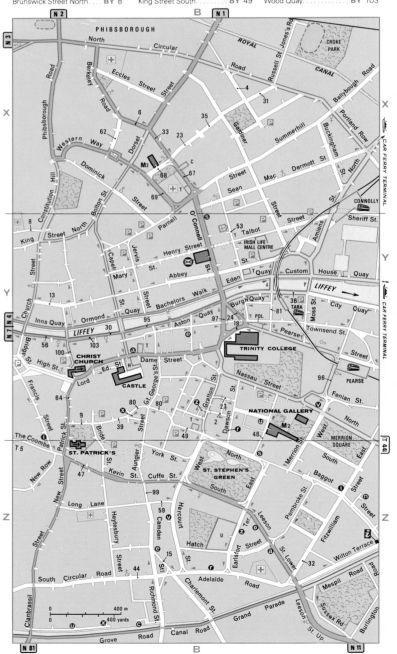

Clonmellon	91 K 7	Colgah Lough	96 G 5	Cora Droma		Creggs	89 G 7	Cúil Aodha/	
Clonmore	87 M 9	Colligan	79 I 11	Rúisc/		Croagh	84 F 10	Coolea	77 E 12
Clonmult	79 H 12	Collinstown	91 K 7	Carrick-on-		Croagh Patrick	94 C 6	Cuilcagh	96 I 5
Clonroche	81 L 10	Collon	92 M 6	Shannon	96 H 6	Croaghnageer	100 I 3	Culdaff	101 K 2
Clontarf	92 N 7	Collooney	96 G 5	Corbally	95 E 5	Croaghnakeela		Culdaff Bay	101 K 2
Clontibret	97 L 5	Comber	99 O 4	Corcaigh/Cork	78 G 12	Island	88 C 8	Culleens	95 F 5
Clontuskert		Comeragh		Corcomroe		Croangar		Cullenagh	88 E 9
Abbey	90 H 8	Mountains	80 J 11	Abbey	89 E 8	(Lough)	100 H 3	Cullin (Lough)	95 E 6
Clonygowan	86 K 8	Commeen/		Cork/Corcaigh	78 G 12	Croghan	96 H 6	Cullybackey	102 M 3
Cloon Lake	76 C 12	An Coimín	100 I 3	Cork (County)	78 F 12	Crohy Head	100 G 3	Cummeragh	76 B 12
Cloonacleigha		Cong/Conga	89 E 7	Cork Harbour	78 H 12	Crois		Curlew	
Lake	96 G 5	Conga/Cong	89 E 7	Corkscrew Hill	89 E 8	Mhaoilíona/		Mountains	96 G 6
Cloonacool	95 F 5	Conlig	103 O 4	Cornamona	88 D 7	Crossmolina	95 E 5	Curracloe	81 M 10
Cloonaghmore	95 D 5	Conn (lough)	95 E 5	Corrandulla	89 F 7	Croithlí/Crolly	100 H 2	Curragh (The)	86 L 8
Cloonbannin	77 E 11	Conna	79 H 11	Corraun		Crolly/Croithlí	100 H 2	Curraghmore	
Clooncoorha	83 D 9	Connemara	88 C 7	Peninsula	94 C 6	Cromane	76 C 11	Gardens	80 J 11
Cloone	96 I 6	Connemara		Corrib (Lough)	89 E 7	Crookedwood	91 K 7	Curraghroe	90 H 6
Cloonee Loughs	76 C 12	National		Corrigeenroe	96 H 5	Crookhaven	76 C 13	Currahchase	
Cloonfad	95 F 6	Park	88 C 7	Corrofin	89 E 9	Crookstown	78 F 12	Forest Park	84 F 10
Cloonfree Lough	90 H 6	Connor Pass	82 B 11	Costelloe/Casla	88 D 8	Croom	84 F 10	Currane/An	
Cloonlara	84 G 9	Convoy	101 I 3	Cottoners	76 C 11	Croos	90 H 7	Corran	94 C 6
Clough	99 O 5	Cookstown	98 L 4	Coulagh Bay	76 B 12	Cross	89 E 7	Currane (Lough)	76 B 12
Cloyne	79 H 12	Coola	96 G 5	Courtmacsherry	78 F 13	Cross Barry	78 G 12	Currans	83 D 11
Cluain Eois/		Coolaney	96 G 5	Courtmacsherry		Cross (River)	88 D 7	Curreel (Lough)	88 C 7
Clones	97 K 5	Coole	97 K 6	Bay	78 G 13	Crossakeel	91 K 6	Curry	95 F 6
Cluain Meala/		Coole (Castle)	97 J 4	Courtown	81 N 10	Crossdoney	97 J 6	Cushendall	103 N 2
Clonmel	85 I 10	Coolea/Cúil		Cousane Gap	77 E 12	Crossgar	99 O 4	Cushendun	103 N 2
Cluainín/		Aodha	77 E 12	Craggaunowen		Crosshaven	78 H 12	Cushina	86 K 8
Manorhamilton	96 H 5	Coolgreany	87 N 9	Megalithic		Crossmaglen	98 M 5	Cutra (Lough)	89 F 8
Coachford	78 F 12	Coolmore	96 H 4	Centre	84 F 9	Crossmolina/			
Coagh	98 M 4	Coolrain	86 J 9	Craigavon	98 M 4	Crois		**D**	
Coalisland	98 L 4	Coomacarrea	76 B 12	Crana	101 J 2	Mhaoilíona	95 E 5		
Cobh/An Cóbh	78 H 12	Coomhola	77 D 12	Cranfield Point	98 N 5	Crow Head	76 B 13	Daingean	86 K 8
Cod's Head	76 B 13	Cooraclare	83 D 9	Cranford	101 I 2	Cruit Island	100 G 2	Dalkey	87 N 8
Coill an		Cootehill/		Cratloe	84 F 9	Crumlin	98 N 4	Dan (Lough)	87 N 8
Chollaigh/		Muinchille	97 K 5	Craughwell	89 F 8	Crusheen	84 F 9	Darragh	83 E 9
Bailieborough	97 L 6	Copeland		Creeslough	101 I 2	Cúil an tSúdaire/		Darty Mountains	96 G 4
Coleraine	102 L 2	Island	99 P 3	Creevykeel	96 G 4	Portarlington	86 K 8		

Davagh Forest		Dingle Harbour	82 B 11
Park	102 L 3	Divis	98 N 4
Dawros Head	100 G 3	Doagh	101 I 2
Deel	84 F 10	Doagh Beg/	
Deel (Mayo)	94 D 5	Dumhaigh	
Delgany	87 N 8	Bhig	101 J 2
Delphi	88 C 7	Doe Castle	101 I 2
Delvin	91 K 7	Dolla	84 H 9
Delvin (River)	92 N 7	Domhnach	
Derg (Lough)	101 J 3	Phádraig/	
Derg (Lough)	84 H 9	Donaghpatrick	92 L 6
Derg (Lough)		Donabate	92 N 7
(Donegal)	97 I 4	Donagh	97 J 5
Dernagree	77 E 11	Donagh Cross	101 K 2
Derravaragh		Donaghadee	99 P 4
(Lough)	91 J 7	Donaghmore	98 L 4
Derreeny Bridge	77 E 13	Donaghmore	
Derriana Lough	76 C 12	Church	85 I 10
Derrybeg	100 H 2	Donaghpatrick/	
Derryclare Lough	88 C 7	Domhnach	
Derrycraff	94 D 6	Phádraig	92 L 6
Derrygonnelly	97 I 4	Donard	87 M 8
Derrylin	97 J 5	Donard (Slieve)	98 O 5
Derrynacreeve	97 I 5	Donegal/	
Derrynane House	76 B 12	Dún na nGall	100 H 4
Derrynane		Donegal (County)	100 H 3
National		Donegal Bay	96 G 5
Historic Park	76 B 12	Doneraile	78 G 11
Derrynasaggart		Donoughmore	78 F 12
Mountains	83 E 11	Doo Lough	88 C 7
Derryveagh		Dooagh	94 B 6
Mountains	100 H 3	Doocharry/An	
Dervock	102 M 2	Dúchoraidh	100 H 3
Devenish Island	97 J 4	Dooega/	
Devilsbit	85 I 9	Dumha Éige	94 B 6
Dingle/		Dooega Head	94 B 6
An Daingean	82 B 11	Doogort	94 B 5
Dingle Bay	76 B 11	Doohooma	94 C 5

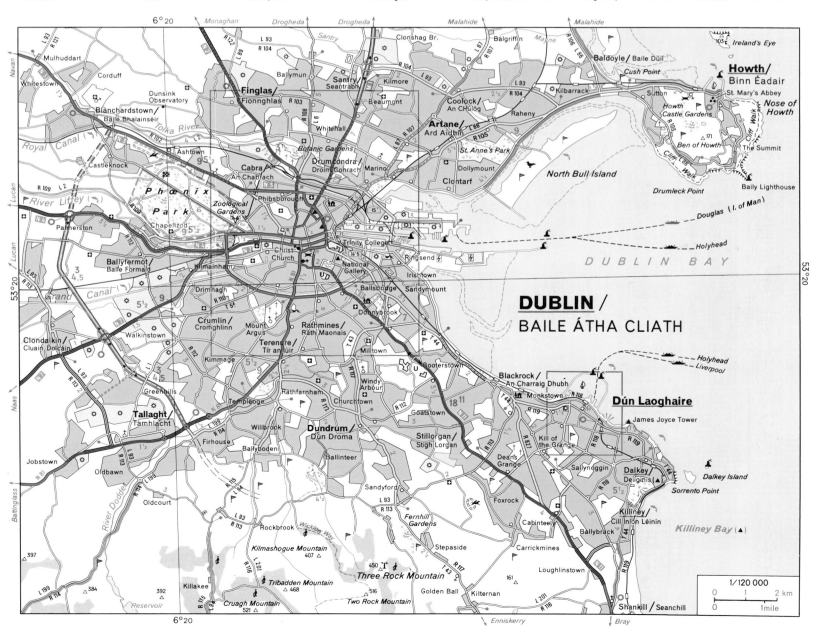

Doon Lough 84 F 9
Doonaha 83 D 10
Doonbeg 83 D 9
Dooncarton 94 C 5
Douglas 78 G 12
Doulus Head 76 A 12
Down (County) 98 N 4
Downhill 102 L 2
Downings/
Na Dúnaibh 101 I 2
Downpatrick 99 O 5
Downpatrick
Head 94 D 5
Downs (The) 91 K 7
Dowra 96 H 5
Dowth 92 M 6
Drangan 80 J 10
Draperstown 102 L 3
Drimoleague 77 E 13
Drinagh 77 E 13
Dripsey 78 F 12
Drishane Bridge 77 D 13
Drogheda/
Droichead Átha 92 M 6
Droichead Átha/
Drogheda 92 M 6
Droichead na
Bandan/
Bandon 78 F 12
Droichead Nua 86 L 8
Dromahair 96 H 5
Dromara 98 N 4
Dromcolliher 84 F 10
Dromin 92 M 6
Dromina 84 F 11
Dromineer 84 H 9
Dromiskin 98 M 6
Dromod 96 I 6
Dromore (Down) 98 N 4
Dromore (Tyrone) 97 J 4
Dromore West 95 F 5
Drum 97 K 5
Drum Hills 79 I 11
Drum Manor
Forest
Park 98 L 4
Drumcliff 96 G 5
Drumcondra 92 M 6
Drumfin 96 G 5
Drumfree 101 J 2
Drumgoft 87 M 9
Drumkeeran 96 H 5
Drumlaheen
Lough 96 I 5
Drumlane Abbey 97 J 5
Drumlish 90 I 6
Drumone 91 K 6
Drumquin 97 J 4
Drumshanbo 96 H 5
Drumsna 96 H 6
Dublin/Baile Átha
Cliath 87 N 8
Dublin Bay 92 N 7
Dublin (County) 92 N 7
Duff 96 H 4
Duleek 92 M 7
Dumha Éige/
Dooega 94 B 6
Dumhaigh Bhig/
Doagh Beg 101 J 2
Dún Á Rí
Forest Park 98 L 6
Dún Chaoin/
Dunquin 82 A 11
Dún Dealgan/
Dundalk 98 M 5
Dún Garbhán/
Dungarvan 80 J 11
Dún Laoghaire 87 N 8
Dún Mánmhaí/
Dunmanway 77 E 12
Dún Mór/
Dunmore 89 F 7
Dún na nGall/
Donegal 100 H 4
Dunaff Head 101 J 2
Dunamase
(Rock of) 86 K 8
Dunany Point 92 N 6
Dunboyne 92 M 7
Dunbrody Abbey 80 L 11
Duncannon 80 L 11
Duncormick 81 M 11
Dundalk/
Dún Dealgan 98 M 5
Dundalk Bay 98 N 6
Dundonald 99 O 4
Dundrum (Down) 99 O 5

Dundrum (Dublin) 87 N 8
Dundrum
(Tipperary) 85 H 10
Dundrum Bay 99 O 5
Dunfanaghy 100 I 2
Dungannon 98 L 4
Dungarvan
Harbour 80 J 11
Dungiven 102 L 3
Dunglow/
An Clochán
Liath 100 G 3
Dungonnell Dam 103 N 3
Dungourney 79 H 12
Dunguaire Castle 89 F 8
Dunkerrin 85 I 9
Dunkineely 100 G 4
Dunlavin 87 L 8
Dunleer 92 M 6
Dunlewy 100 H 2
Dunloe Castle 77 D 11
Dunloe (Gap of) 77 D 11
Dunluce Castle 102 M 2
Dunmanus Bay 76 C 13
Dunmanway/
Dún Mánmhaí 77 E 12
Dunmore/Dún
Mór 89 F 7
Dunmore Cave 86 K 9
Dunmore Head 82 A 11
Dunmore East 80 L 11
Dunmurry 98 N 4
Dunnamanagh 102 K 3
Dunowen Head 78 F 13
Dunquin/Dún
Chaoin 82 A 11
Dunshaughlin 92 M 7
Durlas/Thurles 85 I 9
Durrow 86 J 9
Durrow Abbey 86 J 8
Durrus 77 D 13
Dursey Head 76 B 13
Dursey Island 76 B 13
Duvillaun More 94 B 5
Dysert O'Dea 83 E 9

E
Éadan Doire/
Édenderry 91 K 7
Eany 100 H 3
Eanymore 100 H 3
Easky 95 F 5
East Ferry 79 H 12
Édenderry/
Éadan Doire 91 K 7
Ederny 97 J 4
Edgeworthstown 91 J 6
Egish (Lough) 98 L 5
Eglinton 102 K 2
Emly 84 G 10
Emo 86 K 8
Emyvale 97 L 4
Ennel (Lough) 91 J 7
Ennis/Inis 84 F 9
Enniscorthy/
Inis Córthaidh 81 M 10
Enniskean 78 F 12
Enniskerry 87 N 8
Enniskillen 97 J 4
Ennistimon/
Inis Díomáin 88 E 9
Eochaill/Youghal 79 I 12
Erne (Lower
Lough) 96 I 4
Erne (River) 97 J 6
Erne (Upper
Lough) 97 J 5
Errew Abbey 95 E 5
Erriff 88 D 7
Errigal Mountain 100 H 2
Erris Head 94 B 5
Eske (Lough) 100 H 3
Eyeries 76 C 12

F
Fahan 101 J 2
Fairy Glen 98 N 5
Fairymount 96 G 6
Falcarragh/
An Fál
Carrach 100 H 2
Fanad 101 I 2

Fanad Head 101 J 2
Fane River 98 M 5
Fanore 88 E 8
Farnanes Cross
Roads 78 F 12
Farran Forest
Park 78 F 12
Farranfore 83 D 11
Fastnet Rock 76 D 13
Feakle 84 G 9
Feale (River) 83 D 10
Fedamore 84 G 10
Fee (Lough) 88 C 7
Feeagh (Lough) 94 D 6
Feeny 102 K 3
Fenagh 96 I 5
Fenit 82 C 11
Feohanagh
(River) 82 B 11
Ferbane 90 I 8
Fergus (River) 83 E 9
Fermanagh
(County) 97 I 4
Fermoy/Mainistir
Fhear Maí 78 H 11
Fern (Lough) 101 I 2
Ferns 81 M 10
Ferrycarrig 81 M 10
Ferta 76 B 12
Fethard/Fiodh
Ard (Tipperary) 85 I 10
Fethard
(Wexford) 80 L 11
Fiddown 80 K 10
Finglas 92 N 7
Finglass 76 C 11
Finn (Lough) 100 H 3
Finn (River) 101 J 3
Finnea 91 J 6
Finny/Fionnaithe 88 D 7
Fintona 97 K 4
Fintown/
Baile na Finne 100 H 3
Fintragh Bay 100 G 4
Fiodh Ard/
Fethard 85 I 10
Fionnaithe/Finny 88 D 7
Fivealley 90 I 8
Fivemiletown 97 K 4
Flat Head 78 G 12
Flesk 77 D 11
Florence Court 97 I 5
Florence Court
Forest Park 97 I 5
Foaty Island 79 H 12
Fontstown 86 L 8
Forbes (Lough) 90 I 6
Fore 91 K 6
Forkill 98 M 5
Forlorn Point 81 M 11
Formoyle
(Lough) 88 D 7
Fota Island 78 H 12
Foul Sound 88 D 8
Foulksmills 81 L 11
Four Mile House 90 I 6
Fourknocks 92 N 7
Foxford 95 E 6
Foxhall 89 E 7
Foynes 83 E 10
Freemount 84 F 11
Frenchpark 96 G 6
Freshford 86 J 9
Fuerty 90 H 7
Furnace 88 D 7
Furnace Lough 94 D 6

G
Gabhla/Gola
Island 100 G 2
Gabriel (Mount) 77 D 13
Gaddagh 76 C 11
Gaillimh/Galway 89 E 8
Galbally 84 H 10
Galey 83 D 10
Gallarus Oratory 82 A 11
Galley head 78 F 13
Gallion (Slieve) 102 L 3
Galty Mountains 84 H 10
Galtymore
Mountain 84 H 10
Galway/Gaillimh 89 E 8
Galway (County) 89 F 7
Galway Bay 88 D 8
Galways Bridge 77 D 12

Gaoth Dobhair/
Gweedore 100 H 2
Gaoth Sáile/
Geesala 94 C 5
Gara (Lough) 96 G 6
Garadice Lough 97 I 5
Garrane 77 E 12
Garristown 92 M 7
Garron Point 103 O 2
Garryvoe 79 H 12
Gartan Lough 100 I 3
Garty Lough 97 I 6
Garvagh 96 I 6
Garvagh 102 L 3
Gearagh (The) 78 F 12
Geashill 86 K 8
Geesala/
Gaoth Sáile 94 C 5
Geevagh 96 H 5
Gerahies 77 D 13
Giant's
Causeway 102 M 2
Giant's Ring 98 O 4
Giles Quay 98 N 6
Gilford 98 M 4
Gill (Lough) 96 G 5
Glanaruddery
Mountains 83 D 11
Glandore 85 I 10
Glandore Harbour 77 E 13
Glangevlin 96 I 5
Glanmire 78 G 12
Glantane 78 F 11
Glanworth 78 G 11
Glasdrumman 98 O 5
Glaslough 97 L 5
Glassan 90 I 7
Glasshouse Lake 97 J 5
Gleann Bhairr/
Glenvar 101 J 2
Gleann Cholm
Cille/Glen-
columbkille 100 F 3
Gleann Domhain/
Glendowan 100 I 3
Gleann na
Muaidhe/
Glenamoy 94 C 5
Glen 101 I 2
Glen Bay 100 F 3
Glen Head 100 F 3
Glen Lough
(Donegal) 101 I 2
Glen Lough
(Westmeath) 91 J 7
Glen (River)
(Donegal) 100 G 3
Glenade Lough 96 H 4
Glenamoy/Gleann
na Muaidhe 94 C 5
Glenamoy (River) 94 D 5
Glenariff 103 N 2
Glenariff Forest
Park 103 N 2
Glenariff
or Waterfoot 103 N 2
Glenarm 103 O 3
Glenavy 98 N 4
Glenbeigh 76 C 11
Glenbrook 78 G 12
Glencar 76 C 11
Glencar Lough 96 G 4
Glencolumbkille/
Gleann Cholm
Cille 100 F 3
Glencree 87 N 8
Glendalough 87 M 8
Glendovan
Mountains 100 H 3
Glendowan/
Gleann
Domhain 100 I 3
Glenealy 87 N 9
Gleneely 101 K 2
Glenelly Valley 102 K 3
Glenfarne 96 I 5
Glenflesk 77 D 11
Glengad Head 101 K 1
Glengarriff/
An Gleann
Garbh 77 D 12
Glengarriff
Harbour 77 D 12
Glengarriff (River) 76 D 12
Glengormley 103 O 3
Glenicmurrin
Lough 88 D 8

Glenmalur 87 M 9
Glenmore (Clare) 83 E 9
Glenmore
(Kilkenny) 80 K 10
Glennamaddy 89 G 7
Glennamong 94 D 6
Glenoe 103 O 3
Glenshane Pass 102 L 3
Glenties 100 H 3
Glenvar/
Gleann Bhairr 101 J 2
Glenveagh
National Park 100 I 3
Glenville 78 G 11
Glin 83 E 10
Glin Castle 83 E 10
Glinsce/Glinsk 88 C 7
Glinsk/Glinsce 88 C 7
Glyde 98 M 6
Glynn 103 O 3
Gob an Choire/
Achill Sound 94 C 6
Gobbins (The) 103 O 3
Gola Island/
Gabhla 100 G 2
Golden 85 I 10
Golden Vale 85 H 10
Goleen 76 C 13
Goold's Cross 85 I 10
Gorey/Guaire 87 N 9
Gormanston 92 N 7
Gort/An Gort 89 F 8
Gort an Choirce/
Gortahork 100 H 2
Gortahork/Gort
an Choirce 100 H 2
Gorteen 96 G 6
Gortin 102 K 3
Gortin Glen
Forest Park 102 K 3
Gortmore/
An Gort Mór 88 D 7
Gorumna Island 88 C 8
Gosford Forest
Park 98 M 5
Gougane Barra
Lake 77 E 12
Gowla 88 C 7
Gowna (Lough) 91 J 6
Gráig na
Manach/
Graigue-
namanagh 80 L 10
Graigue-
namanagh/
Graig na
Manach 80 L 10
Gránard/Granard 91 J 6
Grand Canal 90 I 8
Graney 86 L 9
Grange (Kilkenny) 80 K 10
Grange (Louth) 98 N 5
Grange (Sligo) 96 G 4
Granny Castle 80 K 11
Gransha 103 O 3
Great Island 78 H 12
Great Blasket
Island 82 A 11
Great Newtown
Head 80 K 11
Great Skellig 76 A 12
Greenan 87 N 9
Greencastle
(Donegal) 101 L 2
Greencastle
(Down) 98 N 5
Greencastle
(Tyrone) 102 K 3
Greenfield 89 E 7
Greenisland 103 O 3
Greenore 98 N 5
Greenore Point 81 N 11
Grey Point 103 O 3
Greyabbey 99 P 4
Greystones/
Na Clocha
Liatha 87 N 8
Grianan of
Aileach 101 J 2
Groomsport 99 P 3
Guagan Barra
Forest Park 77 D 12
Guaire/Gorey 87 N 9
Gulladoo Lough 97 J 6
Gullion (Slieve) 98 M 5
Gur (Lough) 84 G 10
Gurteen 89 G 7

Gwebarra
Bridge 100 H 3
Gweebarra Bay 100 G 3
Gweedore/
Gaoth Dobhair 100 H 2
Gweestin 77 D 11
Gyleen 79 H 12

H
Hacketstown 87 M 9
Hags Head 88 D 9
Headford/
Áth Cinn 89 E 7
Healy Pass 76 C 12
Helvick Head 80 J 11
Herbertstown 84 G 10
Hillsborough 98 N 4
Hilltown 98 N 5
Hog's Head 76 B 12
Hollyford 85 H 10
Hollyfort 87 M 9
Hollymount 89 E 7
Hollywood 87 M 8
Holy Island 84 G 9
Holycross 85 I 10
Holycross Abbey 85 I 10
Holywood 103 O 4
Hook Head 80 L 11
Hore Abbey 85 I 10
Horn Head 100 I 2
Horseleap 91 J 7
Hospital 84 G 10
Howth/Binn
Éadair 92 N 7
Hugginstown 80 K 10
Hungry Hill 76 C 12
Hurlers Cross 84 F 9
Hyne (Lough) 77 E 13

I
Ilen 77 E 13
Inagh 83 E 9
Inagh (Lough) 88 C 7
Inch 82 C 11
Inch Abbey 99 O 4
Inch Island 101 J 2
Inchigeelagh 77 E 12
Inchiquin Lough
(Kerry) 77 D 12
Inchydoney
Island 78 F 13
Indreabhán/
Inverin 88 D 8
Inis/Ennis 84 F 9
Inis Bó Finne/
Inishbofin 100 H 2
Inis Córthaidh/
Enniscorthy 81 M 10
Inis Díomáin/
Ennistimon 88 E 9
Inis Meáin/
Inishmaan 88 D 8
Inis Mór/
Inishmore 88 C 8
Inis Oírr/Inisheer 88 D 8
Inishbofin/Inis Bó
Finne (Donegal) 100 H 2
Inishbofin
(Galway) 88 B 7
Inishcarra
Reservoir 78 F 12
Inishcrone 95 E 5
Inisheer/Inis Oírr 88 D 8
Inishfree Bay 100 G 2
Inishglora 94 B 5
Inishkea North 94 B 5
Inishkea South 94 B 5
Inishkeen 98 M 5
Inishmaan/
Inis Meáin 88 D 8
Inishmore/Inis
Mór 88 C 8
Inishmurray 96 G 4
Inishnabro 82 A 11
Inishowen 101 J 2
Inishowen Head 102 L 2
Inishshark 88 B 7
Inishtrahull 101 K 1
Inishtrahull
Sound 101 K 1
Inishturk 94 B 6
Inistioge 80 K 10
Innfield 92 L 7

Inny (River) 91 J 6
Inver 100 H 4
Inver (Mayo) 94 C 5
Inverin/
Indreabhán 88 D 8
Ireland's Eye 92 N 7
Irishtown 89 F 7
Iron (Lough) 91 J 7
Iron Mountains 96 I 5
Irvinestown 97 J 4
Iveragh 76 B 12

J
Jamestown 96 H 6
Japanese
Gardens 86 L 8
Jerpoint Abbey 80 K 10
Johnstown 86 J 9
Johnstown
Castle 81 M 11
Jonesborough 98 M 5
Joyce 88 D 7
Joyce Country 88 C 7
Julianstown 92 N 6

K
Kanturk/
Ceann Toirc 78 F 11
Katesbridge 98 N 5
Keadew 96 H 5
Keady 98 L 5
Kealduff 76 C 12
Kealkill 77 D 12
Kearney 99 P 4
Keel 94 B 6
Keel Lough 94 B 6
Keem Strand 94 B 6
Keimaneigh
(The pass of) 77 E 12
Kells (Antrim) 103 N 3
Kells (Kerry) 76 B 12
Kells (Ceanannus
Mor)/Ceanan-
nas (Meath) 92 L 6
Kells Bay 76 B 11
Kenmare/Neidín 77 D 12
Kenmare River 76 B 12
J. F. Kennedy
Park 80 L 11
Kerry (County) 77 D 11
Kerry Head 82 C 10
Kerry (Ring of) 76 B 12
Kesh 97 I 4
Key (Lough) 96 H 5
Key (Lough)
Forest Park 96 H 6
Kilbaha 82 C 10
Kilbeggan 91 J 7
Kilbeheny 84 H 11
Kilberry 92 L 6
Kilbricken 86 J 9
Kilbride (near
Blessington) 87 M 8
Kilbrittain 78 F 12
Kilcar 100 G 4
Kilcreest 89 G 8
Kilclief 99 P 5
Kilcock 92 M 7
Kilcolgan 89 F 8
Kilconly (Galway) 89 F 7
Kilcoo 98 N 5
Kilcormac 90 I 8
Kilcrohane 76 C 13
Kilcullen 86 L 8
Kildare/Cill Dara 86 L 8
Kildare (County) 86 L 8
Kildorrery 78 G 11
Kilfenora 89 E 9
Kilfinnane 84 G 10
Kilgarvan 77 D 12
Kilglass 95 E 5
Kilglass Lough 90 H 6
Kilgobnet 76 C 11
Kilgory Lough 84 F 9
Kilkee/Cill Chaoi 83 D 9
Kilkeel 98 N 5
Kilkeeran
High Crosses 80 J 10
Kilkenny/
Cill Chainnigh 80 K 10
Kilkenny (County) 80 J 10
Kilkieran/
Cill Chiaráin 88 C 8
Kilkishen 84 F 9

Kill 80 J 11
Killadoon 94 C 6
Killadysert 83 E 9
Killala 95 E 5
Killala Bay 95 E 5
Killaloe/Cill Dalua 84 G 9
Killamery 80 J 10
Killann 81 L 10
Killard Point 99 P 5
Killarga 96 H 5
Killarney/Cill Airne 77 D 11
Killarney National Park 83 D 11
Killary Harbour 88 C 7
Killashandra 97 J 5
Killavally 94 D 6
Killavullen 78 G 11
Killeagh 79 H 12
Killeigh 86 J 8
Killenagh 81 N 10
Killenaule 85 I 10
Killerrig 86 L 9
Killeshin Church 86 K 9
Killeter 101 I 3
Killeter Forest 101 I 3
Killevy Church 98 M 5
Killimer 83 D 10
Killimor 90 H 8
Killinaboy 89 E 9
Killiney Bay 87 N 8
Killiney (Dublin) 87 N 8
Killinick 81 M 11
Killinure Lough 90 I 7
Killkelly 95 F 6
Killmuckbridge 81 N 10
Killone Abbey 83 E 9
Killorglin/Cill Orglan 76 C 11
Killough 99 P 5
Killucan 91 K 7
Killurin 81 M 10
Killybegs/Na Cealla Beaga 100 G 4
Killygordon 101 I 3
Killykeen Forest Park 97 J 5
Killylea 98 L 4
Killyleagh 99 P 4
Kilmacduagh Monastery 89 F 8
Kilmacow 80 K 11
Kilmacrenan 101 I 2
Kilmacthomas 80 J 11
Kilmaganny 80 K 10
Kilmaine 89 E 7
Kilmalkedar 82 B 11
Kilmallock/Cill Mocheallóg 84 G 10
Kilmanagh 80 J 10
Kilmeage 86 L 8
Kilmeedy 84 F 10
Kilmessan 92 M 7
Kilmichael 77 E 12
Kilmichael Point 87 N 9
Kilmihil 83 E 9
Kilmore 81 M 11
Kilmore Quay 81 M 11
Kilmurry (mear Kilkishen) 84 F 9
Kilmurvy 88 C 8
Kilnaleck 91 K 6
Kilrane 81 M 11
Kilrea 102 M 3
Kilree 80 K 10
Kilreekill 89 G 8
Kilronan/Cill Rónáin 88 C 8
Kilrush/Cill Rois 83 D 10
Kilshanny 88 E 9
Kilsheelan 80 J 10
Kiltamagh 95 E 6
Kiltealy 81 L 10
Kiltegan 87 M 9
Kilternan 87 N 8
Kiltoom 90 H 7
Kiltormer 90 H 8
Kiltyclogher 96 H 4
Kilworth 79 H 11
Kilworth Mountains 79 H 11
Kinale (Lough) 91 J 6
Kincasslagh 100 G 2
Kings River 80 J 10
Kingscourt 97 L 6
Kinlough 96 H 4
Kinnegad 91 K 7
Kinnitty 90 I 8
Kinsale/Cionn tSáile 78 G 12
Kinsale (Old Head of) 78 G 13
Kinvarra 89 F 8
Kinvarra Bay 89 F 8
Kinvarra (near Screeb) 88 D 7
Kippure 87 N 8
Kircubbin 99 P 4
Kitconnell 89 G 8
Knappagh 94 D 6
Knappogue Castle 84 F 9
Knight's Town 76 B 12
Knock (Clare) 83 E 10
Knock (Mayo) 95 F 6
Knockadoon Head 79 I 12
Knockainy 84 G 10
Knockalongy 95 F 5
Knockcroghery 90 H 7
Knockferry 89 E 7
Knocklayd 103 N 2
Knocklong 84 G 10
Knockmealdown 79 I 11
Knockmealdown Mountains 79 H 11
Knockmoy Abbey 89 F 7
Knocknadobar 76 B 12
Knocknagree 77 E 11
Knockraha 78 G 12
Knocktopher 80 K 10
Knowth 92 M 6
Kylemore Abbey 88 C 7
Kylemore Lough 88 C 7

L

Labasheeda 83 E 10
Labbacallee 79 H 11
Lack 97 J 4
Ladies View 77 D 12
Lady's Island Lake 81 M 11
Ladysbridge 79 H 12
Lagan (River) 98 N 4
Lagan Valley 98 O 4
Laghy 100 H 4
Lahinch/An Leacht 88 D 9
Lamb's Head 76 B 12
Lambay Island 93 N 7
Lanesborough 90 I 6
Laois (County) 86 J 9
Laragh 87 N 8
Larne 103 O 3
Larne Lough 103 O 3
Laune (River) 76 C 11
Lauragh 76 C 12
Laurencetown 90 H 8
Lavagh More 100 H 3
Lawrencetown 98 N 4
Laytown 92 N 6
League (Slieve) 100 F 4
Leamaneh Castle 89 E 9
Leane (Lough) 77 D 11
Leannan 101 I 2
Leap 77 E 13
Leap (The) 81 M 10
Lecarrow (Leitrim) 96 H 5
Lecarrow (Roscommon) 90 H 7
Leckanvy 94 C 6
Leckavrea Mountain 88 D 7
Lee 82 C 11
Lee (River) 78 G 12
Leenane 88 C 7
Legananny Dolmen 98 N 5
Leighlinbridge 86 L 9
Leinster (Mount) 81 L 10
Leitir Ceanainn/Letterkenny 101 I 3
Leitir Mealláin/Lettermullan 88 C 8
Leitir Mhic an Bhaird/Lettermacaward 100 H 3
Leitrim 96 H 6
Leitrim (County) 96 I 6
Leixlip 92 M 7
Lemybrien 80 J 11
Lene (Lough) 91 K 7
Letterfrack 88 C 7
Letterkenny/Leitir Ceanainn 101 I 3
Lettermacaward/Leitir Mhic an Bhaird 100 H 3
Lettermore 88 D 8
Lettermore Island 88 C 8
Lettermullan/Leitir Mealláin 88 C 8
Licky 79 I 11
Liffey (River) 87 M 8
Lifford 101 J 3
Limavady 102 L 2
Limerick/Luimneach 84 G 9
Limerick (County) 84 F 10
Limerick Junction 84 H 10
Lios Dúin Bhearna/Lisdoonvarna 88 E 8
Lios Mór/Lismore 79 I 11
Lios Póil/Lispole 82 B 11
Lios Tuathail/Listowel 83 D 10
Lisbellaw 97 J 5
Lisburn 98 N 4
Liscannor 88 D 9
Liscannor Bay 83 D 9
Liscarroll 84 F 11
Lisdoonvarna/Lios Dúin Bhearna 88 E 8
Lismacaffry 91 J 6
Lismore/Lios Mór 79 I 11
Lisnacree 98 N 5
Lisnarrick 97 I 4
Lisnaskea 97 J 5
Lispole/Lios Póil 82 B 11
Lissadell House 96 G 4
Lissatinnig Bridge 76 C 12
Lisselton 83 D 10
Lissycasey 83 E 9
Listowel/Lios Tuathail 83 D 10
Little Island 78 G 12
Little Skellig 76 A 12
Littleton 85 I 10
Lixnaw 83 D 10
Loch Garman/Wexford 81 M 10
Loch Gowna 97 J 6
Loghill 83 E 10
Londonderry 102 K 3
Londonderry (County) 102 K 3
Long Island 77 D 13
Longford (County) 90 I 6
Longford/An Longfort (Longford) 90 I 6
Longford (Offaly) 85 I 8
Loo Bridge 77 D 12
Loop Head 82 C 10
Lorrha 90 H 8
Loughgall 98 M 4
Loughbrickland 98 N 5
Loughglinn 96 G 6
Loughinisland 99 O 4
Loughrea/Baile Locha Riach 89 G 8
Loughros More Bay 100 G 3
Loughshinny 92 N 7
Louisburgh 94 C 6
Loup (The) 102 M 3
Louth 98 M 6
Louth (County) 98 M 6
Lower Ballinderry 98 N 4
Lucan 92 M 7
Lugnaquillia Mountain 87 M 9
Luimneach/Limerick 84 G 10
Lung 96 G 6
Lurgan 98 N 4
Lusk 92 N 7
Lyracrumpane 83 D 10

M

Maam Cross/An Teach Dóite 88 D 7
Maas 100 G 3
Macgillycuddy's Reeks 76 C 12
Macnean Upper (Lough) 96 I 5
Macroom/Maigh Chromtha 78 F 12
Maganey 86 L 9
Magee (Island) 103 O 3
Maghera (Donegal) 100 G 3
Maghera (Down) 98 O 5
Maghera (Londonderry) 102 L 3
Magherafelt 102 M 3
Magheralin 98 N 4
Maghery 98 M 4
Magilligan 102 L 2
Magilligan Strand 102 L 2
Maguiresbridge 97 J 5
Mahee Island 99 P 4
Mahon 80 J 11
Mahoonagh 83 E 10
Maigh Chromtha/Macroom 78 F 12
Maigh Cuilinn/Moycullen 89 E 7
Maigh Nuad/Maynooth 92 M 7
Maigue (River) 84 F 10
Main 103 N 3
Maine (River) 82 C 11
Mainistir Fhear Maí/Fermoy 78 H 11
Mainistir Laoise/Abbey Leix 86 J 9
Mainistir na Búille/Boyle 96 H 6
Mainistir na Corann/Midleton 79 H 12
Máistir Gaoithe/Mastergeehy 76 B 12
Mal Bay 83 D 9
Mala/Mallow 78 G 11
Malahide/Mullach Íde 92 N 7
Málainn Bhig/Malin Beg 100 F 3
Malin 101 K 2
Malin Bay 100 F 3
Malin Beg/Málainn Bhig 100 F 3
Malin Head 101 J 1
Malin More 100 F 3
Mallow/Mala 78 G 11
Mamore (Gap of) 101 J 2
Mangerton Mountain 77 D 12
Mannin Bay 88 B 7
Mannin Lake 95 F 6
Manorcunningham 101 J 3
Manorhamilton/Cluainín 96 H 5
Mansfieldstown 92 M 6
Manulla 95 E 6
Maothail/Mohill 96 I 6
Marble Hill 101 I 2
Markethill 98 M 5
Mask (Lough) 88 D 7
Mastergeehy/Máistir Gaoithe 76 B 12
Matrix (Castle) 84 F 10
Mattock 92 M 6
Maum 88 D 7
Maumeen Lough 88 B 7
Maumtrasna 88 D 7
Maumturk Mountains 88 C 7
Maynooth/Maigh Nuad 92 M 7
Mayo 95 E 6
Mayo (County) 95 E 6
Mayo (Plains of) 95 E 6
Mealagh 77 D 12
Meath (County) 92 L 7
Meela (Lough) 100 G 3
Meenaneary/Mín na Aoire 100 G 3
Meenavean 100 F 3
Meeting of the Waters 87 N 9
Mellifont Abbey 92 M 6
Mellon House 101 J 4
Melmore Head 101 I 2
Melvin (Lough) 96 H 4
Menlough 89 G 7
Mew Island 99 P 3
Middletown (Armagh) 98 L 5
Middletown (Donegal) 100 H 2
Midleton/Mainistir na Corann 79 H 12
Milestone 85 H 9
Milford 84 F 10
Millford 101 I 2
Millisle 99 P 4
Millstreet 77 E 11
Milltown (Cavan) 97 J 5
Milltown (Galway) 89 F 7
Milltown (Kerry) 76 C 11
Milltown Malbay/Sráid na Cathrach 83 D 9
Mín na Aoire/Meenaneary 100 G 3
Minane Bridge 78 G 12
Minard Head 82 B 11
Mine Head 80 J 12
Mitchelstown/Baile Mhistéala 79 H 11
Mizen Head 76 C 13
Moate/An Móta 90 I 7
Moher (Cliffs of) 88 D 9
Moher Lough 94 D 6
Mohill/Maothail 96 I 6
Móinteach Mílic/Mountmellick 86 K 8
Moll's Gap 77 D 12
Monaghan/Muineachán 97 L 5
Monaghan (County) 97 K 5
Monasteraden 96 G 6
Monasteranenagh Abbey 84 G 10
Monasterboice 92 M 6
Monasterevin 86 K 8
Monavullagh Mountains 80 J 11
Mondello Park 86 L 8
Monea 97 I 4
Moneygall 85 I 9
Moneymore 102 L 3
Monivea 89 F 7
Monkstown (Antrim) 103 O 3
Monkstown (Cork) 78 G 12
Mooncoin 80 K 11
Moone 86 L 9
Moore Bay 83 C 9
Moorfields 103 N 3
Morley's Bridge 77 D 12
Moroe 84 G 10
Mosney 92 N 7
Moss-Side 102 M 2
Mossley 103 O 3
Mostrim 91 J 6
Mount Bellew/An Creagán 89 G 7
Mount Melleray Monastery 79 I 11
Mount Nuggent 91 K 6
Mount Stewart Gardens 99 P 4
Mount Usher Gardens 87 N 8
Mountcharles 100 H 4
Mountfield 97 K 4
Mountmellick/Móinteach Mílic 86 K 8
Mountnorris 98 M 5
Mountrath 86 J 8
Mountshannon 84 G 9
Mourne (Lough) 103 O 3
Mourne Mountains 98 N 5
Mourne River 101 J 3
Moville/Bun an Phobail 101 K 2
Moy 98 L 4
Moy (River) 95 E 5
Moyard 88 B 7
Moyasta 83 D 9
Moycullen/Maigh Cuilinn 89 E 7
Moylough 89 G 7
Moynalty 92 L 6
Moyne Abbey 95 E 5
Moyvally 92 L 7
Moyvore 91 J 7
Muck (Isle of) 103 O 3
Muckamore 103 N 3
Muckanagh Lough 84 F 9
Muckish Mountain 100 H 2
Muckno Lake 98 L 5
Muckros Head 100 G 4
Muckross 77 D 11
Muff 101 K 2
Muggort's Bay 80 J 11
Muinchille/Cootehill 97 K 5
Muineachán/Monaghan 97 L 5
Muine Bheag 86 L 9
Muing 94 D 5
Muingnabo 94 C 5
Mulkear 84 G 10
Mullach Íde/Malahide 92 N 7
Mullagh (Cavan) 92 L 6
Mullagh (Meath) 92 M 7
Mullaghareirk Mountains 83 E 10
Mullaghcleevaun 87 M 8
Mullaghmore 96 G 4
Mullet Peninsula 94 B 5
Mullinahone 80 J 10
Mullinavat 80 K 10
Mullingar/An Muileann gCearr 91 J 7
Mulrany/An Mhala Raithní 94 C 6
Mulroy Bay 101 I 2
Multyfarnham 91 J 7
Mungret 84 F 10
Muntervary or Sheep's Head 76 C 13
Murlough Bay 103 N 2
Murntown 81 M 11
Murrisk 94 D 6
Mussenden Temple 102 L 2
Mutton Island 83 D 9
Mweelrea Mountains 88 C 7
Myshall 86 L 9

N

Na Cealla Beaga/Killybegs 100 G 4
Na Clocha Liatha/Greystones 87 N 8
Na Dúnaibh/Downings 101 I 2
Na Sceirí/Skerries 92 N 7
Naas/An Nás 87 M 8
Nacung (Lough) 100 H 2
Nad 78 F 11
Nafooey (Lough) 88 D 7
Nagles Mountains 78 G 11
Naminn (Lough) 101 J 2
Namona (Lough) 76 B 12
Nanny 92 M 7
Naran 100 G 3
Narrow Water Castle 98 N 5
Naul 92 N 7
Navan/An Uaimh 92 L 7
Neagh (Lough) 98 M 4
Neale 89 E 7
Neidín/Kenmare 77 D 12
Nenagh/An tAonach 84 H 9
Nephin 95 D 5
Nephin (Glen) 95 D 6
Nephin Beg 94 D 5
Nephin Beg Range 94 C 5
New Inn (Cavan) 97 K 6
New Inn (Galway) 89 G 8
New Kildimo 84 F 10
New Ross/Ros Mhic Thriúin 80 L 10
Newbawn 81 L 10
New Birmingham 80 J 10
Newbliss 97 K 5
Newbridge 86 L 8
Newcastle (Down) 98 O 5
Newcastle (Dublin) 87 M 8
Newcastle (Tipperary) 79 I 11
Newcastle (Wicklow) 87 N 8
Newcastle West/An Caisleán Nua 83 E 10
Newgrange 92 M 6
Newinn 85 I 10
Newmarket 84 F 11
Newmarket on Fergus 84 F 9
Newport/Baile Uí Fhiacháin (Mayo) 94 D 6
Newport (Tipperary) 84 G 9
Newport Bay 94 C 6
Newry 98 N 5
Newtown (Laois) 86 K 9
Newtown (Offaly) 90 H 8
Newtownabbey 103 O 4
Newtown-Crommelin 103 N 3
Newtown Forbes 90 I 6
Newtown Gore 96 I 5
Newtown Mount Kennedy 87 N 8
Newtownards 99 O 4
Newtownbutler 97 J 5
Newtownhamilton 98 M 5
Newtownshandrum 84 F 10
Newtownstewart 101 J 3
Nier 80 J 11
Ninemilehouse 80 J 10
Nobber 92 L 6
Nohaval 78 G 12
Nore 86 J 9
Nore (River) 80 K 10
North Sound 88 C 8
North Ring 78 F 13
Nurney 86 L 8
Nurney (Carlow) 86 L 9

O

O'Brien's Tower 88 D 9
Offaly (County) 90 I 8
O'Grady (Lough) 84 G 9
Oileán Ciarraí/Castleisland 83 D 11
Oily 100 G 4
Old Head 94 C 6
Old Kildimo 84 F 10
Oldcastle/An Seanchaisleán 91 K 6
Oldleighlin 86 K 9
Old Ross 81 L 10
Omagh 97 K 4
Omeath 98 N 5
Omey Island 88 B 7
Oola 84 H 10
Oorid Lough 88 D 7
Oranmore 89 F 8
Ossian's Grave 103 N 2
Ougher (Lough) 97 J 6
Oughterard/Uachtar Ard 88 E 7
Ovens 78 G 12
Owel (Lough) 91 J 7
Owenascaul 82 B 11
Owenator 100 H 3
Owenavorragh 81 M 10
Owenbeg (River) 96 G 5
Owenboliska 88 E 8

Owencarrow 101 I 2
Owenea 100 G 3
Owengarve 94 D 6
Owenglin 88 C 7
Oweniny 94 D 5
Owenkillew 101 J 2
Owenkillew 102 K 3
Owenriff 88 D 7
Owentocker 100 H 3
Owey Island/
Uaigh 100 G 2
Owvane 77 D 12
Oylgate 81 M 10
Oysterhaven 78 G 12

P
Pallasgreen 84 G 10
Pallaskenry 84 F 10
Paps (The) 77 E 11
Park's Castle 96 H 5
Parkmore
Point 82 A 11
Parknasilla 76 C 12
Partry 95 E 6
Partry
Mountains 88 D 7
Passage East 80 L 11
Passage
West 78 G 12
Patrickswell 84 F 10
Peake 78 F 12
Peatlands 98 M 4
Pettigoe 97 I 4
Phoenix Park 92 M 7
Piltown 80 K 10
Pluck 101 J 3
Plumbridge 102 K 3
Pomeroy 97 L 4
Pontoon 95 E 6
Port Durlainne/
Porturlin 94 C 5
Port Láirge/
Waterford 80 K 11
Port Laoise/
Portlaoise 86 K 8
Port Omna/
Portumna 90 H 8
Portacloy 94 C 5
Portadown 98 M 4
Portaferry 99 P 4
Portarlington/
Cúil an
tSúdaire 86 K 8
Portavogie 99 P 4
Portballintrae 102 M 2
Portglenone 102 M 3
Portlaoise/
Port Laoise 86 K 8
Portlaw 80 K 11
Portmagee 76 A 12
Portmagee
Channel 76 A 12
Portmarnock 92 N 7
Portmuck 103 O 3
Portnablagh 101 I 2
Portnoo 100 G 3
Portrane 92 N 7
Portroe 84 G 9
Portrush 102 L 2
Portsalon 101 J 2
Portstewart 102 L 2
Portumna/
Port Omna 90 H 8
Porturlin/
Port Durlainne 94 C 5
Poulaphouca
Reservoir 87 M 8
Poulnasherry
Bay 83 D 10
Powerscourt
Demesne 87 N 8
Poyntz Pass 98 M 5
Prosperous 87 L 8
Puckane 84 H 9
Puffin Island 76 A 12

Q
Quigley's Point 101 K 2
Quilty 83 D 9
Quin 84 F 9

R
Rae na nDoirí/
Reananeree 77 E 12
Raghly 96 G 5
Raharney 91 K 7
Ram Head 79 I 12
Ramor (Lough) 91 K 6
Randalstown 103 N 3
Raphoe 101 J 2
Rasharkin 102 M 3
Rath 90 I 8
Ráth Caola/
Rathkeale 84 F 10
Ráth Droma/
Rathdrum 87 N 9
Rath Luirc
(Charleville)/An
Ráth 84 F 10
Rathangan 86 L 8
Rathcool 78 F 11
Rathcoole 87 M 8
Rathcormack 78 H 11
Rathcroghan 90 H 6
Rathdangan 87 M 9
Rathdowney 86 J 9
Rathdrum/
Ráth Droma 87 N 9
Rathfriland 98 N 5
Rathgall Stone
Fort 87 M 9
Rathgormuck 80 J 11
Rathkeale/
Ráth Caola 84 F 10
Rathlackan 95 E 5
Rathlin Island 103 N 2
Rathlin Sound 103 N 2
Rathmacknee
Castle 81 M 11
Rathmelton 101 J 2
Rathmolyon 92 L 7
Rathmore 83 E 11
Rathmullan 101 J 2
Rathnew 87 N 9
Rathowen 91 J 7
Rathvilla 86 K 8
Rathvilly 87 L 9
Ratoath 92 M 7
Raven Point
(The) 81 M 10
Ray 100 H 2
Rea (Lough) 89 G 8
Reananeree/
Rae na nDoirí 77 E 12
Rear Cross 84 H 9
Recess/
Sraith Salach 88 C 7
Red Bay 103 N 2
Red Castle 101 K 2
Redcross 87 N 9
Redhills 97 K 5
Ree (Lough) 90 I 7
Reelan 100 H 3
Relaghbeg 92 L 6
Rhode 91 K 7
Richhill 98 M 4
Ringabella Bay 78 H 12
Ringsend 102 L 2
Ringville/An Rinn 80 J 11
Rinn Lough 96 I 6
Rinvyle 88 C 7
Rinvyle Castle 88 B 7
Riverstown 96 G 5
Roadford 88 D 8
Roaringwater
Bay 77 D 13
Robert's Head 78 H 12
Robertstown 86 L 8
Rochestown 80 K 11
Rochfortbridge 91 K 7
Rockabill 93 N 7
Rockchapel 83 E 11
Rockcorry 97 K 5
Rockhill 84 F 10
Rockmills 78 G 11
Roe 102 L 3
Roonah Quay 94 C 6
Roosky 90 I 6
Ros an Mhil/
Rossaveel 88 D 8
Ros Comáin/
Roscommon 90 H 7
Ros Cré/Roscrea 85 I 9
Ros Láir/Rosslare 81 M 11

Ros Mhic
Thriúin/New
Ross 80 L 10
Rosapenna 101 I 2
Roscommon/
Ros Comáin 90 H 7
Roscommon
(County) 96 G 6
Roscrea/Ros Cré 85 I 9
Rosegreen 85 I 10
Rosenallis 86 J 8
Rosmuck 88 D 7
Rosnakill 101 I 2
Ross Abbey 89 E 7
Ross Port 94 C 5
Ross Lake 89 E 7
Rossaveel/
Ros an Mhil 88 D 8
Rossbeg 100 G 3
Rossbehy Creek 76 C 11
Rosscarbery 77 E 13
Rosscarbery Bay 77 E 13
Rosserk Abbey 95 E 5
Rosses (The) 100 G 2
Rosses Point 96 G 5
Rossinver 96 H 4
Rosslare/Ros Láir 81 M 11
Rosslare Bay 81 M 11
Rosslare
Harbour/
Calafort Ros
Láir 81 M 11
Rosslare Point 81 M 11
Rosslea 97 K 5
Rossmore Forest
Park 97 L 5
Rossnowlagh 96 H 4
Rostrevor 98 N 5
Rough Point 82 B 11
Roughty 77 D 12
Roundstone 88 C 7
Roundwood 87 N 8
Rower (The) 80 L 10
Royal Canal 90 I 7
Royaloak 86 L 9
Rue Point 103 N 2
Runabay Head 103 N 2
Rush/An Ros 92 N 7
Russborough
House 87 M 8
Rylane Cross 78 F 12

S
Saggart 87 M 8
St. Columbkille 100 F 3
St. Doolagh's 92 N 7
St. Fachtnan's 88 E 9
St. Finan's Bay 76 A 12
St. John's Lough 96 I 5
St. John's Point
(Donegal) 100 G 4
St. John's Point
(Down) 99 P 5
St. Johnstown 101 J 3
St. Macdara's
Island 88 C 8
St. Mochta's
House 98 M 6
Saintfield 99 O 4
Sallins 87 M 8
Sally Gap 87 N 8
Sallybrook 78 G 12
Saltee Islands 81 M 11
Salthill 89 E 8
Santry 92 N 7
Saul 99 O 4
Sawel Mountain 102 K 3
Scarriff/An
Scairbh 84 G 9
Scarriff Island 76 B 12
Scartaglin 83 D 11
Scarva 98 M 5
Schull/Skull 77 D 13
Scolban (Lough) 96 H 4
Scotshouse 97 K 5
Scotstown 97 K 5
Scrabo Hill 99 O 4
Scramoge 90 H 6
Screeb/Scriob 88 D 7
Screen 81 M 10
Scriob/Screeb 88 D 7
Scur (Lough) 96 I 5

Seaforde 99 O 5
Seven Heads 78 F 13
Seven Hogs or
Magharee
Islands (The) 82 B 11
Shanagarry 79 H 12
Shanagolden 83 E 10
Shanballymore 78 G 11
Shanes Castle 103 N 3
Shankill 87 N 8
Shannagh
(Lough) 98 N 5
Shannon 84 F 9
Shannon Airport 84 F 9
Shannon
(River) 90 H 8
Shannonbridge 90 I 8
Shannon Harbour 90 I 8
Shantonagh 98 L 5
Sheddings (The) 103 N 3
Sheeffry Hills 94 C 6
Sheelin (Lough) 91 K 6
Sheep Haven 101 I 2
Sheever (Lough) 91 K 7
Shehy Mountains 77 D 12
Shercock 97 L 6
Sherkin Island 77 D 13
Shillelagh 87 M 9
Shinrone 85 I 9
Shrule 89 E 7
Silent Valley 98 O 5
Sillan (Lough) 97 L 5
Silvermine
Mountains 84 H 9
Silvermines 84 H 9
Single Street 96 H 4
Sion Mills 101 J 3
Six Towns
(The) 102 L 3
Sixmilebridge 84 F 9
Sixmilecross 97 K 4
Skannive (Lough) 88 C 8
Skerries/Na
Sceirí 92 N 7
Skibbereen/
An Sciobairín 77 E 13
Skreen 95 F 5
Skull/Schull 77 D 13
Slane 86 K 9
Slane (Hill of) 92 M 6
Slaney (River) 81 M 10
Slea Head 82 A 11
Slemish
Mountain 103 N 3
Slieve Anierin 96 I 5
Slieve Aught
Mountains 89 G 8
Slieve Bernagh 84 G 9
Slieve Bloom
Mountains 86 J 8
Slieve Gamph or
the Ox
Mountains 95 F 5
Slieve Mish
Mountains 82 C 11
Slieve Miskish
Mountains 76 C 13
Slieveanorra 103 N 2
Slievefelim
Mountains 84 H 9
Slievenamon 80 J 10
Slievetooey 100 G 3
Sligeach/Sligo 96 G 5
Sligo/Sligeach 96 G 5
Sligo Bay 95 F 5
Sligo (County) 95 F 5
Slievedagh Hills 80 J 10
Slyne Head 88 B 7
Smearlagh 83 D 11
Smerwick 82 A 11
Smerwick
Harbour 82 A 11
Smithborough 97 K 5
Snaght (Slieve)
(Inishowen) 101 J 2
Snaght (Slieve)
(Derryveagh
Mts.) 100 H 3
Snave 77 D 12
Sneem 76 C 12
Sord/Swords 92 N 7
South Sound 88 D 8
Spa 82 C 11
Spanish Point 83 D 9

Spelga Dam 98 N 5
Sperrin
Mountains 102 K 3
Spiddle/An
Spidéal 88 E 8
Spink 86 K 9
Spring Hill 102 M 3
Srah/An tSraith 95 E 6
Srahmore 94 D 6
Sráid/An
Cathrach/
Milltown
Malbay 83 D 9
Sraith Salach/
Recess 88 C 7
Stack's
Mountains 83 D 11
Staigue Stone
Fort 76 B 12
Stamullin 92 N 7
Stewartstown 98 L 4
Stonyford 80 K 10
Strabane 101 J 3
Stracashel 100 H 3
Stradbally (Kerry) 82 B 11
Stradbally (Laois) 86 K 8
Stradbally
(Waterford) 80 J 11
Strade 95 E 6
Stradone 97 K 6
Straffan 87 M 8
Straid (Antrim) 103 O 3
Straid (Donegal) 101 J 2
Strandhill 96 G 5
Strangford 99 P 4
Strangford Lough 99 P 4
Stranorlar 101 I 3
Stratford 87 L 9
Streamstown
Bay 88 B 7
Strokestown 90 H 6
Stroove 101 L 2
Suck 96 G 6
Suck (River) 96 G 6
Suir 85 I 9
Suir (River) 79 I 11
Summerhill 92 L 7
Sunderlin (Lough) 90 I 7
Swan 86 K 9
Swan's Cross
Roads 97 K 5
Swanlinbar 97 I 5
Swatragh 102 L 3
Swilly 101 I 3
Swilly (Lough) 101 J 2
Swilly (River) 101 J 2
Swinford/
Béal Atha na
Muice 95 F 6
Swords/Sord 92 N 7
Sybil Head 82 A 11

T
Table Mountain 87 M 8
Tacumshin Lake 81 M 11
Taghmon 81 M 11
Tagoat 81 M 11
Tahilla 76 C 12
Tallaght 87 M 8
Tallanstown 98 M 6
Tallow 79 H 11
Tandragee 98 M 4
Tang 90 I 7
Tara (Hill of) 92 M 7
Tarbert 83 D 10
Tarker (Lough) 97 L 5
Tarsaghaunmore 94 C 5
Tay 80 J 11
Tay (Lough) 87 N 8
Teelin 100 G 4
Temple
of the Winds 99 P 4
Temple (The) 98 O 4
Templeboy 95 F 5
Templeglentan 83 E 10
Templehouse
Lake 96 G 5
Templemore/
An Teampall
Mór 85 I 9
Templenoe 76 C 12
Templepatrick 103 N 3

Templetouhy 85 I 9
Tempo 97 J 4
Terenure 87 N 8
Termon/An
Tearmann 101 I 2
Termonfeckin 92 N 6
Terryglass 85 H 8
Thomastown/
Baile Mhic
Andáin 80 K 10
Thoor Ballylee 89 F 8
Three Castle
Head 76 C 13
Thurles/Durlas 85 I 9
Timahoe (Kildare) 86 L 8
Timahoe (Laois) 86 K 9
Timoleague 78 F 13
Timolin 86 L 9
Tiobraid Árann/
Tipperary 84 H 10
Tiobraid Árann 84 H 10
Tipperary
(County) 84 H 10
Tobar an Choire/
Tobercurry 95 F 5
Tobercurry/
Tobar an
Choire 95 F 5
Toberscanavan 96 G 5
Toe Head 77 E 13
Tollymore Forest
Park 98 O 5
Tomhaggard 81 M 11
Toombeola 88 C 7
Toome 102 M 3
Toomyvara 85 H 9
Toormore 76 D 13
Toraigh/
Tory Island 100 H 2
Torr Head 103 N 2
Tory Island/
Toraigh 100 H 2
Tory Sound 100 H 2
Tourig 79 I 11
Tourmakeady/
Tuar Mhic
Éadaigh 88 D 7
Tower 78 G 12
Trá Lí/Tralee 82 C 11
Trá Mhór/
Tramore 80 K 11
Trafrask 76 D 12
Tralee/Trá Lí 82 C 11
Tralee Bay 82 C 11
Tramore/Trá
Mhór 80 K 11
Tramore Bay 80 K 11
Tranarossan
Bay 101 I 2
Trean 88 D 7
Trillick 97 J 4
Trim/
Baile Átha
Troim 92 L 7
Trostan 103 N 2
Tuaim/Tuam 89 F 7
Tuam/Tuaim 89 F 7
Tuamgraney 84 G 9
Tuar Mhic
Éadaigh/
Toormakeady 88 D 7
Tulach Mhór/
Tullamore 86 J 8
Tulla 84 F 9
Tullaghan 96 G 4
Tullaghobegly 100 H 2
Tullamore/
Tulach Mhór 86 J 8
Tullaroan 80 J 10
Tullig Point 82 C 10
Tullow/An
Tulach 86 L 9
Tully 97 I 4
Tully Cross 88 C 7
Tully National
Stud 86 L 8
Tullyallen 92 M 6
Tullyhoge 98 L 4
Tullynally
Castle 91 J 6
Tulsk 90 H 6
Turloughmore 89 F 7

Turner's Rock
Tunnel 77 D 12
Tuskar Rock 81 N 11
Twelve Pins
(The) 88 C 7
Tynagh 89 G 8
Tyrella 99 O 5
Tyrone (County) 97 J 4
Tyrrellspass 91 J 7

U
Uachtar Ard/
Oughterard 88 E 7
Uaigh/Owey
Island 100 G 2
Ugga Beg
(Lough) 88 D 8
Ulster American
Folk Park 102 J 4
Union Hall 77 E 13
Unshin 96 G 5
Upper
Ballinderry 98 N 4
Upperchurch 85 H 9
Urlingford 86 J 9

V
Valencia Island 76 A 12
Valley 94 C 5
Ventry 82 A 11
Ventry Harbour 82 A 11
Villierstown 79 I 11
Virgina 91 K 6

W
Ward 92 N 7
Waringstown 98 N 4
Warrenpoint 98 N 5
Water Garden
(The) 80 K 10
Waterfoot or
Glenariff 103 N 2
Waterford/
Port Láirge 80 K 11
Waterford
(County) 80 J 11
Waterford
Harbour 80 L 11
Watergrasshill 78 G 11
Waterville/
An Coireán 76 B 12
Wellington
Bridge 81 L 11
Wesport Bay 94 C 6
Westmeath
(County) 91 J 7
Westport/
Cathair na Mart 94 D 6
Westport House 94 D 6
Wexford/
Loch Garman 81 M 10
Wexford Bay 81 N 10
Wexford (County) 81 L 10
Wexford
Harbour 81 M 10
Wheathill 97 I 5
Whiddy Island 77 D 12
White Park Bay 102 M 2
Whitechurch 78 G 12
Whitegate 78 H 12
Whitehead 103 O 3
Wicklow/
Cill Mhantáin 87 N 9
Wicklow (County) 87 M 9
Wicklow Gap 87 M 8
Wicklow
Mountains 87 N 8
Wilkinstown 92 L 6
Williamstown 96 G 6
Windgap 80 J 10
Woodenbridge 87 N 9
Woodford 97 J 5

Y
Youghal/Eochaill 79 I 12
Youghal Bay 79 I 12

Notes

Notes

First published 1990 by Manufacture Française des Pneumatiques Michelin
Société en commandite par actions au capital de 2 000 000 000 de Francs
Place des Carmes-Déchaux – 63 Clermont-Ferrand (France) – RCS Clermont-Fd B 855 200 507
© Michelin et Cie, propriétaires-éditeurs ; 1990, 1991
Second edition 1991

Great Britain : the maps and town plans in the Great Britain Section of this Atlas are based upon the Ordnance Survey of Great Britain with the permission of the Controller of Her Majesty's Stationery Office. Crown Copyright reserved.

Northern Ireland : the maps and town plans in the Northern Ireland Section of this Atlas are based upon the Ordnance Survey of Northern Ireland with the sanction of the Controller of H.M. Stationery Office, Permit number 363

Republic of Ireland : the maps and town plans in the Republic of Ireland Section of this Atlas are based upon the Ordnance Survey of Ireland by permission of the Government of the Republic, Permit number 5340

In spite of the care taken in the production of this book, it is possible that a defective copy may have escaped our attention. If this is so, please return it to your bookseller, who will exchange it for you, or contact

Michelin Tyre Public Limited Company
Davy House - Lyon Road - HARROW - Middlesex HA1 2DQ – Tel. (081) 861-2121 to 2143

The representation in this atlas of a road is no evidence of the existence of a right of way.

ISBN Hardback 2.06.701.120-0 - ISBN Spiral 2.06.701.122-7 - ISBN Deluxe 2.06.701.123-5

Dépôt légal 1er trimestre 1991 – Printed in France 02-91-58

Impression : Aubin imprimeur à Ligugé-Poitiers n° 36813.